SERMONS FROM THE SWORD

SERMONS FROM THE SWORD

by
TOM WALLACE

SWORD of the LORD
PUBLISHERS
P. O. BOX 1099, MURFREESBORO, TN 37133

Printed and Bound in the United States of America

Foreword

I heard Dr. John R. Rice the first time in the fall of 1953 while I was a student at Tennessee Temple University (then College) in Chattanooga. He was hurrying up and down the aisles before one of the services, giving out SWORD subscription envelopes. I took one and scraped together $2.50 for a subscription.

My first issue came October 23, 1953. I still have that copy and every copy published since. I now have eight file drawers full. Later, I came in contact with an older copy published December 7, 1945, which contained sermons by D. L. Moody, Dr. Hyman Appelman and, of course, one by Dr. Rice. It is still a treasured possession.

Since then, the ministry of Dr. John Rice and THE SWORD OF THE LORD has had a great influence on my life. In the late fifties, my little church in Elkton, Maryland, had grown in such an unbelievable way that I got up courage enough to invite Dr. Rice to come for a Sword Conference. He did come and later brought Dr. Jack Hyles and Bill Harvey with him.

In one of our conferences at Elkton, a record number of 166 preachers came from Maryland, Delaware, Virginia, New York, New Jersey and Pennsylvania. The church was packed to capacity. The whole area was influenced. Preachers all over the East Coast testify of changed lives and ministries multiplied.

It was in one of these meetings that Dr. Rice invited me to send a sermon for THE SWORD OF THE LORD. I was flabbergasted! I sent it, and he printed it. I sent another and another, and he printed them all. When Dr. Rice was called Home, Dr. Curtis Hutson continued to print my messages. Both Dr. Rice and Dr. Hutson have graciously used me as a speaker in Sword Conferences. I am honored also to serve as a member of the Cooperating Board of Sword of the Lord Foundation.

Twenty-five of these messages are presented in this volume, *Sermons From THE SWORD*, just as they appeared in the original printings. I make no claim to originality but, in many cases, have passed along illustrations and quotes from others.

It is my prayer and great desire that the Lord will use them again and again to challenge, inspire, instruct and bless those who read them.

TOM WALLACE
1988

Table of Contents

Chapter 1

"Man on Fire"

"And in hell he lift up his eyes, being in torments, and seeth Abraham afar off, and Lazarus in his bosom. And he cried and said, Father Abraham, have mercy on me, and send Lazarus, that he may dip the tip of his finger in water, and cool my tongue; for I am tormented in this flame."—Luke 16:23,24.

I unfolded a metropolitan newspaper and glanced at the bold two-inch headline, "Man on Fire." It was an incident where a midwestern union official had been forced into a car, taken to the outskirts of town, drenched with gasoline or some highly flammable fluid, and set on fire.

His picture was on the front page of every newspaper in the country. The newspaper described the painful misery of his charred body, and millions of people sympathized with the man. People are naturally sympathetic, and their hearts go out to those who are the victims of tragedy.

On December 1, 1958, the news of the Chicago school fire burning eighty-nine children and three nuns to death raised the sympathy of the whole nation. Fire and tragedy are two words that go together. One New York newspaper called this particular fire "A Glimpse of Hell."

Some time ago two ships collided somewhere out at sea off the New York coast. One was loaded with a million gallons of gasoline. The explosion and fire which followed resulted in many merchant seamen going down in what the newspaper called an "Unquenchable Fiery Grave."

On March 18, 1937, some 294 school children and teachers died in a fire explosion in New London, Texas.

On March 4, 1908, a total of 176 children perished in the Collingswood school fire at Cleveland, Ohio.

On November 28, 1942, when the cry "Fire!" was screamed out in the Cocoanut Grove Night Club in Boston, several hundred people tried to rush through a revolving door at one time, and 498 were burned to death.

On December 30, 1903, the great fire disaster at the Iroquois Theater in Chicago brought tragedy when 575 lives were burned to death.

In all these incidents we have seen how horrible and awful it is to burn to death. I certainly agree that in each of the twenty-six major fire disasters in which, in each instance, more than fifty people have been killed in the last one hundred years, this is a horrible, hysterical way to die.

But I want to warn you that it is far more horrible to share the fate of the rich man of Luke 16 in our text who cannot die and get it all over with, but must go on in the scorching, crackling flames of eternal Hell forever and forever. The circumstances and details of Hell are more horrible than all the above mentioned fire tragedies put together.

I. WHY PREACH ON HELL?

Some have wondered why we preach on the horrible subject of Hell. I preach on Hell because I know that some of you who listen to this sermon or read these lines will spend eternity there. So it is my duty to warn you to flee the wrath to come.

Hell is a terrible subject, and the thought of burning flesh brings chills to us all. Nothing is more painful or carries a more nauseating odor than burned flesh.

I was visiting in our local hospital not long ago, and I stepped into a room where a man was on his knees with his head down on his folded arms on the bed. I walked up to him and asked, "Sir, are you praying?" He answered, "No, preacher. My back is burned so bad that this is the only position I can get in to get any relief." For several days I went there to see him, and every time he was on his knees. I was reminded that in Hell relief won't come on the knees.

We have read how, in days of history, people used to tie a man to a stick and build a fire under him, then roll him over and over again and roast him alive, like a barbecue chicken, as a means of torture. How horrible! But still not as bad as Hell.

In *Foxe's Book of Martyrs*, we have the account of many Christians being burned at the stake, and we read of great men like John Knox being tortured to death by fire.

The thoughts of death by fire are so horrible that no state in America will allow capital punishment on this basis. Some states allow that a criminal may be executed by the firing squad; some, by the gas chamber; others, by hanging; still others, by the electric chair. But no state law will allow burning a man to death. The people of the United States would rise up in rebellion if such a law were even suggested.

Again, I preach on Hell because many people do not believe it is real. The modernist has discarded the old-fashioned doctrine of Hell on the basis of human reasoning. The Jehovah's Witnesses, Christian Scientists, Seventh-day Adventists, Mormons, and multitudes of others have thrown it out. The Roman Catholics have substituted a purgatory, even though the word *purgatory* is not found anywhere in the Bible.

You, too, might find yourself doubting the reality of Hell, but I remind you that Jesus said there is a Hell. In Matthew 10:28 He said, "And fear not them which kill the body, but are not able to kill the soul: but rather fear him which is able to destroy both soul and body in hell."

Jesus told the story of the rich man in Hell in our text; and again in Matthew 13:49,50 He said, "Angels shall come forth, and sever the wicked from among the just, And shall cast them into the furnace of fire: there shall be wailing and gnashing of teeth."

In Matthew 25:30 Jesus said, "And cast ye the unprofitable servant into outer darkness: there shall be weeping and gnashing of teeth."

In Matthew 25:41 He said, "Depart from me, ye cursed, into everlasting fire, prepared for the devil and his angels."

In Psalm 9:17, "The wicked shall be turned into hell, and all the nations that forget God."

Isaiah 14:15, "Yet thou shalt be brought down to hell."

Again in Revelation 20:15, "And whosoever was not found written in the book of life was cast into the lake of fire."

The Bible is our only source of information on this subject, and the Bible declares that there is a Hell.

Great preachers of the past have declared a real Hell!

R. A. TORREY—"I claim to be a scholarly preacher, and I believe the old-fashioned Bible doctrine regarding a Bible Hell."

D. L. MOODY—"The same Christ that tells us of Heaven with all its glories, tells us of Hell with all its horrors."

H. W. BEECHER—"The thoughts of future punishment for sinners which the Bible reveals is enough to make an earthquake of terror in a man's soul."

T. DE WITT TALMAGE—"Not having intellect enough to fashion an eternity of my own, I must take the word of the Bible."

C. H. SPURGEON—"Hell the saved one will not know, that wrath he will not feel."

BILLY SUNDAY—"You will not have to be in Hell for five minutes until you will believe there is one."

SAM JONES—"The legitimate end of a sinful life is Hell."

You may say, "I still don't think so." I will say, it doesn't matter what you think or what I think; it's what God says that counts.

Someone says, "The scholars have rejected the idea of Hell." But when a "scholar" disagrees with God, that doesn't make God a liar and the "scholar" right. The Bible says, "Let God be true, and every man a liar."

Someone else says, "I believe Hell is here on earth." If you are lost, this is all the heaven you will ever know. If you are saved, this is all the hell you will ever see. I will agree that there is plenty of hell on earth, but this has nothing to do with the Hell that those who reject Christ will be cast into.

Finally those who have carefully reasoned the matter out in their mind say, "God is too good to condemn man into a fire of Hell."

The Bible says, "God is a consuming fire." Let me point out incidents where God did and will use fire.

Genesis 19 tells how God rained down fire and brimstone on Sodom and Gomorrah.

In Leviticus 10:2 the two wicked sons of Aaron the priest put strange fire on the altar. And the Bible says, "There went out fire from the Lord and devoured them, and they died before the Lord."

In Numbers 11:1 the children of Israel complained and grumbled until God sent fire and consumed them unto the uttermost parts of the camp.

In Numbers 16:35 God opened the earth and swallowed Korah and others. Then the Bible says about those who remained alive, "And there came out a fire from the Lord, and consumed the two hundred and fifty men that offered incense."

In II Kings 1:10 fire was sent down from God in answer to Elijah's prayer and devoured fifty men on two different occasions who were trying to capture him for King Ahaziah.

Then in the New Testament, in II Thessalonians 1:7,8, we read that "the Lord Jesus shall be revealed from heaven with his mighty angels, In flaming fire taking vengeance on them that know not God, and that obey not the gospel."

Again in II Peter 3:10, ". . . the heavens shall pass away with a great noise, and the elements shall melt with fervent heat."

Finally, in Revelation 20:15, "And whosoever was not found written in the book of life was cast into the lake of fire."

Now God has not changed, and He has shown in the Old Testament history and in the New Testament prophecy that fire is His medium of judgment.

I preach on Hell because it's a moral necessity. In Dr. John R. Rice's book, *Hell—What the Bible Says About It*, we read on page 25:

If God didn't send anybody to Hell, when we get to Heaven we would have to preach revivals to get sinners saved. We couldn't leave the door unlocked on our mansion because all the thieves, crooks, bums, burglars and such would be there. We couldn't let our daughters walk down the street unescorted because all the lustful sex maniacs would be there. We would witness funeral processions because, where there is sin, there is death. We would find policemen to curtail crime, vice, and drunkenness; see jails; war being waged by Hitler; and insane asylums for the crazy.

Brother Rice goes on to say, "God in Heaven, is that possible! No, thank God, it is not."

God does have a Hell because of a need for a Hell.

II. WHAT IS HELL LIKE?

If the incidents of real life and newspaper accounts of tragedy by fire make us cringe when we read them, then what will the misery and torment of Hell really be like! Our human mind is not capable of understanding either the blessing of Heaven or the horrors of Hell. Paul said, "Eye hath not seen, nor ear heard, neither have entered into the heart of man, the things which God hath prepared for them that love him" (I Cor. 2:9). I believe it is also true of Hell that it has not entered into a man's mind the things that God has prepared for them that reject Him.

According to the Scripture, both body and soul will be there. Says Matthew 10:28, "And fear not them which kill the body, but are not able to kill the soul: but rather fear him which is able to destroy both soul and body in hell." The Scripture teaches that the wicked dead shall be raised to be judged and condemned to Hell.

It will be a place of wailing. Webster defines wailing as a cry or sound arising from grief or pain.

When I heard a man, in his last hours before death, crying with a hair-raising mournful wail in the hospital in Elkton some time ago, I immediately thought of this Bible term for the cry of Hell: "There shall be wailing and gnashing of teeth" (Matt. 13:42).

A dentist often tells a patient to grit his teeth before he injects a needle. People constantly grit their teeth because of pain. When I was a boy and had an aching tooth, I would bite myself on the hand or finger to distract my attention from the pain. In Hell, men will grit their teeth and gnaw on their flesh to try to ease suffering and pain. How awful! Yet men blindly race on toward the pit.

Hell is a place of weeping. "There shall be weeping and gnashing of teeth." I don't believe tears will flow; but dry, uncontrollable sobs will be heard ringing from every spot in Hell. Tears would mean water, and certainly there is no water in Hell.

Hell is a place of torment. The rich man cried out, "I am in torment in this flame." There will be the torment of bodily pain, blinding darkness, and memories of the past.

Hell is a place of pitch darkness. Jesus said, "Cast ye the unprofitable servant into outer darkness" (Matt. 8:12). The man who stands in the barroom or pool hall and loudly boasts that he wants to go to Hell because his friends will be there, needs to be reminded that if he bumped head on into his best friend, he would not know who it was. The darkness will cause fright and uncertainty; and there will be stumbling, falling, and a lost sense of balance. Jesus is the Light of the world, and without Him there will be only darkness.

Hell is a place of unquenchable fire. In Mark 9:43-46 we find these words: ". . . fire that never shall be quenched." The hydrogen reaction of the sun continually erupting and never cooling is an example of a fire built by the Lord.

Hell is a place of memory. Abraham said to the rich man of our text, "Son, remember that thou in thy life time receivedst thy good things." The lost man in Hell will remember the sermons he heard, the invitations he stood through, the many tracts handed to him, the plea of loved ones to repent, and the many opportunities God allowed for him to be saved. These memories will haunt him forever.

Hell is a place of thirst. The rich man cried, "Send Lazarus, that he may dip the tip of his finger in water, and cool my tongue." Not only will a man thirst for water, but every drinking man will crave liquor; the users of tobacco will cry out for just one cigarette; the lustful will have an uncontrollable desire that cannot be satisfied. For all eternity men will reap what they have sown.

Hell is a place of passion for souls. The desire of the rich man was for someone to talk to his brothers, to warn them not to come to that horrible place.

A mother in Hell does not want her boy to be there with her. She has the same cry, "Somebody tell my boy not to come here!" If the ones who love you the most are in Hell, they are pleading that you might be saved and miss the torment they are suffering.

Hell is a place of unanswered prayer. The rich man made his plea, but his prayer was never answered. Men may not pray now, but they will in Hell. Continually the cry of sinners in Hell will ring out; but, as in the days of Noah, God has shut the door and judgment has fallen.

The hypocrites will be there. Men excuse themselves from God's house because of the hypocrites that are there. Yet they buy groceries for their families, gas for their car, work on the same jobs and belong to the same clubs that the hypocrites do; but they are not about to go to church with them. This should be ever the more reason to be saved and escape spending eternity with them.

Finally, Hell is forever. Men are not thinking about the length of eternity. "How long is it?" you ask. This is a crude example; but if you should be able to sum the number of grains of wheat that have ever grown from the beginning of time; and multiply that enormous figure times all the leaves that have ever grown on all the trees since Adam's time; then multiply that figure times all the grains of sand on all the beaches of the world; then multiply that figure times all the stars in the sky; then multiply that figure times all the people who have populated the earth since Adam's time; then multiply that times the number of inches to the sun; then multiply that times all the drops of rain that have ever fallen; times all the snowflakes that have floated to earth; then multiply that times any number you can imagine times anything and everything that crosses your mind—when you are all finished, the number of years will not equal the end of eternity but merely the beginning.

The tragedy of it all is that some of you will spend all that time in Hell!

Someone has written this poem about Hell:

HELL! THE PRISON HOUSE OF DESPAIR

Hell! the prison house of despair,
Here are some things that won't be there:
No flowers will bloom on the banks of Hell,
No beauties of nature we love so well;
No comforts of home, music and song,
No friendship of joy will be found in that throng;
No children to brighten the long, weary night;
No love nor peace nor one ray of light;
No blood-washed soul with face beaming bright,
No loving smile in that region of night;
No mercy, no pity, pardon nor grace,
No water; O God, what a terrible place!
The pangs of the lost no human can tell,
Not one moment's ease—there is no rest in Hell!

Hell! the prison house of despair,
Here are some things that will be there:
Fire and brimstone are there, we know,
For God in His Word hath told us so;
Memory, remorse, suffering and pain,
Weeping and wailing, but all in vain;
Blasphemers, swearers, haters of God,
Christ-rejectors while here on earth trod;
Murderers, gamblers, drunkards and liars,
Will have their part in the lake of fire;
The filthy, the vile, the cruel and mean,
What a horrible mob in Hell will be seen!
Yes, more than humans on earth can tell,
Are torments and woes of eternal Hell!

III. HOW TO ESCAPE HELL

In Matthew 23:33 Jesus, talking to the scribes and Pharisees, said, "How can ye escape the damnation of hell?" This question can only be answered one way—by accepting Jesus Christ as your personal Saviour.

Let us remember that God never intended any of us to end up in Hell. According to Matthew 25:41, everlasting fire was prepared for the Devil and his angels. Neither let us forget that the Lord is "not willing that any should perish, but that all should come to repentance" (II Pet. 3:9). John 3:16 also carries this same wonderful thought.

Jesus said if necessary a man should pluck out his eye if it offended and was causing him to be lost. He added that it would be better for a man to cut off his hand and go to Heaven than have them in this life and go to Hell because of them.

The greatest problem is not offending eyes, hands, or feet but neglect, procrastination and rejection. More people will be in Hell over these than the sins of murder, adultery and stealing.

In Hebrews 2:3 we are warned, "How shall we escape, if we neglect so great salvation?" And again in Proverbs 29:1, "He, that being often reproved hardeneth his neck, shall suddenly be destroyed, and that without remedy." God help you not to delay or neglect but respond to the knock of the Saviour by opening your heart's door and inviting Him in.

The way of escape is, in simple, childlike faith, turn to Christ in repentance. Commit your past, present and future into His hands and by faith claim His promise of forgiveness and cleansing. Confess to Him that you are a sinner, call upon Him for forgiveness through the blood, claim the promise of salvation by faith, confess Him before men, and I'll meet you in Heaven.

This is the rich man's testimony: "And in hell he lift up his eyes, being in torment."

This can be yours: "And in Heaven he lift up his eyes, being in glory."

Chapter 2

The Rottenness of the Liquor Traffic

"Woe unto him that giveth his neighbour drink."—Hab. 2:15.

On the way to my church to preach one Sunday morning, I was attracted by a group of buzzards circling over a spot near the road. I assumed that something was dead and the buzzards were waiting to pull the rotting flesh off the bones of the carcass; but when I approached the spot, I found nothing there but an empty whiskey bottle that some liquor-soaked sot had thrown out of a car. I readily agreed with the buzzards that the liquor business was the rottenest thing in sight.

The process of distilling booze is simply securing the liquid off rotting grain and mash, anyway; so the word *rotten* applies well to Devil brew, whether it is made in a billion-dollar distillery or cooked in the woods by a bootlegger.

I am aware, too, that I am slurring the number one source of income for town, county and state. If someone gets mad, just remember that the Devil doesn't like it either, and you are siding up with him.

I intend to twist his tail on this issue until he gets good and mad. I hope to give the liquor racket a black eye to go along with its red nose.

Good solid preachers and men of God have always been against red liquor, white liquor, legal liquor, bootleg liquor, beer, wine, rubbing alcohol, strained shoe polish, canned heat and anything else that will make a man smell like a slop barrel and act like a fool.

Billy Sunday called the booze business "a rat hole for the wages of men." He told "Ma" Sunday one time, "Nell, when I die, let them skin me and make a drum out of my hide and rally folks and parade down the street beating on my hide fighting the liquor crowd."

A famous preacher calls it "the curse of America."

Abraham Lincoln called it "a cancer eating society."

Lord Chesterfield called it "an artist in human slaughter."

Robert Hall called it "distilled damnation."

Evangelist Jack Shuler referred to it as "destroyer of men and nations."

Pastor Luzene Lamerson marks it as the "damning sin of America."

Evangelist Joe Miller calls it "the Devil in liquid form."

In his book, *Gospel Seeds for Busy Sowers*, J. Ellis has recorded a poem entitled, "Because and But."

Because

A little drop of drink,
  Because I am so old;
A little drop of drink,
  Because the weather's cold;
A little drop of drink,
  To make me soundly rest;
  To make my food digest;
Because I am so sad;
Because I am so bad;
Because the weather's warm;
Sure it can do no harm;
Because my neighbor's wed;
Because my uncle's dead;
Because 'tis Christmas Day;
Because I can't say "Nay"—
It cures them every one.
Was ever such a remedy
E'er found beneath the sun?

But

A little drop of drink
May lead to many more;
And the man becomes a sot
Ere many months are o'er.
A little drop of drink

Brings many a heartache;
Makes the little child to quake;
May make bright eyes grow dim;
Takes the manhood out of him;
Brings "the wolf" to many a door;
Makes bare the cottage floor;
Takes the money from the bank;
Brings down the highest rank;
Sinks the man below the brute;
Brings forth but sorry fruit—
Ponder it, neighbor, well,
A little drop of drink
Can bring a soul to Hell.

One night at a meeting a black man prayed earnestly that he and his brethren might be preserved from what he called their "upsetting sins."

"Brudder," one of his friends said, "you ain't got the hang of dat dere word. It's 'besettin,' not 'upsettin.'"

"Brudder," replied he, "if dat's so, it's so. But I was prayin' de Lord to save us from de sin of 'toxication,' and if dat ain't a upsettin' sin, I dunno what is."

Sure enough, the old black fellow was right. Drink is the upsetting sin. It upsets homes and characters, manhood, womanhood, childhood, hopes, loves and joys.

An old ragged man with a bottle peeping out of his coat pocket met a fine Christian doctor walking along the street. "Is this the way to the poorhouse, sir?" asked the old man, pointing in the direction he was walking.

"No," said the doctor, "but that bottle is."

I want to say with Billy Sunday, "I am sworn eternally against it."

I. THE MORAL ROTTENNESS OF LIQUOR

Anything that would make a man lie to his own mother, beat his good wife, sell the shoes off his dead baby's feet, break up homes, starve his children and damn souls to Hell, like liquor has, cannot be called anything but rotten.

1. Bible warns against it. In Proverbs 20:1, the Bible says, "Wine is a mocker, strong drink is raging: and whosoever is deceived thereby is not wise."

Proverbs 23:31,32 says, "Look not thou upon the wine when it is red, when it giveth his colour in the cup, when it moveth itself aright. At the last it biteth like a serpent [devil], and stingeth like an adder."

Isaiah 5:11: "Woe unto them that rise up early in the morning, that they may follow strong drink; that continue until night, till wine inflame them!"

Proverbs 23:29,30: "Who hath woe? who hath sorrow? who hath contentions? who hath babbling? who hath wounds without cause? who hath redness of eyes? They that tarry long at the wine; they that go to seek mixed wine."

And our text: "Woe unto him that giveth his neighbour drink, that puttest thy bottle to him, and makest him drunken . . . the cup of the Lord's right hand shall be turned unto thee, and shameful spewing shall be on thy glory."

Noah's life was marred, and reproach came upon his family because of drink.

Lot's shameful, immoral acts of fathering the children of his own daughters was due to drink.

In the account of King David's sin of adultery and murder, liquor played its part.

Belshazzar's doom, announced by the handwriting on the wall, came about during a drunken party.

The Apostle Paul gave a scorching rebuke to those who got drunk at the Lord's table in Corinth.

Yes, the Bible is against booze. It sums up the matter in I Corinthians 6:9 and 10 by saying that drunkards shall not inherit the kingdom of God. Here the drunkard is put into the same class as adulterers and murderers. Society calls God a liar by saying it's a disease.

2. Blight on society. America spends thousands of dollars chasing criminals and combating crime, then gives operating license to public enemy number one—whiskey.

If Russia should attack America, millions and billions of dollars would be spent in defense and in an all-out fight to the last man. War would be under way overnight. Yet the liquor traffic kills many more than war, and nothing is being done.

Seventy-five percent of idiots come from drinking parents; ninety percent of all criminals committed their crimes while under influence of alcohol. About all of our poverty and broken homes are brought on by booze. In the last ten years there were 53,463 murders in saloons.

A little lad, when walking by a gin mill and seeing one of its patrons lying on the sidewalk muttering something about more liquor, was right when he opened the door of the tavern and yelled to the bartender, "Hey, mister, your sign fell down."

3. Blindness of mankind. Millions of dollars are spent each year in the upkeep of jails, asylums, hospitals, state farms, social programs and welfare agencies because of the burden of alcohol. The tax burden gets heavier each year.

Billy Sunday told the story of the room in the insane asylum where the doctors tested the sanity of those in question. A water faucet and mop were the only things in the room. The person in question was put into the room, and the faucet was turned on and the door closed while the doctors observed the action of the inmate.

If he took the mop and began frantically to mop up the water, he was determined crazy. But if he turned off the spigot, he was released as sane.

This furnishes an adequate picture of our system of government. Our legislatures are busy building hospitals, organizing clinics, expanding jail facilities, hiring more policemen, training more social workers—all in an effort to mop up the mess that booze is making in our country. Why don't they shut off the faucet!

II. RUIN BY LIQUOR

In 1952 there was poured out of the bottle 3,500 murders, 11,000 rapes, 45,000 assaults, 200,000 divorces, 3 million cases of venereal disease. These statistics are very old, and it has been worse each year, until the 1959 figures would shock us more than these do. (The figures are much greater twenty-seven years later, in 1987.)

1. Disease of sin. The real trouble behind the blindness of the world about liquor lies in the fact that man has a wicked heart. Says Jeremiah 17:9, "The heart is deceitful above all things, and desperately wicked." And again in Matthew 15:19 we read, "For out of the heart proceed evil thoughts, murders, adulteries, fornications, thefts, false witness, blasphemies."

The tragic result of it all is that man does not even remember the wickedness and vile things that he has done. Nevertheless, he will still have to give an account to God. The excuse, "I was drunk and don't remember," will not hold when a man stands before God.

Shakespeare said, "O God, that men should put an enemy in their mouths to steal away their brains!"

2. Disturbing facts. In 1933, one and one-half gallons of distilled spirits were consumed per person in the United States. In 1935 the figure rose to 11 1/4 gallons per person.

In 1937 it went up again to 15 gallons. By 1945 it increased to 20 gallons.

In 1957 America consumed 150 million gallons of wine, 200 million gallons of whiskey and 500 million gallons of beer.

In 1939 there were 39 million drunkards in America. In 1957 there were 69 million; and at this present rate, in forty years everybody in the United States will be drunkards. (Figures given when preached in 1964.)

Sixty-nine percent of the nation's police force is maintained because of liquor. Our liquor bill for last year would have built 2 million average American homes. One dollar bills lying side by side and end for end would have paved a 16-foot highway 18 times around the earth just with liquor money. There are three saloons for every church. Every fifth home must furnish a boy to fill the gin mills.

Alex Cairns has written a poem:

> If you knew that your boy with eyes so blue,
> With manly trend and heart so true,
> Should enter yonder barroom bright,

And stain his soul in one wild night,
What would you do then, what would you do?

If you knew that your girl with silken hair,
With winsome way and face so fair,
By felon drink at last were seen
To follow the steps of Magdalene,
What would you do then, what would you do?

If you knew that your wife through weary years,
Should drown her grief in bitter tears
Because her boy of tender care
Was lured to death by liquor's snare;
What would you do then, what would you do?

But you know, somebody's boy must lie
In drunken stupor and must die;
Some girl go wrong in tender years—
Somebody's wife must sob in tears.
What will you do then, what will you do?

3. Drink and crime and accidents. I read of a Thomas Ball of Sevierville, Tennessee, a thirty-eight-year-old father of two children, a girl four and a boy six. Sleeping off a drunken stupor, he was awakened by their laughter and playing. In a whiskey-mad frenzy, he beat them with a broom until it broke, then took the arms of the rocking chair and beat the boy to death. Arrested and charged for murder, all he could say was, "Honest to God, Sheriff, I loved my children. I never whipped them." Booze turned this man into a crazed demon.

A preacher told the pitiful story of a knock at his door. A skinny boy about twelve years old was standing there on a crutch. The child pleaded, "Preacher, please go to the jail and talk to Daddy. He killed Mommy, and the sheriff says we can have his body after they hang him." Drink was to blame.

What made twenty-five-year-old Harold Roberts stomp his seventeen-month-old baby to death? Drink.

Several years ago here in Elkton a family of five coming out of a drive-in theater was suddenly struck by a speeding car. As the wreckage was cleared away, leaving four dead and two injured, a little five-year-old orphaned girl broke many hearts with her cries of "Mommy! Mommy!"

Three things stood out clearly: bodies, blood, beer. In a big pool of blood in the speeding car was a scattered carton of beer.

III. REDEMPTION FROM IT

The radio personality (dead now) Arthur Godfrey stated that he was sorry they didn't allow advertisements for liquor on TV. (They do advertise beer.) He stated that they could put on a very helpful educational program against drunkenness and alcoholism.

Millions of dollars of advertising by liquor companies in magazines and newspapers are not trying to lift the standards. Their only concern is to sell more liquor and make more money. Nobody was fooled by Godfrey's subtle statement.

The solution to the rotten mess of the alcohol racket will not come by educating people on how to drink gracefully. Cutting off the liquor supply is the only answer to drunkenness.

Actually, it's an individual problem. The way to keep a man from being a drunkard is to get him saved, then teach him the Word of God. The fact that many churches have thrown out the Bible and put in a bar does not change the answer to the problem. When Christ comes in, the Bible will be honored, and its outright stand against booze will be adhered to.

Joseph Malin's poem illustrates the point:

THE FENCE OR THE AMBULANCE

'Twas a dangerous cliff, as they freely confessed,
  Though to walk near its crest was so pleasant;
For over its terrible edge there had slipped
  A duke and full many a peasant;
So the people said something would have to be done,
  But their projects did not at all tally.
Some said, "Put a fence round the edge of the cliff";
  Some, "An ambulance down in the valley."

But the cry for the ambulance carried the day,
  For it spread through the neighboring city;

A fence may be useful or not, it is true;
   But each heart became brimful of pity
For those who slipped over the dangerous cliff,
   And the dwellers in highway and alley
Gave pounds or gave pence, not to put up a fence
   But an ambulance down in the valley.

"For the cliff is all right if you're careful," they said,
   "And if folks even slip and are dropping,
It isn't the slipping that hurts them so much
   As the shock down below when they're stopping."
So day after day as these mishaps occurred,
   Quick forth would the rescuers sally,
To pick up the victims who fell off the cliff,
   With their ambulance down in the valley.

Then an old sage remarked: "It's a marvel to me
   That people give far more attention
To repairing results than to stopping the cause
   When they'd much better aim at prevention.
Let us stop at its source all this mischief," cried he;
   "Come, neighbors and friends, let us rally;
If the cliff we will fence, we might almost dispense
   With the ambulance down in the valley."

Better guide well the young than reclaim them when old,
   For the voice of true wisdom is calling;
"To rescue the fallen is good, but 'tis best
   To prevent other people from falling."
Better close up the source of temptation and crime,
   Than deliver from dungeon or galley;
Better put a strong fence round the top of the cliff
   Than an ambulance down in the valley.

Friend, the way to settle this business in your own heart forever is:

First, be saved and know it.

Second, be right with God and show it.

Third, be a crusader against liquor and sow it.

Chapter 3

Word From the Lord

"When Jeremiah was entered into the dungeon, and into the cabins, and Jeremiah had remained there many days; Then Zedekiah the king sent, and took him out: and the king asked him secretly in his house, and said, IS THERE ANY WORD FROM THE LORD? And Jeremiah said, THERE IS."—Jer. 37:16, 17.

There certainly is a word from the Lord. Jeremiah didn't realize it but he was speaking for all ages when he said, *THERE IS A WORD FROM THE LORD.*

In the Old Testament alone there are more than 3,800 places which say, "The word of the Lord came unto me. . . ." or some phrase parallel to it. There is a word from the Lord—in fact, 773,692 words from the Lord recorded in 31,173 verses, 1,189 chapters, 66 books, and divided into two major divisions, the Old and New Testaments.

The Apostle Paul declared with great authority that "all scripture is given by inspiration of God" (II Tim. 3:16).

There is great power in the message of the Lord. Paul declared, "I am not ashamed of the gospel of Christ: for it is the power of God unto salvation to every one that believeth" (Rom. 1:16). Again he states, "For the preaching of the cross is to them that perish foolishness; but unto us which are saved it is the power of God" (I Cor. 1:18).

Ezekiel was commanded to preach the word of the Lord to a valley full of dry bones (Ezek. 37). No preacher ever had it any harder with a congregation than did Ezekiel. A lot of crowds are dead and unconcerned but none could beat this. Every preacher who has thoughts of resigning because of a hard field needs to read again Ezekiel 37. There was no unity, the bones were scattered. There was no usefulness, for the lifeless pile of dusty bones was not going to accomplish anything. There wasn't any unction, either. The Spirit had long since departed.

You can't help but notice the similarity between this pitiful picture and a lot of dead, dry, lifeless, formal churches going through the motions of worship. The crowd in the pew has little idea of what is going on, and people are glad when the service is over so they can get home to cut grass or wash the car. Usually the clergy is glad to get the chore over with so he can get an early start to the golf course or down to the boat.

But that can all be fixed by a good clear word from the Lord. Ezekiel preached as he was commanded, and the bones began to unify. He preached again—this time to the wind, just like God told him, and breath entered into the bodies and they came alive.

What we need more than anything else is for preachers and teachers to let people know what God has said, because THERE IS A WORD FROM THE LORD.

Jeremiah had the word of the Lord burning in his heart. He knew there was a word from the Lord, but on one occasion he got upset and quit, vowing to never preach again or even mention the Lord's name. But God's message began to burn in his soul—"His word was in mine heart as a burning fire shut up in my bones, and I was weary with forbearing, and I could not stay" (20:9).

I. IT WILL SAVE THE DOWN-AND-OUT

No drunkard or harlot was even too hard for God to save. Testimony is given around the world by those who lived vile, wicked, ungodly lives until a message from God went to work in their heart and brought conviction and concern.

The Samaritan woman at the well was no Sunday school girl. She had changed husbands for the fifth time and finally just didn't bother to marry the sixth.

The message from Jesus about the water of life that would wash away all her sins was like a lightning bolt. She quickly pleaded, "Give me this living water." What she was saying was, "I'm tired of all this sin. If anyone was ever a down-and-outer, I am she." But a word from the Lord fixed her up!

Blind Bartimaeus was a down-and-outer, begging and pleading for physical health. He was unhappy, bitter and pitiful. But a word from the Lord sure changed things for him.

I tried to talk to an alcoholic who was sitting in a dirty black Ford with four or five more drunks. He wouldn't work steady. His family suffered, but he didn't seem to care. He was a typical down-and-outer. When he saw me coming, he slowly pulled away while I was yelling for him to stop. He pretended not to see nor hear me. Later I caught up with him. We talked. I gave him a message from the Lord. He was saved and was soon baptized and joined our church.

He got a good job, bought a car and home. He was elected superintendent of our Sunday school, then bus director, and finally treasurer. He is one of the best-loved and most-respected men in our church today. The word of the Lord will save the down-and-outer.

II. IT WILL SAVE THE UP-AND-OUT

John Wanamaker, J. C. Penney, Andrew Kraft, Cyrus McCormick and J. Pierpont Morgan were all millionaires and were said to have been born-again Christians.

Nicodemus, a rich, religious ruler, came to Jesus to talk about being saved. He was an up-and-outer in the strictest sense. Jesus explained that "as Moses lifted up the serpent in the wilderness, even so must the Son of man be lifted up" (John 3:14). The message did its work, and Nicodemus was saved.

Lydia, a seller of purple, listened to the preaching of Paul and Silas and became the first convert of Europe. This up-and-outer got in.

Jairus listened carefully to the message of Jesus after his daughter was raised, and another up-and-outer became a believer.

The nobleman, seeking help for his dying son, found help for himself and his whole house.

During a revival meeting in a Southern state I noticed a very dignified man sitting in the choir. He was there every night. He seemed to be the busiest man in the church. I asked the pastor who he was. "Oh, he's a banker."

Praise the Lord for the salvation of up-and-outers!

III. IT WILL STABILIZE THE IN-AND-OUT

Every pastor knows too well the problem of the loose, careless, lukewarm, in-and-out type of church member. This kind is not regular in prayer, Bible study, or attendance. This one goes in spurts and seasons. He or she needs something, and it's not easy to tell whether it's conversion or rededication.

The remedy for this problem is the same—plain preaching. Paul advised Timothy, "Preach the word, be instant in season and out of season."

Look what it did to *denying Peter*. He meant well but he cursed and swore, then vowed that he had never before seen Jesus. After some contact with the words of a departing Saviour, he went to the Upper Room and obeyed orders. Pentecost shows the difference as three thousand came to Christ through a simple message from the word and other witnesses.

Look again at *doubting Thomas*. He was an in-and-outer. At a very significant time he was out. He would not believe anything, but a few words from the Lord caused him to cry out, "My Lord and my God!"

Look at *deceitful Ananias and Sapphira*. Barnabas had the real thing, but these folks were in-and-outers. They were only doing their deed because he had set the example. Then they backed out on their commitment to the Lord. The word from the Lord did not help them, but it certainly did stabilize the rest of the early church. We read that "great fear came upon them all."

A local man went to the store to get a $69.00 check cashed. The clerk gave him the money but later, in counting, he discovered she had given him $96.00. Somehow the clerk had read the figures upside down.

The man had been saved several years, and even though he had not been regular in church attendance, he maintained the standard instilled into him during his walk with the Lord. After discussing it with his wife, he decided to return the money. The next day he died suddenly.

Don't you know that at the judgment seat he'll sure be glad he did right. The Word of God had stabilized him in time of testing.

IV. IT WILL STIR THE OUT-AND-OUT

Jeremiah was a good man of God. One day while meditating on the word from the Lord, he cried out, 'The word was like a fire in my bones.' The words of the Lord are spirit and life. They will stir and arouse out of lethargy and complacency and feed and bless the faithful.

Contact with the message of the Lord will create a stronger burden in the heart of the saint. It will also clean up sinful tendencies and patterns. Then it will comfort the troubled and bereaved. Paul told the Christians at Thessalonica to "comfort one another with these words."

The story was told of a happy family of a father, mother and two beautiful little girls. They wanted a little baby brother for the girls, and soon the desire was met. After the baby was born, the doctor took the parents aside and gave them the saddest word they had ever heard: the little fellow was crippled and deformed.

It was a hard blow but they were soon busy planning and caring for their family. After about three years the boy learned to walk in a faltering way.

One day when it was time for Daddy to come home, Mother suggested the girls meet him at the gate. They decided to pick a love bouquet for Daddy. Soon each had one ready. The little fellow saw what his sisters had done, so he went into the yard, found a dandelion, crushed it in his hand, then found a broken stick, and placed it into his bouquet using a dirty string to tie them together.

"There's Daddy!" squealed one of the girls; so down the sidewalk and into his arms they went. He hugged them to him—with a Daddy-joy. Then he saw the little fellow hobbling toward him with his love bouquet. With tears streaming down his cheeks he ran to the boy and picked him up in his arms. This was the best gift of all!

Friend, we may not have much to offer, but if we give our best, God will be pleased and will accept it with great reward.

THERE IS A WORD FROM THE LORD. Let us hear it, heed it and hurry.

Chapter 4

Unwrapping God's Gift

"Thanks be unto God for his UNSPEAKABLE gift."—II Cor. 9:15.

"For the wages of sin is death; but the GIFT OF GOD is eternal life."—Rom. 6:23.

"And she brought forth her firstborn son, and WRAPPED him in swaddling clothes."—Luke 2:7.

It's Christmastime again. It is the time to give and receive gifts. Man has learned all that he knows about giving from God. God is in the giving business.

God gave Adam and Eve a piece of skin from an innocent animal to replace the fig leaves and cover their shame of nakedness.

God gave Noah a plan for the ark that would provide for the saving of his household when judgment came.

God gave Abraham a promise concerning his seed. It would be as the sands of the sea, as the dust of the ground, as the stars of the sky.

God gave Sarah a precious miracle child in her old age, and she named him Isaac. He became a mighty man of God.

God gave Isaac the promised ram to take his place on the sacrifice altar on Mount Moriah as Abraham raised the dagger up.

God gave Jacob the privilege to father twelve sons who were destined to become heads of the twelve tribes of Israel, the people of the Lord.

God gave Joseph a position as prime minister in Egypt that he might rescue his own from sore famine in the days ahead.

God gave Moses the power to work miracles before Pharaoh

and prove that God's hand was still with His own.

God gave Joshua the proposition to cross the Jordan and lead the armies of Israel to victory in Canaan.

God gave the Israelites possession of the land flowing with milk and honey.

God gave kings to preside over His chosen people and blessed those who walked in His ways.

God gave prophets to plead with His people and tell them of amazing things to come.

God gave the Scriptures to prophesy of a Messiah, a Scepter, a Shiloh, a Branch, a Prophet, a Priest, a King and a Saviour who would come to deliver and save.

God gave the shepherds a pronouncement by the angels that Jesus was born.

God gave the Wise Men a preview by the star to lead them to the young Child with their gifts.

God gave Bethlehem the preeminence of all cities of the earth. There Jesus was born.

God gave Joseph the patience to understand the strange circumstances of a virgin with child.

God gave Mary the present coveted by all young girls of Jewish history—the Christ Child.

God gave the world the Prince of Peace, the answer to all ills of all time, in all places.

God gave Jesus the place of the sinner on the cross to bear the sorrow and shame.

God gave all men the pardon for their sins that they might know the joy of everlasting life.

Surely God is a great Giver. Mankind can learn a lot about giving from Him.

John tells us that "God so loved the world, that he gave his only begotten Son, that whosoever believeth in him should not perish, but have everlasting life" (John 3:16).

James states, "Every good gift and every perfect gift is from above, and cometh down from the Father of lights" (James 1:17).

Jesus told the woman at the well, "If thou knewest the gift of God, and who it is that saith to thee, Give me to drink; thou wouldest have asked of him, and he would have given thee living water" (John 4:10).

Paul states, "He that spared not his own Son . . . shall he not with him also freely give us all things?" (Rom. 8:32).

He stated to Timothy, "Neglect not the *gift* that is in thee" (I Tim. 4:14), and "stir up the *gift* of God, which is in thee" (II Tim. 1:6).

To the Ephesians he said, "For by grace are ye saved through faith; and that not of yourselves: it is the *gift* of God" (Eph. 2:8).

It is very obvious that Jesus is God's greatest gift to us. Let us unwrap the gift to behold just what God has for us.

I. GOD WRAPPED UP HIS GIFT IN OLD TESTAMENT MYSTERY

Jesus can be found in every book, every chapter and every verse of the Bible. In the Old Testament He is found everywhere when you begin to consider or unwrap the types, shadows, pictures and symbols.

You can find Him in the sacrificing of the animals, the metals of the Tabernacle, the colors of the garments, and a thousand other places; but you will need to unwrap Him by meditation and study.

He is the "Seed" spoken of in Genesis 3:15. His heel shall bruise the head of the serpent.

He is the source of blessing in God's promise to Abraham in Genesis 12:3—"In thee shall all families of the earth be blessed."

He is the Shiloh mentioned in Genesis 49:10 who would come and gather the people to Him.

He is the "Sceptre" spoken of in Numbers 24:17 to rise out of Jacob and smite the corners of Moab.

He is the "Prophet" of Deuteronomy 18:15 to be raised up out of the midst of the brethren, to be hearkened unto.

He is the one conceived by a virgin according to Isaiah 7:14, the "Immanuel" of Isaiah 9:6 that shall be called "Wonderful, Counsellor, The mighty God, The everlasting Father, The Prince of Peace."

He is the "Messiah" that shall come forth only to be "cut off" according to Daniel 9:26.

He is the "ruler" in Israel to be born in Bethlehem of Judaea according to Micah the prophet in chapter 5, verse 2.

He can be found everywhere if we only take time to unwrap the gift.

II. MARY WRAPPED UP GOD'S GIFT
IN THE STABLE

"She . . . wrapped him in swaddling clothes." These are precious words. They can be felt best by a mother who has felt what Mary felt.

But there is more wrapped up in those swaddling clothes than a little baby.

First, wrapped up in this little Baby is the *fulfillment* of all the Old Testament. Every truth, every teaching, every type concealed in the Old Testament is being held in the arms of Mary. To understand the story of Moses smiting the rock, the brass serpent on a pole, the manna in the wilderness, Jonah and the whale, or to get any sense from the Psalms of David or the Proverbs of Solomon, you will have to watch closely the thing that happens to this little Baby.

Second, wrapped up in this little Baby is the *fullness* of Almighty God. The God who created the heaven and earth, divided the Red Sea, appeared in the burning bush, delivered Daniel from the lions and the three Hebrew boys from the fiery furnace, is sleeping in the arms of Mary, wrapped in swaddling clothes.

John explains that "the Word was made flesh, and dwelt among us." Paul declares, "In him dwelleth all the fulness of the Godhead bodily" (Col. 2:9). He said Himself, "I and my Father are one" (John 10:30).

Third, wrapped up in this little Baby is the *future* of all Christians. The destiny of all men rests in their attitude and relationship to the little Baby. He has come to be their Saviour or their Judge. He is only a little Baby in Mary's arms, but He will soon confound the doctors in the Temple. He will be introduced and baptized by John. He will work miracles and call disciples. He will die on a cross, be buried in a borrowed tomb, be resurrected the third day. He will ascend to the Father to become our Intercessor, Advocate, Mediator and great High Priest.

III. SATAN WRAPPED UP GOD'S GIFT IN IGNORANCE

Man will never know what is wrapped up in the gift if Satan has his way.

First, Satan has *blinded* the minds of men to the true value of the gift (II Cor. 4:4). To the natural eye God's Gift looks just like any other gift (I Cor. 2:14). The spiritual eye can see through the Devil's wrapping and see that Christ is more than a great teacher and reformer. He is the Son of God.

Second, Satan had *bound* men in tradition and religious customs. Thousands who have realized that the modernistic, social gospel has no hope of Heaven are still tied to it by fear to step out and stand. Scores have accepted the religion handed down to them by ancestors, and they proceed through meaningless formalities and never unwrap the gift.

Third, Satan has *built* up barriers to Christ by sin and confusion. The more sin and rebellion in the life, the harder it is to repent. Evil habits and social sins tighten their grip, and the obstacles to Christ get higher each day. Satan is wrapping up God's Gift to keep poor sinners from knowing God's love.

IV. THE HOLY SPIRIT UNWRAPS GOD'S GIFT TO ALL WHO BELIEVE

Jesus promised that, when He went back to the Father, He would send one to teach and reveal the truth to all. The blessed Spirit of God has come to unwrap the Gift and help us understand.

God's Gift was unwrapped for the shepherds to see.

He was unwrapped for the Wise Men to meet and present their gifts to.

He was unwrapped for Anna and Simeon to behold.

He was unwrapped to John the Baptist by the descending dove in order that he might introduce Him publicly.

He was unwrapped to the disciples by His miracle-working so that they might believe.

He was unwrapped to Mary Magdalene at the tomb; and after talking to a stranger, she suddenly said, "Rabboni."

He was unwrapped for Thomas to see the prints in His hands and feet; and he who could not believe cried out, "My Lord and my God!"

The same Holy Spirit will unwrap Him to any sincere heart and show plainly that He is God's Gift to you and me. Praise God for His unspeakable Gift!

During the Second World War the allied army was advancing through France. The Germans were making a last stand wherever they could. During a night of very heavy fog the opposing armies moved very close. Only a long green meadow and one farmhouse separated them.

As dawn came the fog lifted. Bullets and bombs began to explode, and men began to die. After some time of severe battle, the house in the green meadow was hit and began to burn. Then someone whispered, "Look." It was unbelievable, but there a small baby was crawling across the field.

As the soldiers saw the child, the shooting began to cease. Soon it became very still. Every eye was on the baby.

Suddenly a soldier raised up from his position, ran out into the open, grabbed the baby up in his arms, and ran back to his line. In a moment a great cheer went up on both sides, and the bullets began to fly again.

The baby brought peace just for a moment.

The war of ages has been in progress since Satan's rebellion against God. Then Baby Jesus was born in Bethlehem of Judaea. He will give eternal peace to all who will put their trust and faith in Him.

Friend, unwrap God's Gift and accept it from God right now!

Chapter 5

A Tale of Two Men

"There was a certain rich man, which was clothed in purple and fine linen, and fared sumptuously every day: And there was a certain beggar named Lazarus, which was laid at his gate, full of sores, And desiring to be fed with the crumbs which fell from the rich man's table: moreover the dogs came and licked his sores. And it came to pass, that the beggar died, and was carried by the angels into Abraham's bosom: the rich man also died, and was buried; And in hell he lift up his eyes, being in torments, and seeth Abraham afar off, and Lazarus in his bosom."—Luke 16:19-23.

In high school I read the *Tale of Two Cities*. In college, I read a poem called "The Tale of Two Churches." Here we have the tale of two men. Jesus told this true story. It is a story filled with lessons and truth about life, death and eternity. The rich man lived for now and was lost for eternity. The poor man's only hope was eternity. He had nothing here.

Please don't misunderstand the point here. Riches had nothing to do with the rich man being lost, and poverty had nothing to do with the poor man going to Heaven.

Many millionaires have testified of faith in Christ, including J. Pierpoint Morgan, J. C. Penney, Cyrus McCormick, Kraft of Kraft Cheese and Mr. R. G. LeTourneau. On the other hand, numberless poor men have lost their souls and gone to Hell because of a lack of repentance and faith. The difference here is not money but men.

Now I want to point out three things from this passage: the Great Contrast, the Great Controversy, and the Great Concern.

I. THE GREAT CONTRAST, HEAVEN OR HELL

Some time ago I read of two men sitting on a log. Suddenly the log dislodged and began to roll down the hill. One man fell over backwards; the other jumped off the other side. The man who fell got to his feet, brushing himself off only to watch in horror as the log rolled over his friend and crushed out his life. One man was on the right side of the log; the other, on the wrong side.

The story of Cain and Abel illustrates this same truth. Cain's vegetable offering was rejected; and Abel's animal, accepted. Abel's offering fulfilled the prophetic picture of a blood sacrifice and suggested God's way. Cain's offering shows man's way. One was right, and one was wrong.

Jacob and Esau were twin brothers. They had the same parents, the same environment, the same opportunities. But one cared for "now" and the physical needs, while the other was concerned for "later." One was on the right side; the other, on the wrong side.

Jesus told of two men who built houses. One built on the rock and the other on the sand. One house stood while the other fell. One man was wise; the other was a fool.

When Jesus comes He will find two men in a field. One shall be taken, the other left. Two men shall be in bed. One will be gone; the other will be left.

Two men went to pray. The one prayed with pride and boasted of his standing and achievements. The other prayed for mercy because of his sin. One was justified; the other was still condemned.

Two men were crucified with Jesus. The thief on one side sought to be set free in this life. The other thief desired to settle the matter of the next life. One died and went to Hell; the other went immediately to Paradise.

Now in the text, our two men are the rich man and the beggar Lazarus. There is a great contrast here. They lived differently, died differently, and ended in different places for eternity.

The very minute they died, things changed around. Now the rich man is a poor, unfortunate lost creature, hopeless, helpless and condemned for eternal damnation. The poor man now is rich and enjoying the benefit of everlasting life. He is an heir of God and joint heir with Jesus Christ.

Jesus gave us this story to show us the difference between the two men. There are only two kinds of people in the world, saved and lost. The few on the narrow road have eternal life, while the multitude on the broad road are headed for Hell. Once the last breath is taken, the destiny of the soul is settled forever and forever.

"I understand you and your wife are going to be separated," said a friend to a well-known judge.

"How dare you insinuate such a thing!" shouted the judge in anger. "My wife and I love each other very much."

"Is that so?" queried the friend. "Well, I heard that she has only a short time to live. I know she is a Christian and will be going to be with her Lord. Where are you going when you die?"

The judge turned pale as the words took effect, "My God, save me!" he cried. "All these years I have turned away from Thee. Forgive me, Lord, and save me right now!"

II. THE GREAT CONTROVERSY: IS THERE AN ETERNAL HELL OF TORMENT?

While driving near Russellville, Pennsylvania, I saw a large billboard-type sign on the front lawn of a house. It pictured a cemetery with several tombstones and large letters written across it which read, THE BIBLE HELL. The inference was that the grave is the end. Several groups hold to this theory.

1. Hell Could Not Be the Grave

Notice that the rich man in Hell "lift" up his eyes. He was in "torments." He "saw," he "cried," he "said," he "heard," and he was able to "remember." Now aren't these strange things for a man to be doing in the grave? These words indicate that this man was involved in life after death. Men do not see, cry, speak and hear in the grave.

A study of the four words translated "Hell" in the Bible, *Sheol, Hades, Gehenna,* and *Tartaros,* will show that there is more after this life.

Back in school days at Tennessee Temple College in Chattanooga, on one particular day I was washing my car when a sweet old lady stopped to chat. She had snow-white hair and was carrying a large black bag. I asked her if she were going to Heaven.

"Oh, no, I'm not worthy," she said.

"Well, I'm not worthy either, but I'm still going," I blurted out.

Rebuking me, she said, "Young man, the Lord will whip you for talking like that!"

My wife was looking out of an upstairs window and soon was down in the driveway with my Bible. I read verse after verse about fire, brimstone and torment; but she kept saying, "That is figurative. God is too good to send anyone to Hell." Of course, I soon realized that she was a Jehovah's Witness and did not believe in Hell at all.

2. God Has Used Fire to Punish Sinners; Will Do So Again

By the way, that leads to a good question. Would a loving God use fire to deal with sin and sinners? The answer is in the Bible.

In Sodom and Gomorrah the Lord used fire and brimstone to judge the people.

Nadab and Abihu, the wicked sons of Eleazer the priest, were devoured by fire from God.

Fire came down from Heaven to consume a group of complainers in Numbers 11:1, and 250 more rebellious people in Numbers 16:35.

King Ahaziah blamed Elijah for his troubles and sent a captain and fifty men to drag him in before the king. Elijah asked the Lord for direction, and fire came from Heaven to destroy them. Another fifty men and their captain were ordered to get Elijah and bring him in. Again God answered by Elijah; and a captain and fifty men went out, devoured in flames, to meet God.

Finally the king asked for another captain and fifty men. Captains were scarce now, and men were, too. They had heard of the strange fiery judgment. This time they came to Elijah pleading, "If it please thee, could you possibly spare a few minutes? The king wants to talk with you."

Elijah went this time. God did use fire two times to destroy two captains and one hundred men.

In all of these places the Lord used fire. There are great numbers of verses in the Scripture that tell us that He will use fire again.

The Lord will return in flaming fire taking vengeance on them that know not the Gospel (II Thess. 1:8).

The crowd at the Great White Throne Judgment will be "cast into the lake of fire."

In Matthew 5:22 Jesus spoke of the "danger of hell fire."

In Matthew 5:29,30 He advised that it would be better to cut off a hand or a foot or pluck out an eye before allowing these to endanger you to Hell.

In Matthew 10:28 He warned, "Fear him that is able to destroy both body and soul in hell."

In Matthew 11:23 Jesus told Capernaum that she would be brought down to Hell.

In Matthew 13:49,50 He told of the angels gathering up the wicked and casting them into the furnace of fire.

In Matthew 23:33 He asked a group of scribes, "How can ye escape the damnation of hell?"

In Matthew 25:41 He tells how He will order some to "depart into everlasting fire."

The cults are wrong, and the Bible is right. God will use fire to judge the wicked.

The Sunday School Times told of a young woman, dying, who said to her father, "Father, why did you not tell me there was such a place?"

"What place?"

"A Hell!"

He said, "Jenny, there is no such place. God is merciful. There will be no future sufferings!"

She said, "Daddy, you are wrong. My feet are slipping in it this moment. I am lost. Why didn't you tell me there was such a place?"

III. THE GREAT CONCERN: LOST BROTHERS!

The rich man who is now the poor man began to remember his

life on earth. His many opportunities to repent and receive Christ were ever before him. Suddenly, he thought of his five brothers who were following his poor example. They were trying to get rich as he did. They did not have time for God, either. He pleaded with Abraham to do something. "Send somebody, send Lazarus to tell them."

"They have the Bible," Abraham said. "If they will not listen to God through the message of the Bible, they wouldn't listen to one from the dead."

1. If Men Will Not Listen to God's Word, They Will Not Repent

I have often thought that, if it were possible to open the hatch of Hell and get the rich man out and let him testify and warn the people, if he could stand on the platform with his flesh melting and dripping off his bones, little fagots of flame leaping out from his body, and his bloodcurdling screams of warning flooding the auditorium, surely the hair would stand on every head, chills would run up the spine, tears would blur the eyes, and every sinner would cry out for mercy. But, according to our Scripture, if men will not repent because of the words of Jesus and the Bible, then they still will not, even if this poor man came from Hell.

Great concern came, but it was too late for that. However, it is not too late for us. It is time for concern.

> After the joys of earth,
> After its song of mirth,
> After its hours of light,
> After its dreams so bright,
> What then?
>
> Only an empty name,
> Only a weary frame,
> Only a conscience smart,
> Only an aching heart,
> After this empty name,
> After this weary frame,
> After this conscience smart,
> After this aching heart,
> What then?

Only a sad farewell
To a world loved too well,
Only a silent bed
With the forgotten dead.
What then?

Oh, then—the judgment throne,
Then all the woes that dwell.
Oh, then—the lost hope—gone!
In eternal Hell!

2. Many of Us Care About Your Lost Soul

Many years ago Evangelist Joe Henry Hankins preached a sermon in Chicago entitled "Who Cares if a Sinner Goes to Hell?" The message was recorded in a 1955 issue of THE SWORD OF THE LORD.

Dr. Hankins points out that God the Father cares, the Holy Spirit cares, Jesus cares, the lost in Hell care, and the saved in Heaven care.

The invitations and pleas flow endlessly from the Bible begging men to escape Hell. A few have been affected by the plea of this pitiful man in Hell and are going up and down the roads and streets of this country seeking for somebody's brothers to tell them not to go to that awful place.

Some have given their life to God for service because they cared. Many have gone to the mission field, some have become pastors, some evangelists, and some teachers to help keep men out of Hell. Others have sacrificed, worked, and given because they caught a vision of keeping a soul out of Hell.

Our Sunday school superintendent has a famous name—Bob Jones, Sr. We also have a Bob Jones, Jr., in our church. Bob, Jr., played big league baseball for the Washington Senators. Bob was Elkton's town drunk. He would not keep a job. The family often went hungry. He hung around on Water Street and drank cheap wine.

We had a prayer meeting at his house one night and prayed for God to save him. He came home and found us calling on God in his behalf. I peeped to see who was coming in. He quietly closed the door and slipped around to the back of the house and came in the back door. I got up from my knees, slipped into the kitchen, and talked to him while the others prayed. Bob got saved and has been one of God's best men.

In a testimony meeting in the church, Bob Jones got up with tears and said, "If it had not been for Brother Tom and you folks who cared enough to come and pray, I'd be in Hell right now."

3. How Long Is Eternity?

If we could only realize what a horrible thing it is for one to lose his soul! The torment, the burning, the crying, the memories, the regret, the payment for sins will never end. How long is eternity? Will there ever be any hope?

Let's try to imagine how long Hell will last. Take a million years and multiply it times all the population since Adam. Now multiply that number times all the angels God created, times all the trees ever grown, times all the leaves on the trees, times all the birds in the trees, times all the feathers on the birds, times all the bees out of the comb, times all the insects in the air, times all the blades of grass, times all the drops of rain that have fallen, times all the snowflakes from the sky, times all the drops of water in the ocean, times all the fish in the sea, times all the sands of the seashore, times all the dust of the earth, times all the stars of the sky, times all the grains of corn ever grown, times all the grains of wheat ever grown, times all the grains of barley, rice, beans, and berries, times all the eggs ever laid, times all the chickens ever hatched, times all the sheep ever herded, times all the cattle ever stocked, times all the bottles ever filled, times all the books ever printed, times all the letters ever written, times everything and anything you can think of for the next ten years! Now, let that unthinkable number represent the number of lifetimes that go by; and after that time passes, listen to the mourning, the pitiful scream of the poor rich man, "CAN I GET OUT NOW?"

The answer is NO. Eternity is just starting. Will you take a chance with your soul? Think it over, friend. Your life is just a tick of the clock, a twinkle of the eye, a single grain of sand on the shore, a vapor that vanishes away in comparison to that awful eternity.

Friend, if you had to be nailed to a cross and hang in suffering for one hundred years in this life to escape the damnation of Hell, it would be well worth your while.

But thank God, it will not be necessary to hang from the cross one hundred years. Jesus has already hung from the cross for you and me. The payment is made. You can escape Hell and enter Heaven through His death.

Will you trust Him in the matter, NOW?

Chapter 6

Learning to Win Souls

"And they that be wise shall shine as the brightness of the firmament; and they that turn many to righteousness as the stars for ever and ever."—Dan. 12:3.

A letter came to me which read:

Dear Bro. Wallace:

I suppose you will not remember me. You were a bus pastor here when my four girls were small. You and your wife stayed after them until they were saved and baptized. You never gave up on me either until I too was saved; that night my girls were so happy for me.

My oldest daughter Faye never forgot you. She married and soon found that she had a cancer. She died just minutes after praying with Dr. Lee Roberson who was such an inspiration to her. I saw your picture in *The Evangelist* and thought you might like to know since you are the one who helped her to Heaven.

Our sorrow could have been so much worse. She could have been lost.

Just a few months after receiving the above letter, word came that the mother had passed away, too. What a tremendous blessing and encouragement that letter was to my entire ministry! How glad I was that I had learned to win souls!

There surely are thousands of people around us who would like to get the matter settled if they just had someone to help them.

Several years ago I flew into Memphis, Tennessee, for a revival meeting. The pastor picked me up and drove toward the church. He mentioned that he would like to make a visit on the way back. He told me three things about the lady we were going to see: her name was Metsger, her Christian husband had just left for Viet Nam, and she was not saved.

We stopped at the house, walked up the sidewalk and rang the doorbell. She answered the door, recognized the pastor and invited us in. The pastor introduced us. I said, "I'm delighted to meet you, Mrs. Metsger. The pastor has just told me that your husband has gone to Viet Nam."

"That's right."

"He told me too that your husband is a Christian man."

"Yes, he is."

"The preacher tells me that you are not a Christian yet."

"That's true."

"Why aren't you a Christian, Mrs. Metsger?"

She began to weep. "I've been down on my knees the last two nights trying to get saved. Could you help me get saved?"

In a matter of minutes she was beaming with joy and that night walked the aisle to profess Christ as Saviour.

Anyone who has succeeded in learning to tie his shoes can learn to win souls. How difficult it is for a little child to get the strings straight and the knots and bows tied right! Once figured out, there is nothing to it. We can do it with our eyes shut.

It's the same with soul winning. Once we find out how to do it and then work at it, we become effective soul winners, and the joy of the Lord comes each time a soul is born again.

Just a few hours before writing this message, a young Christian fellow came to ask me to preach the funeral for his father. As I set out to comfort him, I soon found that he needed Christ. It was the most natural thing to lead him to the greatest of all comforters. He was saved within minutes.

I want to set forth five steps that can be followed by anyone who really wants to learn to win souls regularly.

I. PUT PEOPLE AT EASE

Many people have a fence built up around them in the form of preconceived ideas, customs and religious notions. Some have endured ugly experiences and various traditions that must be reckoned with. We must somehow get them to relax.

When Jesus talked to the woman at the well, there were some extremely difficult barriers. He was a Jew; and she, a Samaritan. And the Samaritans had no dealings with Jews. Then she was a wicked, immoral woman, and He was the perfect, sinless Lamb of God.

Jesus began by asking for a drink of water. She was surprised and asked about His approach. They got quickly into religion, and then the question of her sin came up. She was wondrously saved in just a short time. Jesus had torn down her wall of resistance and difference, and the Gospel did its work.

I remember so well the case of the woman who was admitted to our local hospital. I had visited the hospital the day before and met the other ladies in her ward. As I entered the room, I spoke to each by name and inquired about her condition. When I came to her bed, I said, "Oh, we have a new lady. What's your name?"

"I'm Mrs. Keyes," she answered quietly.

"Where do you live, Mrs. Keyes?"

"I live out near your church."

"That's wonderful," I remarked. "Then you will be coming to visit us soon."

"No, I will not," she blurted out.

"Oh, you don't mean that," I said. "Everybody comes to our church sooner or later."

"Not me," she coldly barked. "I will not be there."

"Why?"

"Because I'm a Quaker."

I tried to ease the situation, but the more I joked and kidded with her, the more sharp and defiant she became.

The lady in the bed next to her was crying by this time and asked if I would help her to be saved. She made a good decision for Christ, and I prayed for all and left.

The next day when I went back, Mrs. Keyes, sitting on the edge of her bed, remarked as I entered the door, "Oh, there you are. I'm glad you came back."

"Why?" I asked.

"Because I want you to change me over."

"Do what to you?"

"You know, make a Baptist out of me like you did for her," pointing to the other lady who had been saved the day before.

Undoubtedly the ladies there had told her that I was sincere in helping folks get to Heaven. Her barriers were gone, and she was ready to start for Heaven. She had been put at ease.

I'm so glad she got saved, because a little while later, a cancer took her out to meet God.

II. PRESENT THE GOSPEL

The Gospel is still the power of God unto salvation unto everyone that believeth. It is like a hammer that breaketh a rock in pieces. The Gospel still works just as it did with Moody and Finney.

After we get a hearing, then we must pour the water of life into the empty stone hearts and watch the change, as in Jesus' first miracle.

Ezekiel gave the Bible message to a pile of dry bones, and life came. What a picture of the power of the Word of God working in hearts!

I had been working with a drunk for a long time and was getting nowhere in bringing him to Christ. Then he developed a bad case of DT's and began to see pink elephants, red snakes and big orange bugs.

He was admitted to the hospital and was shackled to a bed. After drying out, he quieted down.

I carefully explained the Gospel to him, but he would not decide for Christ. I went back again, again and again until I had given him the message twelve times. A preacher friend tried four or five times, but still he would not break.

Finally he was discharged. Several weeks went by. One day my phone rang; and a boy's voice said, "Preacher Wallace, my daddy wants to talk with you."

I had a bad cold and had not been making calls, but I felt I should go. When I arrived at his home, he was drunk and asleep. I woke him and asked what he had called me for.

"I called you because I wanted you, that's why," he mumbled.

"But what do you want?"

"I just want you, that's why," he mumbled again.

I figured I might as well put some words in his mouth; so I said, "Did you call me because you wanted to be saved?"

"Yeah! That's what I wanted."

I reasoned that, since he had heard the messages sixteen times when he was sober, it was foolish to try to explain it again. So I told him we ought to pray. "That's what I want to do," he hollered out.

"Now, I will pray first," I explained.

"You don't need to pray," he muttered. "I am the one who needs to pray."

I certainly agreed with that. "O.K., pray," I suggested.

"Lord, I'm going to pray, and I don't know how," he mumbled.

"Tell Him you are a sinner," I volunteered.

"He knows that, Preacher," he snapped. "He's got eyes, and He can see that I am a sinner."

"Go ahead, tell Him you are a sinner and want Him to save you," I coaxed.

"Yeah! Lord, that's what I want. Please come into my heart and save me."

Sure enough, he got saved there on the spot.

He showed up Sunday and was baptized. The message had done its work. He couldn't ignore God any longer.

It seems strange that a man would need to get drunk to get enough nerve to get saved, but that's what happened.

III. PLAN YOUR APPROACH

A definite plan gives direction and authority to the soul winner. As a salesman uses a presentation, so a Christian ought to know the road to salvation so he can lead a person to Jesus over a familiar path.

It is my usual practice to start on common ground and to proceed to the Romans Road. I will begin at the Ten Commandments. Normally, I will read all ten and explain how most people try to get to Heaven by climbing up a ladder with these ten rungs on it.

I usually go quickly to the Sermon on the Mount and relate what Moses said about murder and adultery, what Jesus said about malice and lust. When a sinner begins to see that inner sin is the same as outward and aggressive sin, a new concern and interest will result.

It is always good to read James 2:10, "Whosoever shall keep the whole law, and yet offend in one point, he is guilty of all."

From there we go to Romans 3:19, 20 where the apostle explains that the Ten Commandments are given to "stop our mouth," and to bring us to "a knowledge of sin."

The Romans Road then comes natural, and we can move from Romans 3:23 to 6:23, then to Romans 5:8 and on to 10:13.

In making a call on one of the back roads near our church, I found that my visit came at a bad time. Supper was almost ready, and the three boys were glued to their favorite TV show. It seemed that they could not care less about salvation; and I knew the sooner I left, the better it would suit everybody.

After offering prayer, I said good-by and left. But the man followed me out the door and down the driveway to my car. I said good-by three or four more times, but he kept following me. Finally he said, "I need to talk to you, Preacher."

He looked back toward the house and up and down the road and then whispered to me, "I broke a commandment."

"You did!"

"I am afraid I did." He was so serious.

"Do you want to tell me about it?"

"I've got to tell somebody," he volunteered.

He told me a messy, wicked story. Sure enough, he had sinned all right.

"I've got bad news for you, Paul," I said.

"That's what I was afraid of."

I quoted James 2:10 and explained that he was now guilty of breaking all the law. "Oh, no!" he exclaimed.

"There is worse news than that," I reminded him.

"There is?" he asked.

"Yes. You must go to Hell now because the wages of sin is death."

"That's terrible!"

"But there is good news, Paul," I quickly reminded him. With that I gave him the Gospel and urged him to trust Christ. He did so and then said, "Come on back in here and tell my wife and three boys about this."

All four of them accepted Christ. Then the whole family came Sunday and were baptized.

Following a plan made it a simple matter indeed.

IV. PARABLE CLOSING

Jesus used parables continually to get across the truth and help His listeners get the message.

So many times I have watched sinners tighten up when I started to draw the net, so I felt something was needed to help get through this crucial step.

Just when we are ready to ask the seeker to pray, I completely change the subject and start telling him about another fellow just like himself that I talked to a few days before. I explain that we were talking about the same thing, and step by step I lead the other man through the decision. I am careful to relate how the other man prayed the sinner's prayer and saw the light. Then I turn immediately and tell my friend that I want to pray for him, too, just like I did for the other fellow.

When he gives me permission to pray, he is actually consenting to do exactly as the other man did.

This parable approach takes the pressure out of the decision and helps the sinner to do what he really wants to do to start with.

V. PRACTICE

Practice makes perfect. Fluency and effectiveness come with experience.

After a soul-winning lesson and quite a number of illustrations, a young woman came to me and said, "Do you win everybody you talk to?"

I had to answer, "No, but I win a lot more than I used to."

I can tie my shoes with my eyes shut. It is as easy as falling off a log, but only because I have been at it for a good while. When a person gets the plan and approach mastered, then it's just a matter of working at it until the timidities and fears are expelled. Then he really enjoys reaching people for Christ.

Some time ago I preached on soul winning near Washington, D.C. Several folks committed themselves to win a soul by the end of the month.

I went back to that general area, but at a different church, about two months later. After the service a man came up to me and asked, "Do you remember me?"

"I am afraid not," I told him.

"I heard you preach two months ago. I stood up and committed myself to win a soul in a month. My friend and I are working together one night each week, and we have won fourteen so far."

The very next lady to speak told me that she was in that same meeting and now had won six girls to the Lord.

The Lord is anxious for us to join in the great task of bringing in the harvest, which is white, plenteous and great.

We might ask, with Cain, "Am I my brother's keeper?" The answer is yes, we are.

Maybe we could join Esther by saying, "How can I endure to see the destruction of my kindred?"

Since forty million people die every year and most are lost, surely we ought to learn to win souls and make it our main business.

Chapter 7

A Thousand Years Extra in the Grave

"But the rest of the dead lived not again until the thousand years were finished. This is the first resurrection. Blessed and holy is he that hath part in the first resurrection: on such the second death hath no power . . . . "—Rev. 20:5,6.

Men have feared the grave since the beginning of death. The thought of dying sends a chill of terror into the soul. And the thought of lying in a coffin, worse yet.

In the misery of his suffering, Job said, "The grave is mine house: I have made my bed in the darkness" (Job 17:13).

Solomon said, "There is no work, nor device, nor knowledge, nor wisdom, in the grave, whither thou goest" (Eccles. 9:10).

But, hallelujah, there is hope! The sting has been removed. The grave has lost its victory. Man will get out of the grave. The glorious truth of the resurrection has taken the sting out of death for millions of souls.

The resurrection will not be the same for everybody. Some have already experienced resurrection; others will soon; but many will have to wait an extra thousand years to get out of their graves.

I want us to examine this Bible subject under four headings: the Resurrections of the Scripture, the Resurrection of the Saviour, the Resurrection of Saints, and the Resurrection of Sinners.

I. THE RESURRECTIONS OF THE SCRIPTURES

On eight different occasions we read of miracle resurrections.

1. Elijah raise the widow's son. This widow had given Elijah her last bit of meal and used the last of her oil to make him a cake. Elijah worked a miracle, and the meal barrel and the oil cruse were never empty again.

But in the midst of rejoicing and victory, the widow's son died. Elijah called out to God, and a physical resurrection took place for the first time in the history of man (I Kings 17:2).

2. Elisha raised the son of the Shunammite woman. This old couple was very gracious and kind to Elisha and his servant, Gehazi. They built a prophet's chamber onto their house. Elisha was so pleased that he prayed to God for them to be blessed with a son.

His prayer was answered. The son became the joy of their lives. One day the son died of a sun stroke, and the woman begged the prophet to pray. Elisha raised the boy from the dead and restored him to his mother (II Kings 4:35).

3. Resurrection by Elisha's bones. The Moabites were invading the land, and a man of Israel died. As they carried the man to his tomb, they saw the Moabites coming. Quickly, they threw the dead man into Elisha's cave. The Bible says that when the dead body fell on the bones of Elisha, life and breath came back into the body (II Kings 13:20).

4. Jairus' daughter raised. Jairus, a man of faith, pleaded with Jesus to come to his home and touch the body of his dead daughter that she might live. Jesus chased off the professional mourners and took the girl by the hand saying, "I say unto thee, arise"; and she did (Matt. 9:25).

5. The widow's son at Nain. At the gate of the city of Nain, Jesus was filled with compassion when He saw the widow in the funeral procession of her son. In obedience to the command of Jesus, the young man arose and began to speak. What excitement must have filled the hearts of the people! What an experience for the mother! The Bible says, "And there came a fear on all: and they glorified God" (Luke 7:16).

6. Lazarus raised at Bethany. After Lazarus died, Jesus came to comfort Mary and Martha saying, "Thy brother shall rise again." Martha answered, "I know that he shall rise again in the resurrection at the last day" (John 11:24).

Jesus went to the grave and called out, "Lazarus, come forth." Jesus asked the disciples then to loose him and let him go. What a wonderful miracle for Mary, Martha, Lazarus and the world!

7. Dorcas raised by Peter. Dorcas was a wonderful woman and a disciple of the Lord. When she died, all her friends came to weep. Peter was notified also about her death. He entered the room where her body was and asked the others to leave. He began to pray and then spoke, saying, "Tabitha, arise." And she sat up very much alive. The news spread quickly over the city of Joppa, and many were saved because of this miracle resurrection (Acts 9:42).

8. Bodies of the saints arose. When Jesus finished His seventh statement on the cross, He gave up the ghost. At that instant the veil was torn from top to bottom in the Temple, and an earthquake broke open the rocks. Many graves opened also, and the bodies of many saints arose and appeared in the city. The leader of the soldiers said, "Truly this was the Son of God" (Matt. 27:54).

Congress once issued a special edition of Thomas Jefferson's Bible. It was simply a copy of our Bible with all references to the supernatural taken out. The resurrections of the Scripture were not included in his Bible. The closing words of his "book" were: "There laid they Jesus, and rolled a great stone to the mouth of the sepulchre."

Thank God, our Bible does not stop at His death! There is another chapter in the story. He arose again!

II. THE RESURRECTION OF THE SAVIOUR

The Moslems say, "We have something you Christians do not have."

"What is that?" asked a Christian of a Moslem.

"We have a body, and you only have an empty tomb."

How right they are, and praise God for it! He is risen!

First, Christ's resurrection is prophesied. Job said, "For I know that my redeemer liveth, and that he shall stand at the latter day upon the earth" (Job 19:25).

David said prophetically, "For thou wilt not leave my soul in hell; neither wilt thou suffer thine Holy One to see corruption" (Ps. 16:10).

Second, Christ's resurrection was proclaimed in the New Testament. He said Himself, "Destroy this temple, and in three days I will raise it up" (John 2:19). He also said, "But after I am risen again, I will go before you into Galilee" (Matt. 26:32). After returning from the Mount of Transfiguration, He charged them not to tell what they had seen "Till the Son of man were risen from the dead" (Mark 9:9).

Third, Christ's resurrection was preached by the apostles. Of the first church at Jerusalem, we read, "And with great power gave the apostles witness of the resurrection of the Lord Jesus: and great grace was upon them all" (Acts 4:33).

Peter preached to Cornelius and his loved ones, "Him God raised up the third day, and shewed him openly" (Acts 10:40).

Paul, preaching at Mars' Hill, spoke of the unknown God whom they worshiped as one that had risen from the dead (Acts 17:31). Some mocked, others were curious, but some believed.

Fourth, Christ's resurrection was proven. In Acts 1:3 we read, "He shewed himself alive . . . by many infallible proofs."

The resurrection is mentioned over one hundred times in the Bible.

In our courts, one witness can establish a murder charge, two witnesses are necessary to prove treason, three witnesses are needed to establish a written will; and seven, for an oral will. Many more than five hundred witnesses were called to verify the personal resurrection of Christ!

He appeared to Mary Magdalene (Mark 16:9); the other women (Matt. 28:9); two disciples (Luke 24:15); eleven disciples (Luke 24:36); Peter (I Cor. 15:5); to the ten with Thomas absent (John 20:19); to the eleven disciples (John 20:26); at the Sea of Galilee (Matt. 28:17); to James (I Cor. 15:7); at the ascension (Luke 24:50); and to Paul at his conversion (Acts 9:5).

During Napoleon's war on England, he came to the battle with Wellington at Waterloo. The battle was heavy and bloody; but eventually the shooting ceased, and the war was over.

There was no telegraph or telephone to send the news home. The only means of communication was signals from metaphor flags. As the ship approached the dock, the signal man waved out the message to the waiting people of the British Isles, W-E-L-L-I-N-G-T-O-N D-E-F-E-A-T-E-D. Just then a cloud of fog hid the signalman. The shocking news spread like fire and the gloom and despair with it.

Later when the fog lifted and the completed signal was read, "W-E-L-L-I-N-G-T-O-N D-E-F-E-A-T-E-D N-A-P-O-L-E-O-N," a cry of victory rang out through the land. The message had been changed from despair to a shout of victory by adding just one word.

The cry went out to the disciples of the Lord, "Jesus is dead and buried." A gloom and despair settled over all His followers. But then came the shout, "He is risen! He is risen!"

> **Rejoice ye Christians, everywhere!**
> **From that dark tomb so sad.**
> **Christ is risen; He's not there!**
> **Rejoice and be ye glad!**

III. THE RESURRECTION OF THE SAINTS

"Marvel not at this: for the hour is coming, in the which all that are in the graves shall hear his voice, And shall come forth; they that have done good, unto the resurrection of life. . . ."—John 5:28,29.

Before Columbus sailed across the Atlantic in 1492, the motto of Spain was: **"Nothing Beyond,"** which motto appeared on the official seal of the country. The meaning of these two words was simply that Spain was the last westward spot on the globe before the vast nothingness. When Columbus later took back gold and living natives from the New World to prove his discovery, the old motto was changed to the new one, **"More Beyond."**

There are still some people who think that the grave ends all, but we have a lively hope in Christ. There is "more beyond." There is life after death and Heaven forever for all believers.

Read what Peter said about this in I Peter 1:3-5:

"Blessed be the God and Father of our Lord Jesus Christ, which according to his abundant mercy hath begotten us again unto a lively hope by the resurrection of Jesus Christ from the dead, To an inheritance incorruptible, and undefiled, and that fadeth not away, reserved in heaven for you, Who are kept by the power of God

through faith unto salvation ready to be revealed in the last time."

Jesus said, "I am the resurrection, and the life: he that believeth in me, though he were dead, yet shall he live" (John 5:25).

John said, "And this is the will of him that sent me, that every one which seeth the Son, and believeth on him, may have everlasting life: and I will raise him up at the last day" (John 6:40).

Paul said, "Knowing that he which raised up the Lord Jesus shall raise up us also by Jesus, and shall present us with you" (II Cor. 4:14).

Now the blessed part of this resurrection is that we shall be given our glorified bodies. This will take place at the time of the rapture. At this time, "the dead in Christ shall rise" (I Thess. 4:16). Those outside of Christ, the unsaved, will remain in the grave and will not come forth for another thousand years.

An army chaplain told of accompanying a regiment of soldiers on an overnight training session. They camped in an open field and bedded down in row after row pattern. That night a light snow fell and turned to freezing rain. Each sleeping soldier snuggled in his sleeping bag formed a white, icy mound on the ground.

The chaplain arose early and, looking out across the sleeping soldiers, remarked that it looked like rows of graves. Just then the bugler blew reveille, and the men came breaking up through the snow and ice. "What a thrilling sight!" exclaimed the chaplain. "It was like witnessing the resurrection."

Someday it will happen just like that for every child of God!

IV. THE RESURRECTION OF THE SINNER

"But the rest of the dead lived not again until the thousand years were finished."—Rev. 20:5.

The people of this second resurrection will appear at the Great White Throne Judgment, a judgment for sinners who have rejected Christ. These people were condemned already even before they died. However, the sentence will not be passed on them until after their resurrection.

The people of this resurrection will be cast into the lake of fire. The beast and false prophet will have already been cast into this same lake of fire (Rev. 19:20). Satan, the old serpent, will also be there in the fire (Rev. 20:10). The second death and eternal Hell are a part of this lake of fire (Rev. 20:14). What a sad, pitiful thing this will be for the poor sinners with no Saviour!

Then, the people of this resurrection will lie in the grave for one thousand years. During the one thousand years, the saints who are already out of the grave will be involved in the wonderful millennium period. Christ will be reigning from Jerusalem from the throne of David. We shall be kings and priests. Those who have been faithful in this life will be ruling over cities with Him and for Him.

To rule and reign with Christ during the thousand years beats lying in the grave during that time. It doesn't make sense to be lost and bound for Hell.

My friend, if you are still not saved, may I urge you to repent today and receive Christ as your Saviour. Let Him get you out of the grave a thousand years early!

Chapter 8

Why Every Christian Should Be Baptized

"Repent, and be baptized every one of you."—Acts 2:38.

The people at Jerusalem listened carefully to Peter's sermon. His subject was the DEATH, BURIAL AND RESURRECTION of Christ. They became deeply troubled and convicted of their sin. Three thousand repented and accepted Christ as their personal Saviour. Almost immediately they began to ask, "What do we do next?" "Be baptized EVERY ONE OF YOU" was the answer they received.

Every new convert should recognize that this straightforward command is intended for them also. It has always been refreshing to meet people who wanted to know what to do next, after they were saved. The Apostle Paul's first words following his dramatic conversion on the Damascus Road were, "Lord, what wilt thou have me to do?"

I remember a man back in Elkton, Maryland, who, I believe, had the right attitude about baptism. Mr. Carl Cain came to our church one Sunday to visit. He had heard about us, and I think he just came to see if all that he had heard was really so. The half had not been told! Mr. Cain came down the aisle looking from side to side at all the people. He had never seen that many people in a church, and I think he was having trouble believing that they were really there.

The service got underway. Mr. Cain sat near the front. As I preached, he glued his eyes on me and listened with great interest. When I asked a question with a negative tone, he shook his head from side to side in agreement. When my message turned to positive truth, he would nod his head up and down in full accord. It was not hard to see just where he stood on every issue.

When I asked the congregation how many realized that they were lost and wanted to get saved, he stretched his hand high into the air and waved it back and forth to make sure I saw it.

He came forward and accepted Christ with much outward expression. When I asked him if he were trusting the Lord Jesus to save him, he said emphatically, "Yes sir, I most certainly am!" I asked him if he wanted to be baptized right there and then to testify of his faith. He quickly answered, "Preacher, that's exactly what I want to do."

In the baptistry he stood erect with his hands folded, just as he had been instructed to do. When I dipped him back into the water and out again, he suddenly splashed up out of the water, clapped his hands and shouted, "Hot dog! Hot dog! Hot dog!" Our people roared with laughter. I quickly quieted them and explained that Mr. Cain undoubtedly had not been around church much. He was just not familiar with words like "Amen!" "Hallelujah!" "Praise the Lord!" "Give him a little time; he'll learn," I assured them.

This man was thrilled with the idea of getting baptized. I really have my doubts about someone who says he is saved but will not get baptized. Like Mr. Cain, a new convert should be thrilled with the thought of baptism. Preachers ought to be like the old preacher who in every service preached about baptism. If he read John 3:16, he would work baptism into it somewhere.

The deacons got together and picked a text they thought would be impossible to get baptism into. One of them requested that he preach on "The axe is laid to the root of the tree." He agreed. He read the text and got into the message. He said, "When the axe was laid to the root of the tree, the chips flew everywhere and the old tree fell. When the tree fell, it fell across the river and dammed up the water, and they had a baptismal service."

Preachers ought to keep baptism on their minds all the time.

Peter's Orders. It would be good for us to notice that Peter did not tell the people to "think it over" or "pray about it." Rather, he commanded them to obey the Lord and be baptized. He did not even ask them to wait until they could learn more about it. In fact, they were baptized right there and then, some 3,000 of them. None had an opportunity to prove faithful. Jesus Himself had been baptized at the first opportunity, "to fulfill all righteousness." Surely every saved person will want to please the Lord by obeying this first command as soon as possible. "Repent, and be baptized EVERY ONE OF YOU."

The People's Obedience. Baptism tests the willingness of the new convert. Baptism is submission and yielding to His divine command. The Lord wants to know if we will do what we are told.

Baptism is likened unto going to school. It is the first grade of the Christian life. It is not good reasoning to think that we can skip on up to junior and senior high school until we have completed the elementary grades. Those "that gladly received his word were baptized" (Acts 2:41). Three thousand were obedient. None wanted to wait or put it off. They had heard Peter's orders, "Be baptized EVERY ONE OF YOU."

The Powerful Outcome. Because of their obedience, a sweet spirit of fellowship grew among them. They began to study the Scriptures, pray together, sell property, and give away their money; and they became steadfast in the doctrine and service. In short, a great revival was on. A gladness and singleness of heart and purpose came upon them. Multitudes were added to the church as friends and neighbors received Christ, too, and were baptized.

There are many wonderful lessons for us in these Bible verses. One of the most important lessons here concerns baptism. In the next few paragraphs, I want to ask five questions and try to answer them about this all-important Bible theme.

I. WHAT DOES BAPTISM MEAN?

The word *baptize* comes to us from the Greek word *baptizo* which means "to immerse," "to submerge," "to dip under." This Greek word was not translated to English because of embarrassment to the Church of England. It was transliterated instead. The word *baptizo* is used 127 times in the New Testament, and not one time does it infer any thought of sprinkling or pouring. The word for *sprinkle* is *rantizo*.

It Is Symbolic. Baptism is a symbol. It pictures the death, burial and resurrection of Christ. The phrases, "Buried with Him in baptism" and "Raised in the likeness of His resurrection," are taken from Romans 6:4. It is really a sermon from the New Covenant to those witnessing the occasion. The sermon says, "I am depending entirely upon the death, burial and resurrection of Christ to get me into Heaven."

In getting this truth across to junior-age children at Beth Haven Baptist Church at Louisville, Kentucky, Brother Gardiner Gentry illustrated baptism by using the index finger on the left hand. By holding the finger straight up, he explained the death of Christ on Calvary. When the finger was laid back flat, he taught the burial of Jesus. When the finger was brought up straight again, he spoke of the resurrection. The boys and girls went home explaining to Mom and Dad all about baptism.

Not Related to Circumcision. Those who hold to covenant theology claim that baptism was a replacement of the Jewish rite of circumcision. For a long time Gentile converts were baptized as well as circumcised. Timothy was such a one. Circumcision was a seal of a covenant, while baptism is a sign of conversion. The baptism of John the Baptist (the dipper), was not the seal of any covenant. It was definitely a sign of conversion. It should be remembered, too, that if baptism was a New Testament carry-over of Old Testament circumcision, there would be no need for baptizing females.

One of the Two Ordinances. Baptism and the Lord's Supper are the only two ordinances given to the local church. They were divinely instituted by Christ. Jesus taught humility by washing feet but did not leave this practice as an ordinance.

II. WHY SHOULD A NEW CONVERT BE BAPTIZED?

The Great Commission was given to us by our Lord. "Go ye therefore, and teach all nations, baptizing them in the name of the Father, and of the Son, and of the Holy Ghost" (Matt. 28:19). This is not a matter of choice; it is a command. We are to teach, direct, urge, and do all we can to get our new converts baptized.

For a number of years at Elkton, Maryland, we baptized 125-130 each year. The strong emphasis was placed on getting professions of faith. Some 600 to 700 were being saved, but only a small percentage were obedient in baptism. Only two or three per week were responding.

It was then that Dr. John R. Rice began to plead with pastors and churches to set goals and baptize two hundred or more in one year's time. After reading the plea, I immediately wrote Dr. Rice and told him to count us in. We set out to get two hundred. We set a goal the next year of three hundred baptisms.

I preached on the subject and asked for thirty people to accept a goal of ten each for the coming twelve months. Thirty-four people responded, and we set out to help our new converts to obey the divine command of Jesus.

By the end of the year, we recorded 404 baptisms. I began to baptize three times each week. I practiced getting into the water and out again as rapidly as possible to conserve time. I can do it now in twenty-two seconds. The next two years the number of baptisms grew again to 513 and 574.

When I became pastor at Louisville, Kentucky, we baptized 522 in ten months. We set out to go well over six hundred for the twelve-month period. The next year we planned to reach and baptize one thousand. God enabled us to reach our goals.

What I'm saying is that the initiative and leadership in this matter is left in our hands, not the new Christian's. It is important that the new convert understand responsibility to submit and obey the command of the Lord.

There are at least three Bible reasons why the new convert should be baptized.

First, it is obedience to His divine command. We need His blessing on our lives. Disobedience will cut us off from all blessings.

Second, it is following the pattern set forth in the Word of God. Immersion pictures the death, burial and resurrection of our Lord and identifies each of us with Him.

Third, it is a factor of unity in the local church. Spiritually, we have all been baptized by the same Spirit into one body. As we identify with Christ and with other Christians in public baptism, we see that we are the same kind as others who do the same.

III. WHO SHOULD BE BAPTIZED?

The answer to this question is very simple: all those who have truly been saved. All believers in the New Testament, as far as we can tell, were baptized except one—the thief on the cross. We cannot imagine any of the three thousand at Pentecost deciding to put it off until later. Can you imagine the eunuch or Cornelius or Paul or Lydia or the Philippian jailor or any of the outstanding New Testament converts taking baptism lightly?

Only Those Who Believe. Baptism is not for the unsaved. Believing or trusting Christ is the basic requirement. No one was baptized until he had intelligently received the plan of salvation offered in the Gospel. There is no case of baptism in the Bible without definite acceptance of Christ.

"He that believeth and is baptized" (Mark 16:16). "They that gladly received his word were baptized" (Acts 2:41). When they believed, they were baptized (Acts 8:13). "Here is water; what doth hinder me to be baptized?" (Acts 8:36). "Whose heart the Lord opened. . . . And when she was baptized" (Acts 16:14,15). "Spake unto him the word of the Lord. . .and was baptized" (Acts 16:32,33). And many of the Corinthians, hearing, believed and were baptized (Acts 19:5). "Teach all nations, baptizing them" (Matt. 28:19). "Repent, and be baptized EVERY ONE OF YOU" (Acts 2:38).

No Infants. Infant baptism is unscriptural. We have no record in the Bible of babies being baptized. Babies are not believers. They have not repented, and they have not received Christ.

I saw a gospel tract recently with the caption on the front page, "What the Bible Says About Infant Baptism." I opened the tract and found two blank pages. The message of those blank pages was driven home effectively. There are no verses in the Bible about infant baptism.

IV. HOW SHOULD WE BE BAPTIZED?

The question of immersion, sprinkling or pouring is one of long standing. The mode of baptism has been a factor of division among church leaders since 250 A.D. when several sick people requested that water be poured over them to relate as closely as possible the act of baptism. This practice was called affusion. Sprinkling came in the thirteenth century officially but had been practiced and tolerated for some time before. John Calvin prescribed sprinkling to the church of Geneva. Then the churches of England and Scotland followed in the practice.

Baptizo and **Rantizo.** The Greek words for *immerse* and *sprinkle* are different. *Baptizo* means to immerse; *rantizo* means to sprinkle. There is little question in the minds of Bible scholars that immersion was the practice of the early church.

John Calvin: "The very word *baptizo* means 'to immerse.' It is certain that immersion was the practice of the early church."

Martin Luther: "*Baptism* is a Greek word and may be translated *immersion*. I would have those who are to be baptized, wholly dipped in the water."

John Wesley: " 'Buried with Him in baptism'—alluding to the ancient method of immersion."

Buried With Him. The phrase "buried in baptism" ought to settle the matter of how it should be done. Sprinkling or pouring dirt on a dead body will not satisfy any of us. When Jesus was baptized, it is said that "he . . . went up straightway OUT OF THE WATER" (Matt. 3:16). Also, John baptized at Aenon, near to Salim, because *"there was much water there"* (John 3:23). Again, let us note that Philip commanded the chariot to stand still while he and the eunuch *"went down both into the water"* (Acts 8:38). "And when they were come up *out of the water*. . . . " (Acts 8:39).

Any form of baptism other than immersion violates the symbol of death, burial and resurrection; goes contrary to the church fathers' example; violates the command of Christ to baptize in the name of the Father, Son and Holy Spirit; takes lightly New Testament teaching; and takes away the true meaning of the word *baptize*.

V. WHEN SHOULD A NEW CONVERT BE BAPTIZED?

According to the Bible, a person should be baptized as soon as he gets saved. The Scriptures do not indicate that anyone waited to prove himself faithful before baptism. The eunuch was baptized on the spot (Acts 8). Cornelius was commanded to get baptized immediately (Acts 10). The Philippian jailor was baptized during the night (Acts 16). Paul did not want to even wait for daybreak.

Age requirements are not factors. If a young boy or girl knows that he or she is really saved, that one can and should proceed to the baptismal waters.

One little fellow off a bus route had been saved at our church and instructed to go forward and tell the preacher. However, somebody forgot to tell him to wait for the invitation. So just before the morning service, he came up to the platform and hollered, "Hey, Mister, I want to get advertised!" He had the right idea, only the wrong word.

Baptism After Salvation. Thousands go forward in churches and are dipped in the water without really getting saved. Later they come to true conversion and are then faced with the decision, *Should I get baptized again?* The answer is "NO," don't get baptized again—just get baptized. The first time it was not baptism; you were just ducked in the water without any meaning.

Years ago I felt that I ought to "join the church." My wife, who was my girlfriend then, took me to see her preacher, who was a modernist. He told me how to come forward on Palm Sunday, how to stand in the water, etc., but he never told me how to be saved.

I went through the motions and felt everything was in order. A year or so later I accepted Christ and was really saved. Mrs. Wallace and I transferred our membership to a fundamental church and were received by letter. I never thought any more about it until we moved to Chattanooga, Tennessee, and joined the Highland Park Baptist Church.

I began to win souls every week. I would bring my converts to church and walk the aisle with them. I would urge every one of them to be baptized.

One particular day I brought four boys forward and filled out the decision slip. Dr. Lee Roberson recognized the decisions and asked the boys if they wanted to be baptized. As he talked with them, a strong conviction set in upon me. I was convicted about the fact that I had not been baptized since I was really saved. I filled out a decision slip for myself and went back to be baptized along with the four boys. Many times before I had been troubled about that matter, but never since. *Baptism* is a beautiful word to me now. I am glad that is settled.

Falling Away in Disobedience. When folks do not follow Christ in the command to be baptized, they become disobedient and fall away from a happy, useful life. They will be put on a shelf and live a life of uselessness.

Years ago I won a man to Christ in Elkton, Maryland. He began to attend all the services and even started tithing his income, but he would not be baptized. Every time I talked to him, he would argue that he had been baptized already. I told him my story and reasoned that since he was not saved at the time, it didn't count. He grew angry and dropped away and wouldn't come to church.

Every time I saw him, I would urge him to settle it with the Lord. He insisted he was saved. Finally he started attending some of the services just before I left Elkton. And finally he submitted the last day of my ministry there and was the last man I baptized there. It was a wonderful victory, but I couldn't help thinking about twelve wasted years.

Thousands are living useless lives because they have not settled this. Reader, may I urge you to check your life and see that you are right with God in the matter of baptism.

"Repent, and be baptized EVERY ONE OF YOU"!!

Chapter 9

What the Bible Says About Salvation

"For by grace are ye saved through faith; and that not of yourselves: it is the gift of God: Not of works, lest any man should boast."—Eph. 2:8,9.

These two verses were my first introduction to God's message. I'll always remember the little converted Catholic woman, Mrs. Josephine Cerrato, an Italian, who asked us to memorize these two verses. I was seventeen at the time. I did memorize them, and the message of salvation began to dawn on me. When the Gospel was presented to me later, I readily accepted it.

Years before, while attending a boys' Sunday school class in West Virginia, my uncle, Edward Wallace, the teacher, suggested that we might all quote a verse from the Bible. I had remembered someone saying that the shortest verse in the Bible was, "Jesus wept." While I was nervously waiting my turn, my first cousin, next to me, gave my verse, "Jesus wept." I was really in trouble. My embarrassment was showing. I felt like a bank robber who had just been caught in the act. Suddenly I blurted out, "And so He did." My uncle, realizing my predicament, quickly passed on to the next boy and let me get by.

What a genuine blessing it was to see that the initiative for salvation was on God's part and that my part was to believe and receive God's gift. When the Bible speaks of salvation, it is talking about conversion, the new birth, regeneration, justification and sanctification. It is speaking of going to Heaven and staying out of Hell.

The Bible term *salvation* is not related to homemade phrases and ideas such as "joining the church," "living right," "doing the best I can," "keeping the Ten Commandments," "living by the Golden Rule," or "being baptized." These things have nothing to do with salvation!

Several years ago I asked a young fellow, "Have you been saved?"

"Oh yes, I've been saved," he said. I was sure he had not, but I asked him to tell me about it. He told of a time that a big bully was ready to beat him and another young fellow saved him from the fellow. It was easy to see that he did not understand what I was talking about.

I read somewhere recently that there are at least five people involved in our salvation.

First, salvation is conceived in the mind of God. *"But when the fulness of the time was come, God sent forth his Son, made of a woman, made under the law, To redeem them that were under the law, that we might receive the adoption of sons."*—Gal. 4:4,5.

Second, salvation was completed by Christ. *"But made himself of no reputation, and took upon him the form of a servant, and was made in the likeness of men: And being found in fashion as a man, he humbled himself, and became obedient unto death, even the death of the cross."*—Phil. 2:7,8.

Third, salvation is continued by the Spirit. *"And when he is come, he will reprove the world of sin, and of righteousness, and of judgment: Of sin, because they believe not on me; Of righteousness, because I go to my Father, and ye see me no more; Of judgment, because the prince of this world is judged."*—John 16:8-11.

Fourth, salvation is contested by Satan. In the parable of the sower Jesus said: *"When one heareth the word of the kingdom, and understandeth it not, then cometh the wicked one, and catcheth away that which was sown in his heart."*—Matt. 13:19.

Finally, salvation is confessed by the believer. *"That if thou shalt confess with thy mouth the Lord Jesus, and shalt believe in thine heart that God hath raised him from the dead, thou shalt be saved."*—Rom. 10:9.

Now let us notice seven things the Bible teaches about salvation.

I. SALVATION IS SIMPLE

Getting into Heaven is easy. It's just like walking through a door. Jesus said, "I am the door: by me if any man enter in, he shall be saved" (John 10:9). Even a child can learn to open the door. God meant for it to be simple.

Several times I've seen gospel tracts speaking of the "ABC of Salvation." They teach the basic facts: All have sinned; Believe on the Lord Jesus Christ, and thou shalt be saved; Confess with thy mouth the Lord Jesus.

The Apostle Paul spoke of the simplicity of salvation when he said, "But I fear, lest by any means, as the serpent beguiled Eve through his subtilty, so your minds should be corrupted from the simplicity that is in Christ" (II Cor. 11:3).

Dr. Ford Porter years ago wrote the famous little tract, *God's Simple Plan of Salvation.* He ordered two thousand by faith and began to give them out. He began to pray that God would bless the tract to the salvation of many souls. The supply was soon exhausted. Another order was placed. Now millions and millions have gone out in more than sixty languages and in Braille. The testimonies of scores of conversions are recorded in Dr. Porter's files. The simplicity of the tract is surely one of the factors of its greatness.

Dr. Thomas Altizer, the Episcopalian clergyman teaching at Emory University in Atlanta, came to the University of Delaware for a lecture on the "God Is Dead" theory. I went to hear what he had to say. As far as I could tell, his goal was to impress people with intellectualism. He used a great number of high-sounding phrases and quite a few $100 words.

When he had completed his discourse, I was disgusted. I went to the front and gave him a copy of Dr. Porter's tract, *God's Simple Plan of Salvation.* He needed the simplicity of the Gospel.

I heard a radio preacher telling the old, old story again recently. He explained that if someone placed a $5.00 bill in a book and gave it to you, the $5.00 would be yours when you received the book. Christ is the Book, and the $5.00 represents salvation. You get salvation by receiving Christ.

II. SALVATION IS BY TRUSTING, NOT BY DOING

There are only two great religious groups in the world today. One crowd is trying to get to Heaven by works. They are joining, giving, offering prayers and a thousand other things; but they will never get to Heaven doing these things. The other crowd is trusting. This is faith. We are to commit the whole matter into His hands and depend on Him to handle it for us.

The Bible is very clear in its teaching of these matters. Our text says, "For by grace are ye saved through faith; and that not of yourselves: it is the gift of God: Not of works, lest any man should boast" (Eph. 2:8,9). Also, "Not by works of righteousness which we have done, but according to his mercy he saved us, by the washing of regeneration, and renewing of the Holy Ghost" (Titus 3:5).

III. SALVATION IS THROUGH CHRIST, NOT A CHURCH

One preacher recently said that the Roman Catholic folks claim to have the keys that were given to Peter. "Well, let them have the keys," he said. "I have the Door!"

Jesus said, "I am the way, the truth, and the life: no man cometh unto the Father, but by me" (John 14:6).

Peter said, "Neither is there salvation in any other: for there is none other name under heaven given among men, whereby we must be saved" (Acts 4:12).

Paul preached this same truth: "For there is one God, and one mediator between God and men, the man Christ Jesus" (I Tim. 2:5). This is a matter of *trans*formation by a Person, not reformation by a church.

IV. SALVATION IS ETERNAL, NOT TEMPORARY

What a blessed joy to be eternally saved! We are sealed by the Holy Spirit until the day of redemption (Eph. 4:30). As long as Jesus lives, we are safe. He is personally caring for the matter of our salvation. Jesus said, "My sheep hear my voice, and I know them, and they follow me: And I give unto them eternal life; and they shall never perish, neither shall any man pluck them out of my hand" (John

10:27,28). Even John 3:16 emphasizes that our salvation is "everlasting"!

Peter speaks of Christians as those "Who are kept by the power of God" (I Pet. 1:5). A threefold deliverance is explained in II Corinthians 1:10: we *have been* delivered, *are being* delivered, and *will be* delivered. Here we see the past, present and future deliverance of the Christian. We are delivered from the penalty of sin, the power of sin and the presence of sin.

One man told me that coming to an understanding of eternal security was like getting saved all over again. Paul, the great Bible preacher, declared, "I. . .am persuaded that he is able to keep that which I have committed unto him against that day" (II Tim. 1:12). Paul knew that Christ would keep him safe.

V. SALVATION BRINGS A CHANGE

"Therefore if any man be in Christ, he is a new creature: old things are passed away; behold, all things are become new" (II Cor. 5:17). Old drunks become deacon material. Harlots are made pure. There is a change when Christ comes into the picture.

Some time ago while visiting in one church, several had gathered around to shake hands after the service. I noticed a little girl looking at me with big eyes. She took hold of my hand, pulled me down to her level and kissed me on the cheek. Just then I noticed her mother and father smiling. They came immediately and shook my hand with great feeling and emotion. Just a few short years before, they were in desperate trouble. I went to see them. He was a heavy drinker, and she was going through a nervous breakdown. Both received Christ. Now everything is different. The girl was just expressing her gratitude for what I had done for her mom and dad. She liked the change she had seen.

I've heard people say that even the grass looks greener and the sky becomes a prettier blue. I don't know about this, but I do know that the change is real.

One man in my church said, "Even the cat knows there is a difference. I used to come home drunk and kick the cat off the porch.

Since I received Christ, I now stop and pet the cat."

I believe all the cats, the dog, the kids, the wife, the boss, the neighbors, even the preacher, ought to be able to see the difference.

VI. SALVATION IS A MIRACLE

Salvation is likened to being raised from death unto life. "And you hath he quickened [made alive], who were dead in trespasses and sins" (Eph. 2:1). It is likened unto a blind man receiving sight. John Newton wrote:

> **Amazing grace! how sweet the sound,**
> **That saved a wretch like me!**
> **I once was lost, but now am found,**
> **Was BLIND, BUT NOW I SEE.**

Every miracle that Jesus worked during His earthly ministry was to teach a lesson in salvation. Every time one receives Christ, a miracle is worked. Every time I look out over the congregation, I see many miracles.

VII. SALVATION IS A **NOW** MATTER

People are lost NOW. People need to be saved NOW. To put it off and delay is wrong. Paul sent word to Corinth saying, "Behold, now is the accepted time; behold, now is the day of salvation" (II Cor. 6:2).

An old legend tells of the time when Satan had a sale. He put a price tag on all his tools. The sin of pride had a large price, and so did the sins of jealousy, gossip and selfishness. Over in the corner of the workbench was one tool with the highest price of all—"procrastination." When Satan was asked why the highest price was placed on procrastination, he replied, "It is my most effective and valuable tool."

When the demons suggest that we should not be saved, we will revolt and let them know that we do not plan to go to Hell; but when they suggest that there is no need to be in a hurry, we are tempted to heed.

Chapter 10

What Is Your Life?

(Sermon preached at baccalaureate service, Tennessee Temple Schools, May 28, 1972)

Eighteen years ago I sat where you sit. Had I known when I sat where you sit that I would stand where I stand, it would have scared me to death! Someone who sits here tonight where you sit will stand someday where I stand. I am glad that you do not know who it is. If we knew the future, we would not be able to enjoy the present. I am glad that God only gives us one page of life at a time.

In a graduation speech this past week someone said, "Let us pay our sons the debt that we owe our father." Tonight let me rephrase that remark and say, "Let us go forth to pay some new convert the debt we owe Dr. Lee Roberson." Or, "Let us go out to pay some church, school or mission project the debt we owe Tennessee Temple Schools."

Let us read now from James 4:14:

"Whereas ye know not what shall be on the morrow. For what is your life? It is even a vapour, that appeareth for a little time, and then vanisheth away."

Here we have the question both asked and answered. Notice the question asked—"What is your life?" and the answer—"It is a vapour that appeareth for a little time."

The question is not, "What *was* your life?"—we know all about that; for Ephesians 2:2,3 teaches us:

"Wherein in time past ye walked according to the course of this world, according to the prince of the power of the air, the spirit that

now worketh in the children of disobedience: Among whom also we all had our conversation in times past in the lusts of our flesh, fulfilling the desires of the flesh and of the mind; and were by nature the children of wrath, even as others."

Some of you may have been drunkards, but we do not care about that. Some of you may have been on drugs, but that is all in the past. Some of you may have been immoral and unclean, but that is under the blood. We are not asking, "What *was* your life?"

Neither are we asking, "What will your life be?" We know the answer to that question also. We read,

"Beloved, now are we the sons of God, and it doth not yet appear what we shall be: but we know that, when he shall appear, we shall be like him; for we shall see him as he is."—I John 3:2.

Now we know how things are going to turn out, for we have read the last chapter of the Book.

The question now before us is, "What is your life?" If you are in the place you ought to be tonight, then it doesn't matter what you were; and if you are where you ought to be, things will turn out like they should. Your life tonight is the foundation on which you will build your future. The words of the Apostle Paul are very fitting: "Let every man take heed how he buildeth thereupon" (I Cor. 3:10).

This is the day of uncertainty. More and more people are coming apart at the seams. Suicide has become the highest killer among teens and college-age young people. If any group of people in the world have the answers to the problems, it is this group sitting before us tonight.

One old country man said the problem with the world is that people are taking too many of them old "transquillers"!

Dr. Jack Hyles says that this is the day of nervous breakdown. "Every woman I know has either had a nervous breakdown or is going through one right now or is planning one real soon."

Someone has said that if you wanted to know what a nervous breakdown felt like, think of a frog sitting on a Los Angeles Freeway with his "hopper" broke!

I heard the other day of a clock that had a nervous breakdown. It went to a clock psychiatrist. When the psychiatrist asked it to tell him about its troubles, he got this answer: "Well Doc, I got to thinking the other day about how I would have to tick 60 times a minute, 3,600 times an hour, 86,400 times a day, 604,800 times a week, 2,592,000 times a month, 31,104,000 times a year, and the Lord only knows how many years, and I got so nervous that I sprung a spring and quit."

The doctor asked the clock, "How many ticks do you tick at one time?"

"Just one," said the clock.

"Well, I suggest that you just take it one tick at a time and do not think about the future."

The clock went out of the office to apply the suggestion, and he has been ticking away happily ever since.

In answer to the question of our text, the dictionary says, "Life is that space of time that passes between birth and death." Another definition is given: "Life is a way of living."

Mr. Robert Wadlow of Alton, Illinois, was billed as America's tallest man. He grew to 8 foot 8 inches tall. He weighed 439 pounds on his 21st birthday. His shoes were size 37AA and 18 1/2 inches long. From his wrist to his fingertips was 12 3/4 inches. This was his life. Everything he did was wrapped up in that great height and size.

Mr. Max Palmer of Oklahoma City is currently America's tallest man. He is 8 foot 1 inch tall. Max is a fine Christian who goes about giving his testimony for Christ. But everything he does is wrapped up in his size. This is his life.

Pauline Munsters, the Dutch midget of years gone by, was 22 inches high. She weighed between 7 and 9 pounds. She died at age 19. This was her life.

Robert Earl Hughes was known as the heaviest man in the world. He was born in the state of Illinois in 1926. He weighed 11 1/4 pounds at birth. At the age of 6 he weighed 203 pounds; at age 10, 378 pounds; at 18, he was up to 693 pounds; then at age 27 he had gained to 1,069 pounds. He died at the age of 32 and had to be buried in a piano case and lowered to his grave with a crane. This was his life.

Chang and Eng Bunker were Siamese twins. At the time of their birth in Siam, they were joined at their breasts. Chang and Eng married sisters; and in spite of their unusual situation, Chang had 10 children by his wife and Eng had 12. Their whole life was wrapped up in this strange twist of nature.

Many people have lived strange lives. They have given themselves entirely to some program or project.

Now we have before us your life and the question of what shall be done with it. In the message tonight I would like to point out three lives that should be avoided by every one of you graduates.

I. A LIFE OF THINGS

In the famous Sermon on the Mount, Jesus spoke to His disciples saying:

"Therefore take no thought, saying, What shall we eat? or, What shall we drink? or, Wherewithal shall we be clothed? (For after all these THINGS do the Gentiles seek:) for your heavenly Father knoweth that ye have need of all these THINGS. But seek ye first the kingdom of God, and his righteousness; and all these THINGS shall be added unto you. Take therefore no thought for the morrow: for the morrow shall take thought for the THINGS of itself. Sufficient unto the day is the evil thereof."—Matt. 6:31-34.

Jesus is warning people here about living for THINGS. In Luke 12:15 He again says, "A man's life consisteth not in the abundance of the THINGS which he possesseth." Earlier Jesus had warned that men could not serve both God and mammon. He indicated that all of us would have to make a choice between spiritual and eternal values in contrast to possessions, money and worldly goods.

William Jennings Bryan said, "Those who live for money spend half of their lives getting it and the other half keeping others from getting it, and they don't enjoy it either."

Someone asked Mr. Rockefeller, "How much does it take to satisfy a man?"

His answer: "Just a little more."

The Apostle Paul, who had forsaken all to follow Christ, said, "Having nothing, yet possessing all things." The word *nothing* is really two words—*no thing*. In spite of the fact that Paul had no possessions, he claimed to possess all things.

The story is told of a man crossing a desert. He disappeared and was never heard of again. Several years later someone found his bones, and beside the skeleton were several bags of money and jewels, but no drinking water. He had been so wrapped up in THINGS that he forgot one of life's most essential needs, water.

Men spend their health getting wealth, then spend their wealth trying to get back their health. Hundreds of people are wrapped up in this silly rat-race and have never learned to live. Jesus warned the unsaved world, "What shall it profit a man, if he shall gain the whole world, and lose his own soul?" (Mark 8:36). During His short ministry, He continually taught, "He that will save his life shall lose it, and whosoever will lose his life will find it."

A rich man died, and some of his friends asked, "How much did he leave?" A wise friend standing nearby said, "All of it."

Recently I heard a story that illustrates this truth. A man had been overseas and found a large diamond for sale the size of a hen egg. He sold all of his possessions and borrowed to the limit and bought the huge diamond. His whole life was wrapped up in its value.

Walking on the deck of the ship on his return voyage and trying to impress his friends, he got to tossing the diamond into the air and catching it as it came down. But once he tossed it high into the air, and a huge wave caused the ship to lurch. The diamond fell just outside the rail and into the ocean and was gone forever.

Thousands are doing the same thing, throwing their life away for THINGS.

II. A LIFE OF THRILLS

The Apostle Paul warned, "She that liveth in pleasure is dead while she liveth" (I Tim. 5:6). Kids are popping dope and sniffing glue, trying to find a new thrill. Young people are trying to find it in sporty automobiles. Sex and revolution have become exciting. Most are completely ignoring God's solemn word, "Whatsoever a man soweth, that shall he also reap."

The Bible tells of Demas who forsook Paul and went after the world. It says of him, "Demas hath forsaken me, having loved this present world" (II Tim. 4:10). Pleasure is a by-product. It is not intended to be the main business of life.

It is said of Moses that he chose "rather to suffer affliction with the people of God, than to enjoy the pleasures of sin for a season" (Heb. 11:25).

Back in Elkton, Maryland, on a Sunday night while we were having a great church service, a car pulled out of a drive-in movie. A young naval officer and his family were making their way home from the movie when suddenly a big car, speeding down the highway at over 100 miles an hour, smashed into the side of their car.

When everything had settled down, there were five dead, one crippled for life and two orphans. I still remember a can of beer sitting in a pool of blood. In the trunk of the young officer's car were some fishing equipment, a tennis racket, a bat, a baseball glove and several other pieces of sports equipment. Wild music was coming out of the radio of the speeding car.

I saw a vivid contrast in the whole thing. While we were in church, they were out living in pleasure. The world wants a life of thrills.

The old black woman bawled out her husband who was getting off the merry-go-round; and she was right when she said to him, "Now look at you! You spent your money and you got off where you got on, and you ain't even been nowhere."

The world is going round and round looking into every new thing, trying to find a thrill. Real thrills are found in Jesus Christ. David put it this way: "At thy right hand there are pleasures for evermore" (Ps. 16:11).

III. A LIFE OF THEORY

The Bible teaches us to "avoid foolish questions, and genealogies, and contentions, and strivings about the law; for they are unprofitable and vain" (Titus 3:9). In this day of intellectualism and deep philosophy, men are chasing after every new theory. They have been busy chasing every theory of evolution. Now we are trying to figure out the origin of the moon. The "under thirty" generation has been trying out all the "occult" and oriental religions.

Someone has said, "Men hunt through libraries for truth and study in microscopes and test tubes for answers, while the janitor sweeping the steps has long found it in Jesus Christ."

One seminary class was said to have spent one whole semester discussing the color of the virgin's eyes. Another favorite topic of some of these folk is the sex of angels or how many angels can stand on the head of a pin.

All false theories have a little truth imbedded somewhere to make them logical or sound reasonable, but it certainly does not make it justifiable to spend one's life chasing these rabbit trails and side roads that lead to nowhere.

Even a broken clock is right twice a day, and rat poison is 98% corn meal.

Herbert W. Armstrong says some good things, but that doesn't make him right. The same could be said for Ellen G. White, Mary Baker Eddy, Charles Taze Russell and many others.

A man's search for truth ends when he opens the Bible. God's advice to Joshua is very appropriate.

"This book of the law shall not depart out of thy mouth; but thou shalt meditate therein day and night, that thou mayest observe to do according to all that is written therein: for then thou shalt make thy way prosperous, and then thou shalt have good success."—Josh. 1:8.

Paul the Apostle warned,

"The natural man receiveth not the things of the Spirit of God: for they are foolishness unto him: neither can he know them, because they are spiritually discerned."—I Cor. 2:14.

In the old story of Ali Baba and the Forty Thieves, they cried, "Open sesame," and the door opened where their treasure was.

When a man opens his Bible, suddenly he finds the treasure of God.

Paul found this treasure; and if you should ask him the question of our text, "What Is Your Life?" he would answer, "For to me to live is Christ."

A famous old preacher of the past said, "If I live, Christ is with me; if I die, I am with Christ."

We must also remember the Bible answer to our question, "What Is Your Life?" "It is even a vapour." Now a vapor is a breath on a cold morning. It disappears as quickly as it appears. Life is like one grain of sand compared to the rest of the seashore and the desert. It is like one snowflake compared to the mountains of snow that have fallen. It is like one raindrop compared to the oceans of the world. It is like one blade of grass compared to all the grass of all the pasture fields, battlefields and the golf courses of the world. It is one tick of a clock compared to all of time and eternity.

As you young people turn the page and enter into a new chapter of your life, I beseech you to consider the teachings of Jesus, "Except a corn of wheat fall into the ground and die, it abideth alone: but if it die, it bringeth forth much fruit" (John 12:24).

If we go after things, thrills and theories, we will lose our life; but if we give our life to God and plant it in the good ground of His work, He will reproduce it and cause it to bring forth much fruit. Every one of you will either depart to get or depart to give. God will take all you give and multiply it for His glory and your good.

Only one life, 'twill soon be past,
Only what's done for Christ will last.

Chapter 11

Peace

"The fruit of the Spirit is. . .peace."—Gal. 5:22.

Longfellow said:

> **And in despair I bowed my head:**
> **There is no peace on earth, I said,**
> **For hate is strong and mocks the song**
> **Of peace on earth, good will to men.**

There is no *world* peace. Conflicts continue in all the places where communism and capitalism clash.

There is no *national* peace: political issues and pressures continually fill our news headlines. Assassinating Presidents, kidnaping ambassadors, news men, and others, continue.

There is no *community* peace: thousands upon thousands of murders, assaults, rapes and robberies continue to call attention to this fact.

There is no *home* peace: half of the marriages still end in the divorce court.

With millions there is no *personal* peace: over 27,000 suicides each year attest to this fact.

Some people in our world hold to strange kinds of peace. They speak of peace maintained by submachine guns, such as the Berlin Wall situation. East Berlin is at peace, but all of the machine guns make us glad that we do not have the same.

Some talk of the peace of death. Hitler exterminated millions of Jews in gas chambers in Germany. Once we get rid of these troublesome people, we will have peace, he contended.

Then there are those who speak of the peace of Tibet. The communists overran the little country of Tibet, and no one dares speak. They are quiet, and the communists say they are at peace; but they would be glad to do away with it tomorrow.

Some talk of the peace of tranquilizers. They drink cocktails, hard liquor, and shoot heroin and other drugs into their veins. They float around in their own world unattached to reality, saying this is peace.

Then there is the peace of the mental hospital. Some are given lobotomy operations, making them imbeciles. They walk around with a silly grin on their faces and a faraway look in their eyes, doing exactly as they are told. But who is interested in that kind of peace?

John D. Rockefeller gave $8 1/2 million to build the U.N. building. There is less peace today than there was when he gave the money.

I. NO PEACE TO THE WICKED

"There is no peace, saith the Lord, unto the wicked" (Isa. 48:22). "The way of peace they know not; and there is no judgment in their goings: they have made them crooked paths: whosoever goeth therein shall not know peace" (Isa. 59:8). Ezekiel said, "Destruction cometh; and they shall seek peace, and there shall be none" (7:25).

An unknown writer has said, "Men seek peace by self-exploitation, drunkenness, sexual excess, drugs and all the rest. Tragically, they, like the Persian poet Omar Khayyam, come out the same door they go in."

In an art gallery two beautiful pictures were hanging side by side. The first was a picture of a terrible storm at sea. The wind and storm clouds were blowing the water into great swells and waves. The waves were crashing over a big rock. The caption over the picture was STORM. The other picture was identical, with the wind, the black clouds, the waves and the rock. But in the cleft of the rock was a little twig and sitting on the twig was a beautiful little dove. The caption over this picture was PEACE.

There is no promise of the stilling of the storm and the easing of trouble and pressure in this life. But there is peace in the storm. This is what Charles Haddon Spurgeon spoke of when he preached his famous sermon, "Songs in the Night."

II. NO PEACE TO THE WORLDLY

"For to be carnally minded is death; but to be spiritually minded is life and peace" (Rom. 8:6). The psalmist said, "Depart from evil, and do good; seek peace, and pursue it" (Ps. 34:14). A Chinese proverb says,

> If there is righteousness in the heart, there will be beauty of character; if there is beauty of character, there will be harmony in the home; if there is harmony in the home, there will be order in the nation; if there is order in the nation, there will be peace in the world.

A man bought a large farm and then went out to take possession. His neighbor wandered over to meet him and said, "Neighbor, you have bought yourself a lawsuit. That fence is ten feet on my side of the property line." The new owner surprised the neighbor by saying, "Sir, let me give you that ten feet and let us have peace."

Surely this attitude is the solution to many of the problems of the world.

III. PEACE WITH GOD

Job said, "Acquaint now thyself with him, and be at peace" (22:21). The Apostle Paul, writing to the Ephesian Christians said, "He is our peace" (Eph. 2:14). Peace with God will keep you out of Hell. Peace of God will keep you out of the mental hospital. Romans 15:33 says, "Now the God of peace be with you all." And again in I Thessalonians 5:23, "And the very God of peace sanctify you wholly." Speaking to the Roman church, Paul said, "Therefore being justified by faith, we have peace with God through our Lord Jesus Christ" (Rom. 5:1).

Dr. B. R. Lakin, the famous old orator and preacher, said, "When we make a personal acquaintance with God, life takes on meaning and purpose." Boredom no longer exists, and the restless Spirit learns to know the meaning of inward peace. In short, one does not really live until one develops a speaking acquaintance with a living, loving, benevolent God.

Isaiah said, "Thou wilt keep him in perfect peace, whose mind is stayed on thee: because he trusteth in thee" (Isa. 26:3).

Laura T. Halsey penned:

> There is a place of peace and rest,
> A place of perfect quietness,
> Within a world of fear and dread,
> Where human blood is being shed.
> There is a peace in God.
>
> Our trials are many in this world,
> And Satan's darts are being hurled
> Against the children of the Lord,
> But His angels stand on guard.
> There is a peace in God.
>
> Through trials we learn to overcome,
> Through Christ our victories are won;
> Come lay your burdens at His feet
> And find this inner peace so sweet.
> There is a peace in God.
>
> Be strong, courageous, unafraid.
> Trust in God, and be not dismayed.
> He has promised never to forsake,
> To guide and guard each step we take.
> There is a peace in God.
>
> Oh, blessed peace; oh, perfect rest,
> With which the child of God is blessed.
> Men's hearts are failing them for fear
> That our redemption draweth near.
> There is a peace in God.

IV. PEACE IN JESUS

Melchizedek, called the "king of peace," was a picture of Jesus Christ. Abraham paid tithes and tribute to this great king. Isaiah the prophet, hundreds of years before Jesus was born, said, "For unto us a child is born, unto us a son is given: and the government shall be upon his shoulder: and his name shall be called Wonderful, Counsellor, The mighty God, The everlasting Father, The Prince of Peace" (Isa. 9:6).

While Jesus was sleeping in the boat, a storm came over the Sea of Galilee. The frightened disciples came crying, "Master, we perish." Jesus rose and said to the sea, "Peace, be still." The winds and the sea obeyed His voice.

In John 16:33 Jesus was ready to ascend into Heaven, and He said unto His disciples before leaving, "These things I have spoken unto you, that in me ye might have peace. In the world ye shall have tribulation: but be of good cheer; I have overcome the world."

Paul said, "For he is our peace, who hath . . . broken down the middle wall of partition" (Eph. 2:14).

Philippians 4:6 admonishes, "Be careful for nothing; but in every thing by prayer and supplication with thanksgiving let your requests be made known unto God. And the peace of God, which passeth all understanding, shall keep your hearts and minds through Christ Jesus."

V. PEACE AND THE BIBLE

David said, "Great peace have they which love thy law: and nothing shall offend them" (Ps. 119:165). Isaiah added to that, "O that thou hadst hearkened to my commandments! then had thy peace been as a river, and thy righteousness as the waves of the sea" (Isa. 48:18).

Forty of the books of the Bible speak of peace, and practically all New Testament books begin or end with the quotation, "Grace be unto you, AND PEACE."

Dr. Smiley Blanton, Director of the American Foundation of Religion and Psychiatry, was once asked if he read the Bible. He replied, "I not only read it; I study it. It is the greatest textbook on human behavior ever put together. If people would only absorb its message, a lot of us psychiatrists could close our office and go fishing. How foolish it is not to make use of the distilled wisdom of three thousand years!"

VI. PEACE AND YOU

Jesus spoke to His disciples in His closing few moments with them and said, "Peace I leave with you" (John 14:27). Paul exhorts us, "Let us therefore follow after the things which make for peace, and things wherewith one may edify another" (Rom. 14:19).

It has been said that peace is a sprout taken from the tree of life and planted by the Holy Spirit in the soil.

Henry Wadsworth Longfellow wrote this second verse to that song mentioned in the earlier part of this message:

> **Then pealed the bells more loud and sweet,**
> **God is not dead nor doth He sleep.**
> **The wrong shall fail, the right prevail**
> **With peace on earth, good will to men.**

Mr. Phillip Bilhorn wrote 2,000 sacred songs. The best known of all told the beautiful story of our text:

> **There comes to my heart one sweet strain,**
> **A glad and a joyous refrain;**
> **I sing it again and again,**
> **Sweet peace, the gift of God's love.**
>
> **Through Christ on the cross peace was made,**
> **My debt by His death was all paid;**
> **No other foundation is laid**
> **For peace, the gift of God's love.**
>
> **When Jesus as Lord I had crowned,**
> **My heart with this peace did abound;**
> **In Him the rich blessing I found,**
> **Sweet peace, the gift of God's love.**
>
> **In Jesus for peace I abide,**
> **And as I keep close to His side,**
> **There's nothing but peace doth betide,**
> **Sweet peace, the gift of God's love.**

The newspaper told of two Japanese soldiers who have been isolated in the hills of the Philippine Islands since World War II. One has killed over one hundred people. A small army went into the hills to seek these men out. They killed one of the Japanese soldiers. The other is still at large. They are dropping leaflets to him and trying to reach him by loudspeaker. His loved ones have come from Japan to try to make contact and explain the situation to him. The war has been over now for many years, but this Japanese is still at war while everyone else is enjoying peace.

What a sad thing that even though peace has been purchased by the blood of Christ and made available to every individual in the world, yet the majority are still at war with their own flesh and with the Lord.

Our Heavenly Father is sitting at the peace table waiting for us to enter and sit down and come to terms.

Chapter 12

Let's Go Get Them

Jesus gave the Great Commission to His disciples saying,

"Go ye therefore, and teach all nations, baptizing them in the name of the Father, and of the Son, and of the Holy Ghost: Teaching them to observe all things whatsoever I have commanded you: and, lo, I am with you alway, even unto the end of the world. Amen."—Matt. 28:19,20.

He also said,

"Go out quickly into the streets and lanes of the city, and bring in hither the poor, and the maimed, and the halt, and the blind."—Luke 14:21.

Then He said again,

"Go out into the highways and hedges, and compel them to come in, that my house may be filled."—Luke 14:23.

Getting people ready for Heaven was His main business; it ought to be ours, also. Many are going out into eternity to meet God every day, most being unprepared. It certainly behooves all Christians to put forth an all-out effort to bring people to a saving knowledge of Jesus Christ.

Dr. A. B. Simpson wrote this famous poem:

> **A hundred thousand souls a day**
> **Are passing one by one away**
> **In Christless guilt and gloom.**
> **Without one ray of hope or light,**

> **With future dark as endless night,**
> **They're passing to their doom.**

His poem has to be altered now to read:

> **A hundred sixty thousand souls a day**
> **Are passing one by one away,**
> **In Christless guilt and gloom.**

We must remember that over 160,000 people die every day, over 68 million every year. Surely the main business is soul winning and aggressive, evangelistic outreach. So "Let's Go Get Them!"

Churches are usually born in time of revival and evangelism when a few who get right with God band together for prayer, Bible preaching and soul-winning efforts. This red-hot evangelism approach usually draws a crowd. Too often when the buildings get full, instead of launching into building programs and solving the space problems, we settle into complacency.

One preacher being urged to participate in an outreach campaign made the statement, "I have more sheep now than I can say grace over." It is sad when so many do not care about the burden of carrying the Gospel to needy souls.

I heard about a football game being played on the home field. The home team was being smeared by the visiting squad. Someone on the sidelines kept yelling, "Give the ball to Calhoun! Give the ball to Calhoun!"

They tried another play, and again the home team was smashed to the ground, losing valuable yardage. Again came the cry, "Give the ball to Calhoun!"

After this happened two or three times more, the familiar cry rang out again, "Give the ball to Calhoun!"

A tall man raised up from the pile of human bodies on the field after the next play and responded, "Calhoun don't want the ball!"

I am afraid this is true of many preachers and Christian leaders. They do not want to carry the ball of evangelism. When the church settles down after a work of revival and evangelism, the members slip into a dead, orthodox teaching position and begin to work with the saints, excusing themselves from the Great Commission. They soon drift into liberalism, compromise and softening up on issues.

Modernism is the next step down on the cycle. Logic and reasoning then begin to replace scriptural teaching and doctrinal exhortation. That usually results in the uprise of radical theology. Everyone seems to feel God must have died.

That is followed by riot and revolution. The burning of cities, shooting policemen, smashing store windows, and marching in mobs down the streets usually shake up the remaining remnant of Christians who go back to the prayer closet and seek God's face for help. That in turn brings back evangelism and revival. We have completed a cycle and are ready to go again.

In our day, we have drifted from evangelism into an aggressive evangelism movement. There is a fresh breath blowing across America. We have entered into what is being termed "super-aggressive evangelism." Churches are starting to push for 1,000, 2,000, 5,000, 12,000, 19,000 in Sunday school.

The big question now is: shall we work with the saints or continue to carry out the Great Commission and gather up sinners? Dr. Walter Hughes said, "God did not call us to cuddle the saints but to collar sinners." Ray Sadler used to say, "Are we to be fishers of men or keepers of the aquarium?"

Dr. Jack Hyles gives a famous illustration about a fire company being organized. He asked the question, "Is the purpose of the fire company to put out fires, or to keep the fire truck shiny and the fireman's uniform neat?" There is surely a need for both. There must be a balance between reaching souls and caring for the saints, but to forsake one for the other must be displeasing to the Lord.

The question now before us is: Shall we build large, aggressive, soul-winning churches, using buses, Christian day schools, Bible colleges, radio outreach, TV, printing presses, camps, book stores, newspapers, etc., etc.? Some are saying we should not neglect the members and the saints.

It seems the early church in Jerusalem had that same problem. It cried out that the widows were being neglected in the daily ministration. This problem was solved by the appointing of deacons who cared for those needs, while the men of God continued to carry on a program of aggressive outreach and the Great Commission.

Suppose a man walking down the street suddenly came upon a burning house. Flames are breaking out under the eaves. The smoke is billowing up into the sky. The man hears screaming and crying from within. He sees the faces of several children pressing against the window panes with frightened, fearful looks. He quickly dashes into the burning house, fighting the flames, fanning the smoke until he locates a beautiful little girl in one of the rooms. He quickly pulls off his coat, wraps it around the little girl, and rushes through the flames out onto the sidewalk. He sets the little girl down and begins to brush off her dress. He wipes the tears from her eyes and dusts off her shoes. Then, he takes his comb and combs out the tangles in her hair. Meanwhile, the rest of the children are screaming and crying and being overcome with the flames.

When we ask him why he doesn't go back and get the other children out of the fire, he excuses himself by saying, "I cannot leave this little girl. I must clean her up and brush off her dress and shoes."

Now the question before us is: Shall we care for the needs of this little girl, or shall we run back into the house and get some more children out of the fire? The answer is yours, my reader friends.

I. LET'S INVITE THEM

"A certain man made a great supper, and bade [invited] many" (Luke 14:16). Let's go get them! Let's go out where they are and bring them in where we are.

But, whom shall we get? Maybe the poor people like Bartimaeus; the rich people like Zacchaeus; religious people like Nicodemus; sick people like the impotent man; wicked people like the woman at the well; black people like the Ethiopian eunuch; working people like James and John who were mending their nets; political leaders like Cornelius; the social people like Lydia; and the little people like the children Jesus spoke of in Matthew 19:14.

The story is told of the little girl in England who came running home from church one day saying, "Mommy! Mommy! My name is in the Bible! My name is in the Bible!"

The mother, answering the child, said, "Edith, honey, your name is not in the Bible."

The little girl persisted, "Yes, it is, Mother. The preacher said, 'Jesus receiveth sinners and Edith with them.'"

What a blessing to know that not only Edith's name is in the Bible but so are yours and mine. It is a "whosoever will" proposition.

When shall we invite them? It is said, "Daily . . . in the temple, and . . . from house to house" (Acts 2:46). Then again, "Son, go work to day in my vineyard" (Matt. 21:28). In another place, "Behold, now is the accepted time; behold, now is the day of salvation" (II Cor. 6:2).

Clement Stone, the famous multimillionaire who edits *Success* magazine, wrote an article called "Do It Now." He pointed out that the sales world was losing billions of dollars because of procrastination by salesmen. He recommended that through a process of psychocybernetics men could repeat out loud every morning, "Do it now," fifty times and at night fifty times more. After a week or ten days the little phrase would be so embedded in the subconscious mind that it would go against the grain to put anything off that needed to be done.

Christians could profit from this tremendously. We know the world is lost, we know people need to be saved, we know that many want to be saved and are waiting for us to come—but we still do not go. Let's go "NOW" and bring them in.

Where should we go to invite them? Jesus said, "Into all the world." He also said, "Into the streets and lanes" (Luke 14:21), and "into the highways and hedges" (Luke 14:23).

Several years ago when I came to visit Louisville, Kentucky, for the first time, we went out to knock on doors and tell people about a new bus route we were beginning. A little fellow came along on a bicycle and said to me, "Hey, Bud, what's you doin'?"

I explained that I was trying to get folk to go to Sunday school with me on the bus.

He followed me down the block asking more questions. "Hey, Bud, how much money you got?"

After several of these questions, I turned to him and said, "Now look, you've asked all the questions so far; it's my turn to ask the questions."

"What do you want to ask?" he said.

"I want to ask if you're going to Heaven when you die?"

He looked up at me and said, "I don't know."

I asked him if he would like to know.

"Sure, I would."

I told him the story of how our boy Timmy had received the Lord as his Saviour.

After hearing the story, he said, "Boy, I'd like to do that!"

And there on the sidewalk we bowed our heads and prayed and he did what Timmy did—he opened his heart and received Jesus Christ as his Saviour.

They are out there, even on the street, waiting for us to come.

There are thousands just waiting for us to come and help them.

II. LET'S INSTRUCT THEM

Jesus said, "Teaching them to observe all things whatsoever I have commanded you" (Matt. 28:20). After inviting folk, we must then instruct them. There are basically only two messages in the Bible. The first is for sinners and deals with how to go to Heaven; the second is for saints and deals with how to be happy. Being happy, of course, involves helping other people get to Heaven, and so it becomes a cycle.

There is such a need to keep the instruction practical and down to earth. It is sad that in so many of our seminaries and Bible instruction centers we have drifted into digging into the deep theology and have missed the practical everyday truths. Someone has said we go down deep, stay down long, and come up dry.

We must admit there is a great void of Bible knowledge in our day, and it seems to be getting worse. As one old man said, "We seem to be getting ignoranter and ignoranter!"

In one adult Sunday school class, when the teacher mentioned as he pointed to a map of Israel, "From north at Dan all the way down south to Beersheba," one of the members raised his hand, saying, "Did I understand you to say that Dan and Beersheba were places? I thought they were man and wife, like Sodom and Gomorrah." There is a real need to teach the Word of God.

III. LET'S INSPIRE THEM

There is a need for Christians to be alive, alert and awake. There is a tremendous need for zeal and inspiration. The message is exciting.

In Beth Haven Baptist Church we have created what we call the "Beth Haven spirit." Hearty singing, warm, friendly people, evangelistic messages, and invitations in every service have helped us to live up to our slogan used on the daily broadcast, "Next to Heaven, it's Beth Haven." Our people have been caught up in the spirit of this thing, and it has greatly helped us in inspiring our people to do a job for God.

It is said that a little country store had a sign hanging out on the front porch,

> THERE IS NO PLACE LIKE THIS PLACE
> SO THIS MUST BE THE PLACE.

Surely every church needs to have that type attitude and spirit about it so that people will want their friends to come and get involved in the greatest business in all the world.

So many people are like a cold fish—all of the strength has drained from them. They carry a frown on their face, walk a little stooped. The weight of their burdens is obvious. When they come to church, we need to charge their battery. We must make a volcano out of them. Some are talking about "getting all excited." There is a great need to get people fired up and filled with enthusiasm for God.

My friend, Jack Wyrtzen, always signs his letters, "Yours on the victory side, Jack." I like that!

IV. LET'S INVOLVE THEM

Jesus said, "Ye shall be witnesses unto me both in Jerusalem, and in all Judaea . . ." (Acts 1:8). Once people are invited to come to

Christ, instructed in the ways of the Lord, and inspired to do the work of God, it is time to involve them in the detailed activity of getting the vast storehouse of God's wealth and blessing to the unprecedented need of man's heart.

Several years ago we decided to have what we called an "August Campaign." We were moving into a new auditorium. The contractors delivered the building at the end of July instead of the spring date we had planned for.

We were quite concerned about the psychological effect of moving into that large auditorium since our people so long had been jammed together for the services. We divided the auditorium into six sections and appointed a group captain over each. These captains in turn had twelve sub-captains each to help them pack the pews Sunday morning, Sunday night and Wednesday night during the hot month of August. We set a goal for a certain number of souls to be saved. We also had an offering goal and a baptismal goal for the month.

To make a long story short, we exceeded every goal and had an old-fashioned, Holy Ghost revival during the month of August. Our people were so excited that our church took on new life and the problem never materialized. Involvement was the key.

When Dr. John R. Rice challenged the preachers of this country to set a goal to try to baptize 200 people in one year, I felt the Lord would have me accept his challenge.

I wrote Dr. Rice and told him we would set out to baptize 200. We worked hard at it, and by the end of the year, the count was 216. I wanted to set a goal of 300 for the next year. At the invitation I asked for thirty people who would accept a goal of ten each for the next twelve months. Over thirty responded, and the count at the end of the year was 404. The next year it was 513.

We have used the same approach in Louisville, Kentucky, for the last two years now; and in the past twelve months we have baptized 1,284. This year (1973) I believe we will go over 1,500, for we are involving our people.

Somewhere recently I read of a tribe of natives in a South American jungle who learned that the leaves of certain trees would give them extra energy and strength and would keep them from getting hungry. So they began to eat them regularly. They seemed strong, energetic and seldom got hungry. A few days later some died. An investigation revealed that they had starved to death. The leaves had tranquilized them and tricked them with false drug-like energy.

It is quite obvious that Satan is busy causing people to be perfectly satisfied with the humdrum routine of going to church, taking part in the formalities of the services, carrying on the functions of a social ministry, and thinking they are pleasing God; but they are really dead spiritually. Surely the only answer is to get back into the mainstream of going after people, carrying out the Great Commission, then solving all the problems that result so that we do not have to stop at any point along the way.

LET'S GO GET THEM!

Chapter 13

The Blessing of Trouble

"For we would not, brethren, have you ignorant of our trouble which came to us in Asia, that we were pressed out of measure, above strength, insomuch that we despaired even of life: But we had the sentence of death in ourselves, that we should not trust in ourselves, but in God which raiseth the dead."—II Cor. 1:8,9.

"We are troubled on every side, yet not distressed; we are perplexed, but not in despair; Persecuted, but not forsaken; cast down, but not destroyed; Always bearing about in the body the dying of the Lord Jesus, that the life also of Jesus might be made manifest in our body."—II Cor. 4:8-10.

While attending a Bible conference several years ago, I heard Dr. Lee Roberson of Chattanooga, Tennessee, announce that he would speak the next evening on "The Secret of Greatness."

I arrived early the next evening with notebook in hand, ready to take down several points of instruction. I wanted to be sure to get the facts straight from the man who knew what he was talking about. Dr. Roberson, of course, is one of the greatest men alive today in the work of God.

After he was introduced to speak, he stood up, announced the text, and repeated his title: "I give you tonight the secret of greatness. It is found in one key word, and that word is 'TROUBLE.'"

I was so disappointed not to get a systematic formula of instruction from Dr. Roberson based upon his years of experience and success. But the more he preached, the more I realized that what he was saying surely was the true secret of greatness.

People react to trouble in several different ways. Some grumble, others gripe, many growl, a few groan; then there are those who grieve and thank the Lord; then some grow. Trouble will never leave one the same.

Someone has said that life is a bowl of cherries but some of the cherries are sour. I think it is necessary that we accept a problem as it is, adjust to it, then approach it with a determination to do something about it.

Trouble is nothing new to God's people. The Bible, of course, is filled with stories of those in trouble. The Hebrew children had their fiery furnace. Daniel had his lions' den. Joseph was cast into prison. Paul was shipwrecked and beaten with stripes. Peter was sent to prison. John was exiled at Patmos. James had his head cut off. David fled from Saul. Samson had his eyes put out. These are just a few.

Clyde Gordon, who is completely paralyzed from his neck down, edits a magazine called *The Triumph*. In it he said recently:

> **Christ is no security against storms,**
> **But He is perfect security *in* storms.**
> **He does not promise an easy passage,**
> **But He does guarantee a *safe* landing.**

Someone said recently, "The road to success is always under construction." It seems that those who have it hard always get more done.

I read in a magazine recently that great civilizations of history have been in the northern hemisphere. On the equator life is easy and comfortable; there have been no lasting achievements. Now let me point out some benefits of trouble.

I. TROUBLE UNIFIES

When someone dies in the family, loved ones gather from far and near for the funeral. People want to be together when in trouble. When someone is seriously ill, their friends and neighbors gather in to check on them and make sure things are all right.

During the serious tornado damage in Louisville, we began to get phone calls from out of state. One call came from our daughter

Debbie in North Carolina, checking to make sure Mom and Dad were all right. Then a call came in from Pennsylvania from more loved ones. Then the phone rang again; a sister in Ohio was checking everything out in Louisville. These were basic family concerns.

Several years ago in Elkton, there was a serious accident. A car passing a truck ran into the back end of one of our school vans, killing two of our kindergarten children and injuring several others. During the ordeal of that tragedy, several families were drawn very close together, and our church was unified and harmonized in a new way. Trouble became a blessing in that it unified and harmonized our people around our church family and program for God.

Trouble not only draws people together, but it also draws them to the Lord. David said, "Before I was afflicted, I went astray" (Ps. 119:67). Many a person has called for a preacher in time of trouble to make things right with God.

Then trouble also draws people to church. It is not uncommon to see a whole family show up at church after a funeral.

Sometimes when people get bad news from the doctor about their physical condition, they take a renewed interest in church. So trouble unifies.

II. TROUBLE IS COMMON

Paul said in I Corinthians 10:13, "There hath no temptation [trouble] taken you but such as is common to man: but God is faithful, who will not suffer you to be tempted above that ye are able; but will with the temptation [trouble] also make a way to escape."

One old preacher said that we ought to be good to everybody because everybody is having a tough time. God is no respecter of persons. He has no pets. In spite of this, we sometimes feel like victims. It seems that we suffer far more than others. But this is simply not the case. I think if all the truth were known, we would probably not trade places with anybody else in the whole world.

Just a few days ago a preacher came to see me who had more troubles than anyone I have seen for a long time. He told me a story of problems in the church, in the community, in his home and in his heart.

I had just talked a few moments before with a preacher's wife in a far-off state. There were serious problems in the life of her preacher-husband and in their church. She was asking for advice.

I talked just two days before that to a preacher who had come to the place where he felt he could no longer effectively serve the Lord in his setting. He wanted to resign and leave his pulpit and find a new place to start again.

And then our increased demand for counseling requests at the church. It seems that pastors are spending more and more time counseling with people about their troubles and problems. Trouble is a very common thing.

III. TROUBLE DEEPENS SPIRITUALITY

David said,

"Thy righteousness also, O God, is very high, who hast done great things: O God, who is like unto thee! Thou, which hast shewed me great and sore troubles, shalt quicken me again, and shalt bring me up again from the depths of the earth. Thou shalt increase my greatness, and comfort me on every side."—Ps. 71:19-21.

Here we find the effect of trouble. It was a blessing in disguise, a benefit to the life of this good servant of God.

Paul emphasized that "all things work together for good to them that love God, to them who are the called according to his purpose" (Rom. 8:28). He also said, "Tribulation worketh patience" (Rom. 5:3). The graduate degree of spirituality comes from attending the *University of Hard Knocks.*

IV. TROUBLE PRODUCES REALITY

The world is filled with veneer, sham, hypocrisy and deceit. After a serious bout with trouble, we don't usually care as much about what people think. Pride is plowed under, the world loses its value, the appetites for sin lose their taste. God could have kept Daniel out of the lions' den, Paul and Silas out of jail, the Hebrew children from the fiery furnace; but it was good for all these to go through these experiences.

Dr. Jack Hudson made this statement in our church: "My soul demands reality." I thought it was interesting since Brother Jack has been through deep waters so many times with his own physical condition, with a serious arthritic condition and two or three hospital bouts for various other things. It doesn't seem strange, then, that Brother Hudson abounds with genuine sincerity.

Several times I have heard preachers remark, "He's for real." What a great attribute for a man of God!

V. TROUBLE FURTHERS THE CAUSE

In Philippians 1:12 Paul states, "That the things which have happened unto me have fallen out rather unto the furtherance of the gospel." The strength of a ship can only be demonstrated by hurricane. The power of God's grace can only be fully known when the Christian is subjected to some fiery trial. If God would make manifest the fact that He gives songs in the night, He must first make the night.

The weather bureau in the Caribbean island area uses planes to help keep check on the weather. These planes have learned how to take advantage of the cyclone winds in that area. When going north, they get out on the fringes of the cyclone winds and take advantage of the tremendous tailwinds. They actually ride the fringe of the storm and save time and gasoline. Then coming back south, they get on the other edge and take advantage of the same storm to go in the opposite direction.

Trouble should become a steppingstone to better understanding of the will of God and the teaching of the Bible, and also to mature and give us experience in our work for God.

VI. TROUBLE PRODUCES A CROWD

We read in James 1:12, "Blessed is the man that endureth temptation [trouble]: for when he is tried, he shall receive the crown of life." Someone has said:

> **For God has marked each sorrowing day**
> **And numbered every secret tear;**
> **And Heaven's long age of bliss shall pay**
> **For all His children suffer here.**

Those who go through fire and water should remember it is God's way of refining and cleansing you for your good and His glory.

Not only will victory and blessing be a result of this life, but a crown is going to be presented to those who endure suffering for His sake here. This, of course, will be presented at the judgment seat of Christ when all Christians will give an account of themselves according to the deeds done in the body. God is surely looking. His recording angels are keeping a good set of books. As in the case of Job, He will return all that we have lost and reward us with an abundant increase.

The purpose of the Lord is to present us faultless before His throne after the last days. Trouble is simply the factory God is using to produce the right type of product in our lives. Someone wrote:

> He sat by a fire of sevenfold heat
> As He watched by the precious ore,
> And closer He bent with a searching gaze
> As He heated it more and more.
>
> He knew He had ore that could stand the test;
> He wanted the finest gold
> To mold as a crown for the king to wear—
> Set with gems with a price untold.
>
> So He laid our gold in the burning fire,
> Though we fain would have said Him nay,
> And He watched the dross that we had not seen
> As it melted and passed away.
>
> And the gold grew brighter and yet more bright,
> But our eyes were so dim with tears
> We saw but the fire, not the Master's hand,
> And questioned with anxious fears.
>
> Yet our gold shone out with a richer glow
> And it mirrored a form above
> Of Him bent o'er the fire, unseen by us,
> With a look of ineffable love.
>
> Can we think that it pleases His loving heart
> To cause us a moment's pain?

Ah, no, but He saw through the present cross
To bliss of eternal gain.

So, He waited there with a watchful eye,
With a love that is strong and sure;
And His gold did not suffer a bit more heat
Than was needed to make it pure.

VII. TROUBLE GLORIFIES GOD

Paul speaks of glory in trouble in Romans 5:3. When Adam and Eve were in trouble, God stepped in and met their need; and of course, we give glory to God for it. Noah's problems were solved by the God who cared. Again we want God to have glory. Joseph was delivered from prison; the children of Israel were delivered as they crossed the Red Sea; Elijah needed God's help in getting some rain; David's baby died; Paul and Silas were locked in the Philippian jail. There was great profit and benefit to these people in the times of their deliverance.

But all the glory goes to God. We are admonished in I Corinthians 6:20, "For ye are bought with a price: therefore glorify God in your body, and in your spirit, which are God's."

Now in summary let me say that trouble is good for a Christian. It may be hard to endure, but in the end it will bring forth peaceful fruit of righteousness and a note of praise. Maybe we can understand now what James meant when he said, "Count it all joy when ye fall into divers temptations [trouble]."

Chapter 14

You Can Be a Soul Winner

1. **Lost people all about us;**
2. **Many are concerned, could be won;**
3. **Be on the alert; watch for opportunities;**
4. **Get a reputation that you win souls, and some will come to you;**
5. **Set a goal and work at it.**

(Preached at Sword Family Conference at the Bill Rice Ranch, July 3, 1974)

I want to give you seven passages of Scripture. First, Dr. John R. Rice's favorite passage, Psalm 126:5 and 6:

"They that sow in tears shall reap in joy. He that goeth forth and weepeth, bearing precious seed, shall doubtless come again with rejoicing, bringing his sheaves with him."

A second verse is Proverbs 11:30:

"The fruit of the righteous is a tree of life; and he that winneth souls is wise."

In the first verse, we go out into the field and we bring back sheaves, the harvest part of the crop. You will soon notice a common denominator in all seven of these passages. We go out into the field, and we bring back the sheaves or the harvest from the crop.

In Proverbs 11:30 we go to the orchard and bring back the fruit. Now the fruit from the tree is the harvest part of the tree.

And then Joel, chapter 3, and verses 13 and 14:

"Put ye in the sickle, for the harvest is ripe: come, get you down;

for the press is full, the fats overflow; for their wickedness is great. Multitudes, multitudes in the valley of decision: for the day of the Lord is near in the valley of decision.''

In this case we go out into the field and bring in the harvest, for it is ripe. The first trip we went into the field and brought the sheaves from the field—that is harvest. Second, we went to the orchard and got the apples from the field—that is harvest. Third, we go into the field and bring in the harvest because it is now ripe.

In Matthew 9:36-38:

"But when he saw the multitudes, he was moved with compassion on them, because they fainted, and were scattered abroad, as sheep having no shepherd. Then saith he unto his disciples, The harvest truly is plenteous, but the labourers are few; Pray ye therefore the Lord of the harvest, that he will send forth labourers into his harvest.''

This time the harvest is plentiful. The first time we brought the harvest in from the field; second, we went to the orchard and got the harvest from the trees; third, we went to the field and put the sickle in and found the harvest was ripe; and fourth, we went to the field and we found that the harvest was very, very plentiful.

In Mark 4:26-29 we read that Jesus said:

"So is the kingdom of God, as if a man should cast seed into the ground; And should sleep, and rise night and day, and the seed should spring and grow up, he knoweth not how. For the earth bringeth forth fruit of herself; first the blade, then the ear, after that the full corn in the ear. But when the fruit is brought forth, immediately he putteth in the sickle, because the harvest is come.''

Now we brought the sheaves from the field, we brought the apples from the trees, we put the sickle in for the harvest is ripe, we saw that the harvest was plentiful. Now we see the harvest is come.

Luke 10:1,2 says:

"After these things the Lord appointed other seventy also, and sent them two and two before his face into every city and place, whither

he himself would come. Therefore said he unto them, The harvest truly is great, but the labourers are few: pray ye therefore the Lord of the harvest, that he would send forth labourers into his harvest.''

Here, the harvest is great.

Now John 4:35:

"Say not ye, There are yet four months, and then cometh harvest? behold, I say unto you, Lift up your eyes, and look on the fields; for they are white already to harvest."

Now let's put it all together. First, we went into the fields and brought the sheaves, or the harvest from the field. Second, we went to the orchards and got the apples or the fruit or the harvest of the trees. Third, we went to the fields and put the sickle in, for the harvest was ripe. Fourth, we went to the field and brought forth the harvest because it was plentiful. Next, we went down into the fields and found the harvest had come. We went again to the field and found that the harvest was now great. And again we went to the field and now found that the harvest is white, or just about through.

Now Jeremiah 8:20:

"The harvest is past. . . and we are [still] not saved."

We see a cycle. Remember there are four sets to a crop. First, we must plow; second, we must plant; third, we must prune or cultivate; fourth, we must pick.

Now, to plow. That would be repenting or calling on people to turn over the hard soil, break up the fallow ground as the prophet put it, in order that we might root up all the weeds, the thistles, the thorns, briars, and all the habits, customs, traditions and all the things that get into the lives of people and into the programs of the local church that cause the ground to be barren. We get in the place where we sing the wrong music and have the wrong kind of program. We don't give the right type of invitations. And the first thing we know, we slide into formalism and procedure and tradition and habit patterns and such things. And the ground soon gets hard. And hard ground won't bear any crop. So we must get out the old gospel plow and break up the fallow ground or turn over all of the procedures.

Dr. Lee Roberson preaches a sermon that he calls "Conversion of a Church." Now, we need the conversion of a church, and we need the conversion of some Christian lives. Plow under the old. Then we can plant the seed. As we plant the seed, some will fall along the wayside, some will fall in the stony places, some will fall on the thorny ground, and some will fall into good ground. So twenty-five percent of the ground will be good ground, and that ground will bring forth fruit, some of it thirtyfold, some sixtyfold, and some one hundredfold.

Now after we get the crop to come forth, there must be the pruning of the vine. The Scripture says, "Let us lay aside every weight, and the sin which doth so easily beset us, and let us run with patience the race that is set before us" (Heb. 12:1).

Most Christians have too many formalities, too many habits, too many clubs, too many activities, too many outside programs to be a very good witness and very good soul winner for the Lord. We allow ourselves to get too wrapped up in too many organizations, too many club meetings, too many group programs within the society in which we live. As a result, there are no nights left after we go to church Sunday morning and Sunday night and Wednesday night. We feel now it is all right to spend our time in all the other activities in our community. And we need to do some pruning of the vines in order that they might bring forth some more fruit.

Now in John, chapter 15, we read about no fruit, then some who have fruit, some who have much fruit, then others who have more fruit, then some who have fruit that remains. Now God help us not to stop with just bearing a little fruit when we could be bearing more fruit and much fruit and a lot of fruit that remains. So we must continually prune on the vine.

Then if we do those three things—plow and plant and prune—then automatically we will pick. There will be a constant picking of the harvest.

I believe we can have revival on a year-'round basis. I don't think we have to have just spring revivals and fall revivals, but I believe every Sunday morning, every Sunday night, every Wednesday night souls ought to come down the aisles who have been won to Christ by the people who sit in the pews, who will come forward with their converts. This is the secret of building a great work for the Lord and keeping God's people in their proper place.

How are you going to get to this and get this to be priority in our lives? We ought to take a new look at it and maybe freshen our vision on this matter of how simple and easy and wonderful and thrilling it is to really win somebody to the Lord Jesus Christ.

I. LOST SINNERS NEEDING CHRIST ARE EVERYWHERE

According to the verses that we have shared together, according to what Jesus said, there is an abundance of sinners. Now nobody would argue with this. People are everywhere.

Over in Louisville, we have them hanging in knots just like grapes. They are everywhere, hanging over the vines. Why, they are in the cars driving up and down our highways. They are in the houses, in the stores, in the places of business—everywhere we go. We find them out in the yard under the trees, waiting for red lights, on the buses, in planes, downtown on the elevators. Everywhere you look, there are sinners, sinners, sinners and sinners—an abundance of sinners.

That is what Jesus said. The field is out there, and the harvest now is plentiful, and the harvest is ready, and there is an abundance of them all over the place.

Everywhere I go, I meet those who say, "Well, Brother Wallace, you must have an abundance of them over in Louisville." We just have more than you can imagine. You know, we have all the liquor factories over here, too. Seventy percent of America's bourbon is made there. You can go out on the back porch early in the morning, take a deep breath and get drunk! I mean you can smell the stuff cooking.

And then we have all these tobacco factories. Then there is Churchill Downs. Sinners everywhere.

But I have a sneaking suspicion that you have almost as many sinners where you are as we have where we are. Everywhere I have ever gone, I have found that there is an abundance of sinners.

Now somebody says, "I don't know where you find them all. I can't find any sinners. Why, I look all around, and I don't see them." But they are out there.

There is a plentiful harvest. There are people all over the place who are waiting and ready to be saved.

II. MANY LOST PEOPLE ARE CONCERNED, WILLING TO BE SAVED

May I point out something else. According to what Jesus said, many, many, many of those people are very, very concerned, interested, willing and ready to be saved.

As I walked down the hall in the hospital in Elkton, Maryland, a nurse said, "Oh, Brother Wallace, right in room 216, behind the door, is a little lady who has been talking about Heaven this morning. I sense that she would like to get saved. I started to talk to her about getting saved, but my head nurse saw what I was doing, and she has been giving me details down on the other end of the hall. Every time I start in that room, she sends me to the other end. If you could get in, I believe you could win that lady."

Well, I went through the doorway and found the sick lady. "Lady, I am Pastor Tom Wallace from over at Baptist Bible Church. One of the nurses tells me that you have been talking about Heaven this morning."

"Well, yes, I have."

"Are you planning to go there?"

"I don't suppose so."

"Would you like to go there?"

"I really would like to go."

"Well, would you like me to sit down beside the bed here and tell you what you will need to do to get ready?"

"That would be so nice of you."

So I sat down beside the bed and explained to her the simple Romans Road of salvation. Then I said, "Would you like to close your eyes while I pray for you and ask the Lord to save you?"

"That would be wonderful."

So I prayed. When I got through I asked her, "Now, would you like to pray, 'Dear Lord Jesus, I am a sinner. . .'?"

She started crying. But she prayed, "O dear Lord, You know I am a sinner. You know I want to be saved. Please come into my heart and save my soul. And I pray in Jesus' name. Amen." She wiped the tears away and said, "Preacher, I have wanted to do that for such a long, long time."

Oh my! I got under conviction as I thought, *That woman lives right here in our city. She has wanted to do that for such a long, long time. I wish I had known that. I wish I had known where she was. Maybe if I had gotten out and knocked on all the doors in that area, I could have found her.*

Then I got to wondering on the way back to the church, *How many hundreds more are there within a five-mile radius of my church who probably feel the same way?*

We have gotten the idea—I guess it came from the Devil—that everybody out there who is still not saved has absolutely no interest in getting saved, that they could not care less, that they are anxious to die and go to Hell.

Jesus said that the harvest is ready. Jesus said that hearts are hungry and that they are waiting. Many of them have been to a recent funeral, and they are thinking, *What will happen to me when I die?*

Some of them have been to church, have heard a sermon and have been wrestling with what they are going to do. People all over are just sitting waiting, ready, if we could but find them.

I tell our people in Louisville, "Let's go out and knock on every door we come to. If you have a card for a certain address and nobody is home, then go next door and find out who those people are. Get acquainted with them. Go on the other side. Make three or four calls while the car is parked. You may find one out of a hundred who will ask you to leave, but you go on and keep knocking, and you will find some little old lady who will say, 'I have been thinking about this all week. You know, it must be of the Lord that you came here today.'"

How many times I have had people say to me, "The Lord must have sent you today. The Lord must have sent you!" And I think literally hundreds and hundreds of people out there would love to be saved, so we must find them.

Sunday night I said to our people, "How many of you have won somebody to the Lord this week? Those who have, please stand to your feet."

Seventy-five or eighty got up. I said, "Let's find out now. How many did you win?"

A man said one; another—three. "How about you?" Another—two; this one—three; this lady—five; others from two to eight.

One fellow got up and said, "Brother Wallace, God gave me a revival this week. I won thirty-three!"

The fellow who was counting them all up said, "Preacher, I counted 215 who were saved this week."

Our people had won them out in the homes. Somebody must have wanted to get saved. Our fellows are not that sharp and not that good, to talk folks into it who didn't want to get saved. I believe with my soul that this country is full of people who are anxious, willing and ready. Many of these people are interested, and the harvest is ready.

III. WE SHOULD BE CONSTANTLY WATCHING TO FIND THOSE WE CAN WIN

Then let me also point out that you and I must allow the Spirit of the Lord to keep us freshly alert because we may bump into somebody who is waiting and ready to be saved.

I was holding a meeting in Baltimore, Maryland. When I got through preaching, I asked, "How many of you folks will join me in trusting the Lord to help you get somebody saved in the next thirty days? I don't know whom you will get, and you don't know whom I will get, so we will just have to go look, wait and pray."

Almost all those in the church stood up. We dismissed the service, asking God to show us whom we could get and where we would find them. Two ladies with white hair came up to me. One said, "Brother Wallace, I have a problem."

I said, "Ma'am, if you would care to tell me about it, maybe I could help you."

"When you said we ought to go win somebody, I said to myself, *That is right. I ought to do it.* You said some of us had never won anybody. That was me. I stood up and promised the Lord I would go get one, but I'm scared to death."

I said, "Join the club, Lady. The rest of us are, too!"

She said, "My friend here, it is the same with her. She has never won anybody either, and she stood up. I am afraid to go by myself, and she is afraid to go by herself. So may we go together tomorrow?"

"Oh, that would be beautiful, and it is scriptural. Jesus said go two by two."

"Well, what the problem is, when we win one tomorrow, whose will it be—hers or mine?" she asked.

"Well, that is quite a problem," I said. "I think you ought not count at all until you get two. Then you can divide them and have one apiece."

Hey, they had not even thought about that!

By this time a third lady was standing by. They introduced me to her and said, "This is Mrs. _____insky." (I never got the first part of her name, but I know it had an "-insky" on the back end!)

I said, "I am happy to meet you, Mrs. _____insky."

About this time, the choir director said, "All right. Everybody who is going to sing in the choir tomorrow night, come on up, and we are going to run over our number."

The two ladies said, "Will you please excuse us? We are both in the choir."

They left me standing there with Mrs. _____insky. As they left, they said to her, "You wait, now. We will be right back."

I said, "Do you come here to church?"

"No. This is my first time."

"Oh. Where do you attend?"

"I go down to St. Peter's."

"How did you like this service tonight?"

She said, "This has just been so interesting. I have enjoyed hearing you talk about Heaven and how to get there."

I asked her, "Are you going?"

"Well, no. I don't suppose so."

"Well, would you like to go?"

"Oh, more than anything in the world," she replied.

I said, "Well, do you have to wait on those ladies?" She said she did.

"Well, why don't we sit down on the front row here, and I will explain to you all about this?"

Do you know what I did? I sat down there on the front row and stole her from both those ladies! Do you know what they were going to do? Tomorrow they were going to go out and try to find a sinner, and here was one right beside them all the time!

You have to get your eyes opened. They are all over the place. You might have one sitting right next to you. There might be one sleeping in the same building with you this week. You ought to ask everybody, "How long have you been saved?" and see who can tell you right off the bat. We have to be alert, have to keep our eyes opened.

Now once we get started on this, the most amazing things will happen. Have you ever seen the wind blow across the wheat field? Have you seen the ripple of that thing? Have you ever seen ways fires spread? You let two or three people in the local church really get active and fired up about soul winning, and watch what will happen. That thing will spread across the congregation, and people who have never won anybody will suddenly begin to realize, *I am the only one here not doing this. Others have been bringing people down the aisle that they have won to the Lord. I better get into this, too.* Soul winning has kind of a fever to it. It will spread like a fire across the field. It is catching.

IV. WHEN IT GETS KNOWN YOU ARE WINNING SOULS, PEOPLE WILL COME TO YOU

You will develop a reputation, and people will start coming up to you and asking, "Will you go with me and help me win So-and-So to the Lord?" Getting a reputation is a beautiful thing. People call up and want to be saved. I have had people come up to me and talk about everything under the sun—the weather, the world situation, animals—about everything. But in a few minutes I will say, "Are you trying to tell me that you would like to talk about some spiritual things?"

"Well, now that you mention it, Preacher, I would like to ask a question."

Really and truly, a lot of people who want to get saved will walk up to you and start talking. If you know what they are doing, you can get them saved right there on the spot—that is, after you get a reputation for being a soul winner. Any layman or lady or young person can do this.

I was driving down the road the other day; and as I pulled up to a red light, I got a really funny feeling, a feeling that I ought to look back.

I did, and behind me was a car that had a big bubble gum machine on the top. The thing was going around and around, and it had a little flashing light in the thing. I pulled over to the curb. I knew I had not done anything wrong. This big policeman got out of his car. He walked up beside my car, and he said, "Good morning, Reverend. My grandmother is over in the hospital, and I wondered if maybe you might go over there and win her to Jesus for me."

I said, "Man, I sure will!"

I went and found this little snow-haired grandmother, and in ten minutes she was born again. Now where did that policeman find out I could win souls? I don't know, but I hope every policeman in Louisville finds it out.

But you have to get the reputation and let the thing spread around. Then remember that other folks will begin to pick it up and it will spread across the congregation.

The very next night after that Baltimore message, I went down to Occoquan, Virginia, to speak to the teachers and officers in the Sunday school, deacons and deacons' wives, pastors, all people from that church, at a banquet, a workers meeting. I said, "Everybody here ought to do this. Everybody here ought to win a soul in the next thirty days. How many will do it? Those who will, please stand."

Everybody in the place stood up. We prayed and asked the Lord to bless us and to help us to know whom to win and help us to know how to start. "Give everybody a soul, Lord. In Jesus' name. Amen."

There was not a soul there to talk to. But shortly the kitchen door opened, those big old swinging doors, and here came a colored boy with a dishpan. He came out of that kitchen, started out to that dining hall, walked right up to my table, and put that dishpan down right in front of me. He reached over and got my plate, my fork, my knife, my spoon, my saucer, my cup. I leaned over the table and asked, "Boy, are you going to Heaven?"

That black boy was scared to death. His eyes got big, and he said, "I don't know."

I said, "Son, you understand that you are a sinner, don't you?"

"Oh, yes, Sir. I know about that."

"Well, you know what happens to sinners when they die, don't you?"

"Yes, Sir. I am afraid I do."

"Do you believe that Jesus came here, was born of a virgin, lived without sin, and died on the cross, was buried in the ground, rose again the third day, and ascended into Heaven?"

"Yes, Sir. I believe every bit of that."

I said, "The Bible says that if you will call on the Lord and ask Him to save you, He would do it. Do you believe that?"

"Yes, Sir."

"Well, I am going to pray for you, and I am going to ask the Lord to save you right now. Is that all right with you?"

"Yes, Sir. That would be fine with me."

We bowed our heads, and I began to pray. That black boy, with a Virginia accent, said, "Dear Lord, You know I is a sinner. . . ." And the angels of Heaven were weeping and smiling while that little boy tried to talk and explain to the Lord. He got saved. It was so simple and easy. But there he was, placed right before me.

Now I believe that out there the fields are ripe and the harvest is now ready and almost past! And we must somehow get out there and get the job done.

V. SET A GOAL AND WORK AT SOUL WINNING

I went to the Naval Base and preached to a bunch of naval officers.

When I got through I said, "Now I want to give you fellows an assign-
ment. I want to commission you. You know how to take orders. You
are trained, disciplined men. I want you to sit up and take this order.
Go win a soul to Jesus Christ in thirty days. If you have done it before,
great. Get another one. If you have never done it, this will be your
first one. Every one of you do it. Will you accept the challenge? If
you will, please stand to your feet."

All of them stood up and saluted. I felt like an Admiral Somebody!
Boy, they were ready to go.

I said, "Now, I want to ask you men, if you will please, to send
me some sort of a notice after thirty days as to how you got along."

About 33 days later I got a letter:

> **Dear Brother Wallace:**
>
> **We the undersigned, officers of the United States Navy,
> would like to report to you that our mission has been
> fulfilled. We won our soul to Jesus Christ in thirty days.**

And there were twenty-two names signed underneath that letter. What
a thrill!

I was visiting in the Delaware State Hospital. When I came out,
I was carrying the gloom of visiting in that mental hospital. My
shoulders were drooped. I started to cross the parking lot and a great
big fellow was walking down the parking lot. When he saw me, his
eyes lit up and his hair was flying. He started waving his hands at
me and saying, "Hey! Hey there! Hey! Hey!" He was running right
toward me. I thought, *Goodness! One of them got out!*

I jumped in my car and pushed down both locks. He kept running
toward me. "Hey there! Hey! Hey! Hey, Preacher! Hey, Tom Wallace!
Hey, Preacher Wallace!"

Goodness! The fellow knows me!

I rolled my window down. He came to the side of my car and said,
"Don't you remember me?"

"No. I don't believe I do."

"So and so. First Baptist Church at . . ." and he named the town
in Delaware.

I said, "Yes, I remember that."

"You know, you preached on getting people saved."

"Yes, I remember that."

"I stood up and said I would get somebody saved. I had never won anybody in my life, and I was scared to death! Twenty-eight days went by, and I was not able to get anybody. I went home, got down on my knees, prayed and cried to the Lord about it, and asked Him to help me in the two days I had left before the deadline.

"Preacher, while praying the telephone rang. It was an old drinking buddy who was having D.T.'s, and he was just about to die.

"I went over there and found him lying in the bed shaking, seeing pink snakes, yellow bugs, lizards and spiders crawling over him. I told him what he needed to do was to get down on his knees and ask Jesus to save him. He got out of his bed and went down on his knees. Preacher, we prayed, and he asked the Lord to come into his heart and save him.

"The next day he died! If I hadn't gotten him saved, he would be in Hell right now. Preacher, the next day I went out and got me two more!"

I was down there about two years later at that same church. I was sitting in my car in the parking lot talking to a preacher when a Fleetwood Cadillac pulled in. There that big fellow was with his hair slicked down and wearing about a $250 suit and $50 shoes and about a $12 shirt and an $8 tie. He walked across the parking lot. I said to the preacher, "Is that who I think it is?"

"That is he."

I said, "What happened to him?"

He said, "It is amazing. Somebody died out on the West Coast and left him a fortune. He came home, bought that big car and another little one for his wife. He bought a new home and some suits like that and shirts and ties and shoes. He retired from his job; and he drives that big car up and down the road, in and out of driveways, winning people to the Lord. Every time I preach he brings somebody down the aisle."

That fellow has learned how to live.

I was back up there about a month ago, and he is still at it, still going strong. That fellow is winning them all over the place—the most unlikely person I ever saw in my life to win souls.

If I never won a soul in my life, I would get Dr. Hyles' book, *Let's Go Soul Winning*, read that through, then go win somebody to the Lord. Get Dr. Rice's book, *How Great Soul Winners Were Filled With the Holy Spirit*, and read that. I believe I could go win somebody then. That great big yellow book by Dr. Rice, *Golden Path to Successful Personal Soul Winning*, with about 15 chapters—get that. I believe I could read that and go out and win somebody.

Anybody can win somebody. And everybody ought to. There is a plentiful harvest. The fields are white unto harvest.

Now listen. The harvest will be past pretty soon. Let's bow our heads together. Let me ask you to think very seriously about your responsibility.

I believe the Lord will give me somebody else in the next thirty days. I hope He will give me one today or tomorrow or at least this week. How many of you will say, "Preacher, I believe the Lord will give me one in thirty days. I will give myself to the Lord and ask Him to use me in the next thirty days. By God's grace and with His help I'll win at least one." Everybody who will give yourself to the Lord to win somebody in the next thirty days, will you stand please, with heads bowed and eyes closed?

Almost everybody is standing. Maybe you have never won anybody but you will say, "Preacher, I will get me a little soul-winning book. I will get me one of these cassette tapes, and I will study how to do it, and I will get somebody saved. God helping me, I will do it."

Now when you win someone, let me encourage you to immediately bring that one to church and introduce him to your preacher. Try to get him down the aisle; try to get him baptized.

Chapter 15

Son of Sam?
Son of God?
Son of Satan?

"And even as they did not like to retain God in their knowledge, God gave them over to a reprobate mind to do those things which are not convenient."—Rom. 1:28.

When the grinning face of the alleged "44 caliber" killer of New York City appeared on National TV from the back seat of a police car, the great city breathed a sigh of relief. The news media shouted, " 'Son of Sam' captured!"

"Six dead, seven wounded," were the headlines that plunged the nation's largest city into a midnight of terror. The deranged killer had been systematically picking off his victims one by one. Everyone waited to see who was next.

Then, suddenly he was arrested. The charge: parking by a fire hydrant! Some of the psychiatric workers said, "He parked there on purpose. He wanted to be caught." Rumor had it that he was preparing to kill a whole nightclub full of folks with a machine gun.

David Berkowitz told his doctors a 6,000-year-old voice from a neighbor's dog told him to do it. He was going to rid the world of sinners.

"That boy's a victim of the crime-infested streets of New York," said one man. "It's the result of watching all that killing on TV and in the movies," testified another. Some blamed it on a broken home; others spoke of drugs, public school exposure, rock-and-roll influence;

and still others associated it with a tour of duty in Korea.

Mark Life, a journalist with the *New York News,* blamed the Beth Haven Baptist Church of Louisville, Kentucky, for the whole thing. In a syndicated news story, Life wrote that Berkowitz had picked up the inspiration to rid the world of sinners while attending services at our church.

Young David was stationed at Fort Knox after his army tour in Korea. At the invitation of Jim Almond, a young Christian buddy, Berkowitz came to Beth Haven and heard the Gospel. Obviously sick and tired of sin and the emptiness of his life, the young Jewish boy responded to the invitation and bowed in prayer at the altar. After a public profession of Christ, he was baptized and united with the church.

Charles Daley, editor of *The Western Recorder,* Kentucky's voice of Southern Baptists, blamed the aggressive outreach evangelism program. He favored the logic-and-reason approach of waiting for a convert to prove out before baptism or church membership. His rationalizing, of course, was in spite of the well-known fact that nowhere in the Bible does it even suggest that. All Bible converts were baptized on the spot. In the nine examples of souls being saved in the early chapters of the book of Acts, all were baptized then and there. In the Gospels, the thief on the cross was an exception.

Was he really saved? Did David Berkowitz get born again? These were questions that would not go away when the news media began to tell the story of Beth Haven Church Member No. 6,256.

May I share with you my thoughts on the matter, under the headings, "Son of Sam? Son of God? or Son of Satan?"

I. SON OF SAM?

Berkowitz gave himself the name "Son of Sam." I took this to mean "Uncle Sam" and surely the "44 caliber" killer was indeed a "Son of Sam," a product of Uncle Sam.

1. He Was a Product of Uncle Sam's Crime-Infested City Streets

New York City's crime increased 300 percent in the last ten years.

Paul Harvey told of a crime survey by *The Wall Street Journal* that revealed a contrast of 300 percent increase for New York City to two percent decrease for Tokyo, Japan. West Berlin increased their crime rate 200 percent, and London 160 percent.

The investigation revealed Tokyo's secret: a family closeness, a two-hour moral and educational teaching time, strict law enforcement, and a requirement that all policemen must visit and become acquainted with all those families in their district. While Japan's crime continues to decrease, ours continues to skyrocket.

Dr. Bertrand Brown, Director of National Institute of Mental Health, wrote, "Repeated exposure to violent programming can produce sensitivity to cruelty and violence and builds the feeling that violent behavior is appropriate under some conditions."

In a society where there is a murder every 26 minutes, a violent crime each 31 seconds, and 21 serious crimes every minute, we are not surprised anymore when some fellow goes berserk and on a killing spree.

A recent psychiatric study of 225 hard-core criminals noted that all had in common the following: anger, pride, sentimentality, moodiness, etc. Half of those committed to institutions for the criminally insane were not insane at all.

One psychiatrist explained, "These men had rejected parents and society long before these institutions had rejected them." Dr. David Oeschger, staff member of Beth Haven Christian School and recent graduate of University of Louisville, associated this case with that of Leo Held. Held, after working for 19 years in a Lock Haven, Pennsylvania, factory, and in spite of the fact that he was a regular church attender and Boy Scout leader, walked into his place of work with two guns blazing. When it was all over, several were dead and others wounded. Resentment, anger and disappointment had been brewing inside for years, and it finally boiled over.

A recent article called "Killer Kids" alerted us that more and more youngsters were going the path from playground to penitentiary. Reasons cited were: erosion of family relationships, unpunished officials in public office, drugs, TV and frustration over war.

2. He Was a Product of Uncle Sam's
Public School System

David Berkowitz did not have the advantage of a Christian school education. While he attended classes, Thomas Altizer was telling all who would listen that "God is dead." During that time, Madalyn Murray O'Hair won her court case in Maryland and put Bible reading and prayer out of school.

Day after day *Darwin's Theory of Evolution* was drilled into his young, impressionable mind. John Dewey's philosophy of education had its grip on the schools and was having its effect. Lester Frank Ward's view of sociology was accepted by almost everybody. William James, father of Modern Psychology, was enjoying an unbelievable following. Charles Beard's program of undermining George Washington and our national heroes in schoolbooks was widely accepted. Dr. Spock became an accepted authority. The Kinsey Report was the final word on sex.

Sex education was being taught by public schoolteachers who laughed at the old-fashioned views of the Bible. The "Son of Sam" was taught naturalistic, secularistic reasoning built upon few facts, much theory and assumption. He was surely a product of Uncle Sam's secular schools.

3. He Was a Product of Uncle Sam's Rock Music Culture

Elvis and The Beatles were in full swing. Hard, acid rock music had its message. It was specifying sex, drugs and suicide.

Bob Larson pointed out the example of "Goat's Head Soup," a rock album of The Rolling Stones. The Stones are considered by some to be the world's greatest rock band. Part of the record was taped live at a voodoo ritual. One by one, you can hear the screams of those who are being possessed by demon spirits. The inside of the album jacket displays a severed goat's head floating in a boiling pot. The goat, of course, has long been recognized as a symbol of Satan.

Larson explains that many parents are concerned about the loudness of the music and insist, "If you must listen to it, go into your bedroom and close the door behind you so I won't have to hear it." But what they think is racket is also a direct line of communication with the philosophy of individuals whose lives are often controlled by Satan.

Hard rock is his tool of propagandizing their thinking—brainwashing them to accept his concept of life. Larson also reminds parents that rock music glorifies promiscuous sex and invites immediate, physical self-indulgence. With heroes like Brian Jones, who drowned after an overdose; Johnny Winters, who ended up in a mental institution; Jimi Hendrix, who collected $100,000 for a one-night performance and suffocated in a pool of his own vomit that same night; Janis Joplin, the lesbian with V.D., who tried suicide six times and finally made it; plus a crowd of others, how was Berkowitz to end up any different?

4. He Was a Product of Uncle Sam's Hollywood Movies and Television

The projector and a screen have proven to be the best teaching tool invented to date. The problem, of course, is the lessons sent out over the celluloid strip. Hollywood propagates the world views on sex, drugs, alcohol and divorce; for hours each day sins of adultery, homosexuality, lesbianism and wife-swapping are glamorized.

Communism is glorified continually, while our leaders are undermined, mocked and put in bad light at the expense of our national image. Killing is the major theme. A youngster at fourteen has witnessed 11,000 murders. By twenty-one he's seen 18,000. Movies and TV belittle preachers and churches. They are presented as "Elmer Gantrys" or "sissy" men. The Bible is distorted by productions such as "David and Bathsheba," "Samson and Delilah," "The Ten Commandments," and "Moses."

Morals and principles of ethics are of no concern to producers of Hollywood films. There's more money in the other approach.

Yes, David Berkowitz was indeed a "Son of Sam."

5. He Was Also a Product of Uncle Sam's Drug Culture

Smoking marijuana or "pot," sniffing cocaine, shooting heroin and morphine and popping pills have become a way of life.

In my visits to mental hospitals, it is shocking to see that the great majority of those being cared for are not old folks suffering from hardening of the arteries or middle-age women enduring the change; but they are teens suffering from drug aftereffects. Suicide, the eventual end of heavy drug use, is accelerating at an unbelievable rate.

Just this week a very expensive folder put out by a group at University of Kentucky at Lexington crossed my desk. It gave seven reasons why Kentucky should legalize marijuana. I was shocked that seemingly educated, intelligent people could be so blind and dumb.

6. He Was a Product of Uncle Sam's Broken Homes

One psychologist told of David Berkowitz's desire to locate his real mother. Broken homes have always had their effect on the children.

With over one million divorces last year [preached in 1977], we are probably in store for some more of these results. Kentucky last year had more divorces than marriages. Could this tragedy in New York have been prevented by a family altar?

Family life seminars are springing up across America to help offset the results of a lack of Bible reading and prayer in the home.

Several reasons given for breakdown in modern homes are: lack of parental authority, permissiveness, lack of discipline, no work ethics and so-called demand for rights. Soap operas and vulgar themes on popular television shows are making their contributions, also.

7. He Was a Product of Uncle Sam's Liberal, Modernistic View of Religion

The young people of America have long ago lost confidence in the diluted, middle-of-the-road, liberal National Council of Churches' approach. We have seen this country pass through the cycle from red-hot evangelism to an evangelistic position, then to an orthodox stand, on to dead orthodoxy. From there, it has gone to liberalism, on to modernism and from that, to radicalism, and finally to revolution and anarchy.

A wave of building-burning, riots and sit-ins brought us to a stark realization that revival was our only hope. A remnant, once again, went to prayer and set into motion a movement of revival and soul winning. We have begun to refer to the result as "aggressive evangelism."

With the excitement of drugs, sex, pornographic literature and rock music, the "Son of Sam" looked upon the sick, anemic, formal religious systems that he knew as a joke. When he saw the reality of young people with changed lives, high standards, good habits and clean language, he was willing to take a second look. The sincere message of the Gospel was different, and he listened to it carefully.

II. SON OF GOD?

WAS HE A SON OF GOD? That is the $64,000 question! This was the question of the Religious News Service of Washington, D.C., a television station from Delaware and news editors from New York City. "Did you notice anything different about him?" asked the television news reporter from one of our local TV stations.

Jesus gave the parable of the sower in Matthew 13. The seed fell on four types of ground. First, the seed fell by the wayside. Second, some fell on stony ground. Third, a part of it fell in the thorns. Finally, twenty-five percent of it fell in good soil. The Lord went on to explain that birds ate the first seed, the sun burned out the second, and the thorns choked the third, leaving only the last one-fourth of the seed to bear fruit.

He further explained that the birds were symbolic of the Devil snatching away the seed before it could root. The seed was able to endure for a short while on the stones, but tribulations and persecutions overcame it. The thorns represented the deceitfulness of riches and cares of the world.

David Berkowitz was sincere when he came to Beth Haven. He saw reality and liked it. The seed went forth. He received it gladly. It was such a welcome contrast to "religion." *Forgiveness, peace, happiness* were appealing words to him. He heard and responded; but obviously, we think, did not repent and exercise faith.

Jim Almond testified that as long as he kept on him and worked with him, it was great; but as soon as he eased up to give him opportunity to show his faith, he turned immediately back to the "girlie" pictures, the drinking buddies and the foul language.

It is possible, of course, for a person to be really born again and then get away from it, like the prodigal son. Paul taught, "Therefore if any man be in Christ, he is a new creature: old things are passed away; behold, all things are become new" (II Cor. 5:17).

David Berkowitz had an interest in getting away from the army base, circulating among the girls in the College and Career Class at Beth Haven, and even enjoyed the music and message of the church services; but he did not become a new creature. I do not believe he was a son of God. He may have been, but this is my personal belief.

III. SON OF SATAN?

One doctor who spent hours on this case remarked, "I have never heard anything so strange in my life." He referred to the stories of the experiences of David Berkowitz.

Did this boy actually hear a voice talking to him from a dog? Was it Satan or maybe a demon? Nobody really knows! However, in this day when we "wrestle not against flesh and blood, but against principalities, against powers, against the rulers of the darkness of this world, against spiritual wickedness in high places" (Eph. 6:12), it would be good for us to "put on the whole armour of God."

In our text Paul speaks of those who did not like to retain God in their knowledge as being turned over to a reprobate mind (Rom. 1:28). Jesus told of the case of a man who had a demon. The demon became restless and departed from the man. It went wandering in dry places and could find no rest. When it returned, the house was empty, swept and garnished. The demon entered back in and brought with it seven more wicked spirits, worse than itself (Matt. 12:44,45).

I personally believe that this poor, unfortunate boy came seeking for peace and help. In the favorable atmosphere of our church, he reformed and threw out some of the wicked things in his life. But because he did not get Christ in to fill the empty place, it all returned and with more wickedness than before! He was obviously overcome by a demon of insanity.

King Saul, the great king of Israel, was plagued by an evil spirit and tried to kill David on several occasions. There is really no way to be sure whether the killings by "Son of Sam" were demon-inspired or not; but we can form opinions as we read the Bible and look to the Lord for spiritual insight.

William B. Young wrote:

> Demons are disembodied, wicked spirits actively engaged in destruction, affliction, uncleanness and tragedy. They are powerful personalities under the control and direction of Satan who operates as an "angel of light." Therefore, with clever deception, he has hidden the truth from many believers as to his wiles, fiery darts and "devices."

Satan uses three approaches to attack and bring about his desired end:

FIRST, HE USES OPPRESSION. Jesus went about doing good and healing all that were oppressed of the devils (see Acts 10:38). The Greek word here means "to exercise harsh control over one; to exercise dominion against one." He pressures and works endlessly to bring about broken homes, broken hearts, or broken bodies.

SECOND, HE USES OBSESSION. Webster says this word means "to besiege; to vex or harass, as an evil spirit."

Luke 6:18 tells of people who were "vexed with unclean spirits." Later, we read of a multitude out of the cities round about Jerusalem bringing sick folks and those which were vexed with unclean spirits (Acts 5:16).

THIRD, SOME ARE POSSESSED. Getting control of the mind is the thought in this word. The Greek word used in Luke 8:36 to tell of some "possessed of devils" is *daimonizomai*. It means "to have a devil or to have demons."

Jesus spoke to a group of people on one occasion and said, "Ye are of your father the devil, and the lusts of your father ye will do. He was a murderer from the beginning. . ." (John 8:44).

It is most likely that the young man in the mental ward accused of being the "44 caliber killer" is still a child of Satan and was possessed by a demon that told him to go kill people.

Every lost sinner is a candidate for this type of circumstance. The only protection one has is to get Christ into the heart by truly repenting and exercising faith in His Word. The beautiful words of John will meet the need then.

"Ye are of God, little children, and have overcome them: because greater is he that is in you, than he that is in the world."—I John 4:4.

Chapter 16

A Word to the Backslider

The word *backslider* has a negative ring to it. Most people cringe or tighten when the name *Judas* or the word *hypocrite* is mentioned. So it is with the term *backslider*. It's like bad breath—most people won't tell you if you have it.

Solomon advises that the *backslider* in heart shall be filled with his own ways (Prov. 14:14).

It is important that we realize that a backslider is one who has lost fellowship, not salvation. The joy and happiness depart but not the Spirit. When King David sinned so grievously and finally came to himself, he prayed, "Restore unto me the joy of thy salvation" (Ps. 51:12). He did not pray for his salvation to return, but his joy.

The prodigal son was still a son and was restored to the fellowship of the home upon his return.

We recently studied in Sunday school the adventures of Simon Peter. One chapter in his book was an experience on backsliding. He became self-confident and boasted, "I will never forsake You, Lord." He was next seen following afar off and soon was warming his hands by the enemy's fire. An old Scottish woman said, "Peter had no business among the flunkies."

A parrot got loose and flew into the cornfield with the crows. When the farmer began to shoot crows, the parrot was wounded. While picking up dead crows, he saw the wounded parrot and picked it up. The parrot began to speak, "Bad company! Bad company!"

When a person lies down with dogs, he's likely to get up with fleas!

Peter's bad company and distance from the Lord's presence soon resulted in cursing and swearing. Finally, he left the Lord to go back to his fishing business. How sad, because it influenced several others to do the same!

I. IDENTIFYING SIGNS OF BACKSLIDING

Dr. H. A. Ironside said, "If you were ever closer to the Lord than you are right now, you're backslidden."

Just yesterday a young executive with the Ford Motor Company came to me and said, "Preacher, what's wrong with me? I don't have what I used to have." He had lost his zeal and intent, had become distracted and was miserable.

There are several identifying signs that reveal a backslidden condition.

1. Loss of heavenly values. When the excitement of Bible truth about the things of God is weak, worldly pleasures get a grip and claim our interest and time. The Bible gets dull, prayer is commonplace, church attendance does not have a pull, and living is hard. The problem is obvious.

2. Loss of conviction of sin. The darkness in a restaurant is not so bad as our eyes adjust to it. The closer to sin we get, the less we see wrong with it.

3. Lazy in service. Initiative and aggressive action is the theme of the Bible Christian. A tombstone in an old graveyard said:

Here rests John Brown. That is all he ever did.

There are thousands like that. Another read:

Here lies the body of a man who did no good,
and if he had lived, he never would.
Where he's gone and how he fares,
nobody knows—and nobody cares.

4. Putting people's word ahead of God's Word. Some are persuaded more by the opinion and advice of others than the plain, clear teaching of the Bible. They have a problem called a backslidden condition.

5. Loss of testimony. We are to let our light shine. Man's Christian character is like a tree, and his testimony is its shadow. It all depends upon his relationship to the Son.

Years ago we were having a street meeting, and several men had given testimony of the joy of the Lord in their life. Several churches were represented. The leader asked a man standing on the edge of the crowd if he would give a testimony. He bluntly answered, "I beg to be excused. I don't have any testimony."

A lot of others don't have one either, but they don't realize it. I'm sure there are many other signs, but let's move on to the . . .

II. INSIGHT INTO THE CAUSES OF BACKSLIDING

Sin for the Christian falls into two categories—sins of omission and sins of commission. One leads to the other. Most of the causes of backsliding are sins of omission.

1. Evil thinking. When a person's heart is not pure, he will begin to think evil. As a man thinketh in his heart, so is he. Paul tells us to "let this mind be in you which was also in Christ Jesus." A Christian would do well to post a guard at the doors and windows of his mind, lest "that which entereth into a man defileth him."

2. Worldly attitude. This problem is not just in things or involvement in pleasures. It is an attitude or spirit of worldliness that we must be alert to.

3. Root of bitterness. How sad to see a bitter person! They have usually slammed the door on a lot of people who love them and are concerned for them. Oh, the misery of a heart filled with grudge and an unforgiving spirit!

4. Self-centeredness. Some live only for themselves. Number One is all that matters! They have never learned the blessing of living for others. Jesus said, "Love thy neighbour as thyself."

5. Prayerlessness. Dr. Leonard Ravenhill said, "If we are not praying, we're playing." A spiritual, victorious person will delight to talk to God in prayer and will do it at every possible opportunity. As one preacher said, "I love to preach, and I'll preach at the drop of a hat. If necessary, I'll drop the hat." It should be that way with us when it comes to praying.

6. Gossip. Surely no one will argue that the gossiper is backslidden. "Let all . . . evil speaking, be put away from you" (Eph. 4:31). Like leaven through bread and a drop of ink in a glass of water, gossip will spread out over the whole area and have its dread effect.

7. Unbelief. To doubt is to drift. A person who is unsure will not boldly charge ahead and accomplish things for God. Where seeds of doubt are planted, backsliding begins to grow.

III. INSTRUCTION TO THE BACKSLIDER

If a Christian sees signs of backsliding and understands the cause of backsliding, he surely will be interested in the pathway home. There are some things you can do.

1. Confess your sin to God. We must come to ourselves like the prodigal and say to the Father, "I have sinned." "If we confess our sins, he is faithful and just to forgive us our sins, and to cleanse us from all unrighteousness" (I John 1:9).

Solomon said, "He that covereth his sins shall not prosper: but whoso confesseth and forsaketh them shall have mercy" (Prov. 28:13).

2. Forsake your sin. It is necessary to break with sin. Let every man be fully persuaded in his own mind. There must be a humbling and seeking after God. "If my people, which are called by my name, shall humble themselves, and pray, and seek my face, and turn from their wicked ways; then will I hear from heaven, and will forgive their sin, and will heal their land" (II Chron. 7:14).

My friend, if you find yourself backslidden and out of the pathway of God's blessing, heed the call of Hosea, "Come, and let us return unto the Lord" (Hosea 6:1).

Chapter 17

The Tattletale

David was on the run. King Saul was trying to kill him. He fled to the land of Nod, where Ahimelech took him into the Temple, gave him bread from the shewbread table, also the sword of Goliath, and sent him on his way.

Doeg saw it all. Later, when Saul complained that his followers were not being loyal to him but were giving their loyalty to his enemy, David, Doeg stood up and told the whole story, jeopardizing the life of Ahimelech and all the priests.

In a fit of anger, Saul demanded his followers to kill the priest and all the young priests in the Temple. They refused. In fury Saul turned to Doeg and demanded he do it. So Doeg took a sword and killed Ahimelech and eighty-five priests, along with their wives and children and all their animals. It was a terrible massacre.

All this is recorded in I Samuel 22:7-23. This was the background for Psalm 52, where David talks about the damage caused by the tongue of Doeg. In this Psalm, David mentions five different types of tongues: (1) the Boasting Tongue, (2) the Blasting Tongue, (3) the Beguiling Tongue, (4) the Bridled Tongue, and (5) the Blessed Tongue.

In speaking at a graduation service in Augusta, Georgia, a young lady was introduced who had been born with an undeveloped nerve in her tongue. The doctor predicted she would never talk, but when she stood to receive highest honors upon graduation, she made a beautiful speech. There was a slight impediment, but tears flowed down the cheeks of almost all present as they saw firsthand a tremendous lesson in discipline, therapy and the ability to control a situation that had been predicted uncontrollable.

There is a great need today to learn to develop a control over the human tongue.

I. THE BOASTING TONGUE

In Psalm 52:1 David says, *"Why boastest thou. . .?"*

Here is a message condemning self-sufficiency. Pride is an awful enemy of the Christian.

Nebuchadnezzar is an example of the man with the boasting tongue. He stood before the great city of Babylon with its Hanging Gardens and said, "Is not this great Babylon that I have built by the might of my power?" Within the hour, he was turned into a wild beast with the judgment of God upon him.

King Uzziah is another example. In his early reign, he sought the Lord. He had a highly-trained army of 307,500 soldiers with 2,600 courageous commanders. Jerusalem was attack-proof. They had artillery that could hurl huge stones at enemy armies. They had thousands of soldiers that could climb up on the wall and shoot a flood of arrows upon those who were trying to attack.

But then came self-confidence, and then self-sufficiency, and finally pride. Uzziah usurped the place of the priest and offered sacrifice upon the holy altar which was forbidden of God. He was smitten with leprosy and died a miserable man.

Pride blinds the eyes. It melts the mind and deceives the heart. It wears a variety of robes. Pride is seen in the long hair of young men trying to prove their point. Pride is found in the immodest dress of women. Pride shows itself in the motives of some businessmen. It is seen in the goal of many athletes.

Pride is everywhere. It's in the king's palace and the pauper's shack. It's in the pulpit and in the pew. You can see it in the choir loft as well as in the deacon's office. Pride is a terrible thing!

A young man was presented an award for some achievement in public. A lot of praise was given to him, causing him to get the big head. After the presentation, he said to his mother, "How many great men are there in the world today?" The wise old mother replied, "One less than you think."

II. THE BLASTING TONGUE

In verse 2 of the Psalm, David says, *"Thy tongue deviseth mischiefs; like a sharp razor, working deceitfully."*

The sin of gossip caused by jealousy and envy brings an awful curse upon humanity.

In North Dakota a man, his wife and two small children were very happy. They lived a quiet, peaceful life. One day the village gossip started a rumor that the man was being unfaithful to his wife. The cruel words soon reached her ears.

On coming home from work one evening, the man could not find his wife and children. He hunted everywhere. Finally, going down into the cellar, he found all three of them hanging from the rafters. The mother had hanged the two small children and herself out of a broken heart because she had believed the malicious rumor. Later, it was revealed that the rumor was completely unfounded. The man was completely innocent, but the damage had been done. The blasting tongue has caused many a heartache.

I recently read an article entitled "Wanted—Dead or Alive." It spoke of a known criminal who attacks without warning, usually coy and subtle. It is a killer to both body and soul. It destroys the esteemed values of life and will destroy all that is good and holy.

This killer turns wives against husbands and husbands against wives, parents against children and children against parents. It has split many a church, causing pastors to turn away in sorrow with their character slandered. It breaks the hearts of saints by destroying Christian standards and influence. It brings nation against nation and kingdom against kingdom, causing hate and distrust. It turns riches to rags and kindness into bitterness.

This killer has such aliases as "Envy," "Temper," "Gossip," "Liar," and "Jealousy." His true name is "The Tongue."

"But the tongue can no man tame; it is an unruly evil, full of deadly poison."—James 3:8.

John Wesley was deeply disturbed about people criticizing others. On one occasion a woman in the service kept glaring at him.

Finally, he realized it was his new bow-string tie.

At the end of the service she came up and said sharply, "Mr. Wesley, the strings on your bow tie are much too long. It is an offense to me."

He asked if any of the ladies present happened to have a pair of scissors. When someone produced a pair, he handed them to the lady and asked her to clip off the strings to her liking. She did so. Then he said, "Now, let me have those scissors. I am sure you wouldn't mind if I gave you a bit of correction. I don't want to be cruel, but I must tell you, Madam, that your tongue is an offense to me. It is too long! Please stick it out. I'd like to take some off!"

III. THE BEGUILING TONGUE

This is the sin of lying and deception. Solomon said:

"Lying lips are abomination to the Lord: but they that deal truly are his delight."—Prov. 12:22.

"He that speaketh lies shall not escape."—Prov. 19:5.

"Thou shalt not bear false witness against thy neighbour."—Exod. 20:16.

According to a UPI news item, the Metropolitan Insurance Company received some unusual explanations for accidents from its automobile insurance policyholders.

One said, "An invisible car came out of nowhere, struck my car and vanished."

Another stated, "The other car collided with mine without warning me of its intention."

Some of the other explanations were:

"I had been driving my car for forty years when I fell asleep at the wheel and had an accident."

"As I reached the intersection, a hedge sprang up obscuring my vision."

"I pulled away from the side of the road, glanced at my mother-in-law, and headed over the embankment."

"The pedestrian had no idea of which direction to go, so I ran over him!"

"The telephone pole was approaching fast. I attempted to swerve out of its path when it struck my front end."

"The guy was all over the road. I had to swerve a number of times before I hit him."

"The indirect cause of this accident was a little guy in a small car with a big mouth."

Someone wrote a poem entitled,

THE WAY OF A LIE

First somebody told it; then the room wouldn't hold it.
So the busy tongues rolled it 'til they got it outside.
Then the crowd came across it and never once lost it,
But tossed it and tossed it 'til it grew long and wide.

This lie brought forth others, both sisters and brothers,
And fathers and mothers—a terrible crew.
And while headlong they hurried, the people they flurried,
And troubled and worried, as lies always do.

And so evil-bodies, this monster lay goaded,
Till, at last it exploded, in smoke and in shame.
Then from mud and from mire, the pieces flew higher,
And hit the sad liar and killed a good name.

IV. THE BRIDLED TONGUE

In verse 8 David speaks of a green olive tree in the house of God. There is a difference between an olive tree in the house of God and one out in the field growing wild. The difference is cultivation. This one is pruned, trimmed, cared for, and disciplined.

James speaks of doing that to the tongue: "If any man among you seem to be religious, and bridleth not his tongue, but deceiveth his own heart, this man's religion is vain" (1:26).

He also spoke these words, "If any man offend not in word, the same is a perfect man [or controlled], and able also to bridle the whole body. Behold, we put bits in the horses' mouths, that they may obey us..." (3:2,3).

Teachers tell us that we have at least 700 occasions to speak daily. Some 12,000 sentences come from our lips involving 100,000 words.

So we speak a very thick book every day. If these were all recorded and put on a shelf, we would have thousands upon thousands of volumes of recorded phraseology to take with us to the Judgment Seat of Christ.

"But I say unto you, That every idle word that men shall speak, they shall give account thereof in the day of judgment."—Matt. 12:36.

Someone said,

> The boneless tongue, so small and weak,
> Can crush and kill, declared the Greek.
> The tongue destroys a greater horde,
> The Turk asserts, than does the sword.
> The Persian proverb wisely saith,
> A lengthy tongue—an early death.
> The tongue can speak a word whose speed,
> Says the Chinese, outstrips the steed.
>
> While Arab sages this impart,
> The tongue's great storehouse is the heart.
> For Hebrews' wit from mouth is sprung,
> Though feet should slip, ne'er let the tongue.
>
> The sacred writer crowns the whole,
> Who keeps the tongue doth keep his soul.

James informs us of the threefold power of the tongue.

There is the power to direct. He speaks of bits in the horses' mouths and rudders to guide the ships.

Then, there is the power to destroy. He speaks of a fire burning and devouring.

Third, there is the power to delight: "Out of the same mouth proceedeth blessing and cursing. . ." (James 3:10).

Recently one of our ladies crossing the parking lot on Sunday morning was on her way to teach a Sunday school class. I gave her a friendly compliment. She smiled and said, "Preacher, you have made my day." Just a little word of blessing can make the day for many a person.

V. THE BLESSED TONGUE

In verse 9 David says, "I will praise thee for ever. . . ."

Praise is the magic word, according to Dr. Kopmeyer of Louisville, a noted writer of psychological help books. He calls it "The Wonder Drug," saying it has an amazing effect of lifting and encouraging people when they are down.

Paul and Silas were in jail on Death Row at midnight. It was cold, dark and damp. Their feet were fixed fast in the stocks. There was no hope. But suddenly, they sang praises to God, and the prisoners heard them.

David said in Psalm 147:1, "Praise ye the Lord: for it is good to sing praises unto our God; for it is pleasant; and praise is comely."

I read somewhere of a group who visited a leper colony. When the lepers were assembled, they were a sad-looking lot. The author of the article said,

> I was sure that they would sing the song, "I must tell Jesus all of my troubles. I cannot bear these burdens alone. . ."; instead, when they broke into song they started with, "Singing I go along life's road, Praising the Lord, Praising the Lord. Singing I go along life's road, For Jesus has lifted my load."

Thank God for the blessed tongue of praise!

Chapter 18

Why Every Town in America Should Have a Christian Day School

"And these words, which I command thee this day, shall be in thine heart: And thou shalt teach them diligently unto thy children, and shalt talk of them when thou sittest in thine house, and when thou walkest by the way, and when thou liest down, and when thou risest up."—Deut. 6:6,7.

"Children are an heritage of the Lord," says David. And parents certainly have a sacred responsibility to care for them in the basic areas of their life.

There are five basic areas of a child that need developing:

The physical: Since the body is the temple of the Holy Ghost, that area needs attention and personal care.

The mental: It is so vitally important that we work toward a positive outlook in a pessimistic and negative world.

The social: Certainly we have a responsibility to teach righteousness and holy relationships in society.

The emotional: All of us understand the great need for balance in this area.

The spiritual: The inner man and his relationship to God.

In the public and government school system, attention to the spiritual is frowned upon and in many cases, outlawed.

One could not imagine the Jews coming out of Egypt and through the wilderness; finally, entering into the Promised Land, fighting the battles, conquering the land, then turning their children over to the Canaanites, the Hittites, the Hivites, the Jebusites, the Amorites and the Perizzites, to teach them of their false gods, worship of images, etc.

A child's mind is an unexposed film—like a photograph plate. What that child is exposed to through the five senses of sight, hearing, taste, feeling and smelling leaves an indelible impression upon the subconscious mind.

Solomon touched on this when he said, "Train up a child in the way he should go: and when he is old, he will not depart from it" (Prov. 22:6).

Children are "copycats." They imitate teachers—their vocabulary, habit patterns, attitudes, philosophies, theories, tone of voice, diction, mannerisms, etc. Then how important it is that they be exposed to the right kind of person.

Maxwell Maltz wrote a book called *Psycho-Cybernetics*. In it he made reference to subconscious storage of the mind and spoke about the fact that everything that we come in contact with is absorbed in our subconscious mind and becomes a part of us.

When the philosophies and the theories of the world continually are exposed to our children, they automatically adopt them and accept them as right. They grow up in rebellion against the over-thirties. In short, they are stolen from their mothers and fathers through the process of brainwashing.

An old farmer had a field full of beautiful sheep. A visitor from the city asked him how he managed to raise such beautiful sheep. His statement touched on this great truth that we've been discussing: "I take good care of my lambs."

I think the problem before us today can be seen clearly in an illustration of the man and woman who took their little five-year-old boy fishing. The purpose of the trip was to get alone to talk about their family problems.

They left the little boy under a tree with his hook in the water and a couple of worms in the can. The parents walked down the bank a couple hundred feet and sat down under another tree. They threw their poles in, not bothering to bait the hooks. They simply wanted to talk about their family problems, not catch fish.

After awhile, a game warden came along. He saw the little boy fishing and asked him if he were catching anything. "No, my fish worms keep biting," the little boy said.

"Let me see those fish worms," the game warden said. Then he asked, "Where did you get these?"

The little boy pointed to a rock and explained, "I turned over that rock, and they just ran everywhere. I grabbed them, put them in my can; but they kept biting me."

He had thirty bites on his hands. The little worms turned out to be little Copperhead snakes.

The man grabbed up the boy, ran to his parents, loaded them all in an automobile, sped away to the city; but the little fellow died before reaching the emergency room, a victim of his own innocence.

So it is with hundreds of thousands of boys and girls who file into the classrooms to be taught by socialistic, communistic, materialistic, anti-Bible, anti-God government schoolteachers.

It has been my privilege to organize and build two large Christian day schools. The first one was in Elkton, Maryland, in relation to the Baptist Bible Church there. It became a very successful program, with approximately 600 day-school students.

I had the joy of giving the commencement address to the first graduating class of seniors. The growth, maturity and development of those young people was worth all of the twenty-odd years I'd put into the ministry. I felt in my heart that evening that this type program was the answer to the ills of our country.

What a joy a few weeks ago to give the graduation message at Beth Haven Christian Schools! Twenty-five seniors walked down the aisle to receive their diplomas. Our school has approximately 1,100 pupils; and to witness the discipline, ethics, principles or morality being taught and enforced by our administrator and teachers brought a real revival to my soul.

As far as I'm concerned, this is the answer to almost everything.

Now why should we have Christian day schools across America? Because of the

I. DRIFT AWAY FROM EVERYTHING CHRISTIANS COUNT PRECIOUS

Jesus said, "Man shall not live by bread alone, but by every word that proceedeth out of the mouth of God" (Matt. 4:4).

There was a time in America when the law required that children memorize the Lord's Prayer and the Ten Commandments. It was required that teachers have daily Bible reading and public praying. Now, that same law forbids all these things.

The first nine colleges organized in America were church-sponsored, with one exception—Harvard in 1636, William and Mary in 1693, Yale in 1701, Princeton in 1743, Columbia in 1754, Brown in 1765, Rutgers in 1766, and Dartmouth in 1769. The one exception was the University of Pennsylvania in 1755.

These first eight were opened for the sole purpose of training young men for the ministry. Now, of course, all of these have been stolen by the secular society, and it frowns upon the very principles for which it was founded.

Schools have gone from religious-sponsored to non-religious, then to anti-religious. They have passed through various stages, from godly, to non-godly, then to ungodly, and finally, to anti-godly.

Since 72 percent of state income is spent for education, and since the largest payroll in the state and the largest employer in the state and the largest number of employees are involved in public education, there is more influence exerted here than in any other area of our society. It is obvious that we have a great need to be concerned and burdened about this and try to get something done about it.

Some think we should stay in and be the "salt of the earth," trying to flavor and hold check on the drift toward anarchy and anti-everything.

It would be wise for us to remember that this same principle did not work for the Methodist church. They still went into modernism, in spite of the old saints who tried to hold the line.

Neither did it work for the Presbyterian church. It did not work for the American Baptist Convention, and it is certainly not working for the Southern Baptist Convention.

The basic principle of the Scripture is: "Come out from among them, and be ye separate, saith the Lord" (II Cor. 6:17).

Schools have always been a place where people gathered to get and to give information on social projects and needs in the community. Now they have become a center for propagating socialism and political reform.

Years ago a Harvard team studying education said, "Education is not complete without moral guidance." Dr. John Dugger said, "Most of America's early success and growth is largely attributed to her Christian fortitude, and her present troubles and confusion to its lack of Christian fortitude."

Before the Revolutionary War, 80 percent of school curriculum was religious in content. Now it is ZERO; and more than that, it is anti-religious. A hundred years ago practically no atheism or materialism was taught in schools; now 90 percent of the content of school curriculum is atheistic or materialistic.

We need to start Christian day schools because of the

II. CONFLICT BETWEEN TWO BASIC PHILOSOPHIES OF EDUCATION

Not long ago Dr. Robert Billings said, "We cannot, we must not allow children of fundamental, Bible-believing people to be poisoned by smart-aleck teachers who pooh-pooh the Word of God."

The basic conflict shows up in all major areas of our life.

In education, the conflict is progressivism versus traditionalism.

In the field of science, it is evolution versus creation.

In religion, it is liberalism versus fundamentalism.

In politics, it is socialism versus capitalism.

In ethics, it is humanism versus theism.

In psychology, it is expression versus discipline.

In philosophy, it is materialism versus other-world-ism, or the eternal versus the temporary.

Someone has wisely declared, "Their music is not our music; in fact, it is not music. Their art is not our art; it's not even art. Their god is not our God, for their god is self, and ours is the God of Heaven."

It is important to remember that an ounce of prevention is still worth a pound of cure. One Christian schoolteacher is worth a dozen policemen. And one year in a Christian school may save a young man ten years in jail.

We should start Christian day schools because of

III. SITUATION ETHICS AND NEW MORALITY

In the government schools, the new morality is nothing but old immorality! Situation ethics is just an excuse for being able to sin and live in the old carnal nature. Their philosophy—"everything is good"; their practice—everything goes; their product—everything gone!

Their philosophy teaches that pre-marital and extra-marital sex are perfectly all right; that people who have a desire to live on abnormal sex or perversion, such as homosexuality and lesbianism, should be just as welcome in our society as anyone else. Their basic teaching is pro-abortion, and the sex education taught in our public school system is usually taught by teachers who hold to these carnal, worldly *Playboy* magazine philosophies. We cannot stand by and see our children exposed to all that filth and trash!

Another reason for Christian day schools is simply

IV. THE ACADEMIC STANDARDS ARE SO MUCH HIGHER

Thousands of high school graduates cannot read. In a 1980 *Reader's Digest* article, examples were given of students who just couldn't handle reading or writing. One junior-high student wrote the sentence:

> The old brige was a swing brige and it was a real old brige. The bords was roten in the brige and you could see right through the brige. In some places bords was missing.

A seventeen-year-old wrote:

> My famous person whom I admire the most is John Wayne. He is a famous person in many peoples eyes of America.

These seventeen-year-olds sound like second graders. In our comparison of Christian day school students to high school students in government schools, we found the Christian school students to be two or three grades ahead.

We must start Christian day schools to

V. PROTECT OUR YOUNG FROM CRIME, DRUGS, DE-STRUCTION OF PROPERTY AND VANDALISM

Two years ago there was over $500 million worth of damage in government schools in America. It is predicted that this year the figure will be $600 million.

Ask any administrator of a Christian day school what their vandalism and property damage figure is, and, almost without exception, you can mark down ZERO!

In the public schools last year, 1979, there were 100 murders by student vandals; 12,000 armed robberies, 270,000 burglaries and 9,000 rapes. Some schools have become public battlefields. One person referred to the public school system as the reign of schoolhouse terror.

In a recent article pointing out the drift of crime and destruction, Paul Harvey emphasized that the public schools had to accept the responsibility for not doing anything to counteract it.

The crime bill in America this past year was $27 billion. There's a fatal shooting every 30 minutes; a rape every 26 minutes; a burglary every 26 seconds; a larceny every 12 seconds; 800,000 have been divorced; and in Kentucky this past month, there were more divorces than weddings! It seems to get worse every year. While the federal government pours millions of dollars into crime prevention and studies, it continues to happen.

It is surely true that "the god of this world hath blinded the minds of them which believe not" (II Cor. 4:4).

We believe that the Christian day school students are not involved in ANY of these things. The percentage is so low in things like drugs, vandalism, crime and the like among Christian day school students that anyone with an ounce of brains will see that this is the answer to our problems in America.

There's another basic reason why Christian schools should be started: because of the

VI. ROTTEN TEXTBOOKS USED IN GOVERNMENT SCHOOLS

The textbooks are filled with cursing and vulgar talk. There are the detailed descriptions of sex acts. The communist and socialistic philosophies are propagated. The books degrade parental authority. They downgrade great heroes of our history. They exalt the women's lib movement. They fight for the rights of radicals, revolutionaries, homosexuals, draft-card burners and all the rest of that crowd.

Max Rafferty recently said, in one of his articles released to newspapers across the country:

> I've been here at Charleston, West Virginia, testifying in the "dirty textbook case," and I'm as frustrated as Bella Abzug with laryngitis. When the TV and the radio boys asked me what words I objected to, I couldn't reply. Oh, it wasn't that there weren't a whole slew of Anglo-Saxon, four-letter, lavatory walls, graffiti expressions crawling through the kiddies textbooks, like boll weevils in a cotton bale. It was just that none of the media could print them or say them because of their own decency codes, so there was no way for the general public to be told what all the fuss was about. After all, the news story about unspecified, improper language assigned to school children has all the impact of a wet noodle, compared to the bombshell of the actual filth, presented in the form of newspaper headlines.
>
> I've got the same problem in writing this column. I know how bad the books are, but I can't share my knowledge with the public because your local family newspaper would refuse to carry my quotations.
>
> The best I can do is bowdlerize the unspeakable, carefully laundered terminology, and leave the actual expressions to your imagination. In this connection, let me add that in this case, no imagination, vivid as it may be, can hold a candle to the real thing.
>
> I finally asked the media this: "If you fellows follow a code which prevents you from using the words and expressions which contaminate and fester in these books, don't you think the educators and textbook publishers should adopt a similar code?"
>
> If the reading and listening public, in general, is entitled to protection from a Niagara of nausea, shouldn't the children be entitled to even more protection; especially since, unlike your customers, school children are a captive audience?

Mr. Rafferty continues by saying,

> Nobody will answer my questions or offer rebuttal. They just give
> hang-dog glances and sheepish silence. There's more here than
> meets the eye, friend. There's big money here and big planning
> by big corporations. "Somebody," to quote Jenkins Lloyd Jones,
> "is tampering with the soul of America."

One couple from Springfield, Missouri, took their children out of
the public school for a number of reasons. The thing came to a head
one day when a play in the school involving the boys was brought
to their attention.

> There was a scene of a pig being killed by slitting its throat. Many
> other details followed, including a woman kissing the blood off the
> man. It was full of cursing, drinking, and smoking. We refused to
> let our son take part in it. He also had to write a slang dictionary
> of words that we had been trying to get out of his mind, like, "the
> old man" for father, "chick" for a young girl, and a few words much
> worse—these words that we feel show disrespect and teach rebellion
> against authority. We couldn't take it, so we removed our children
> and transferred them to a Christian school.

We need Christian day schools because of the

VII. STRONG DISCIPLINE PROGRAMS

Solomon said, "Foolishness is bound in the heart of a child; but
the rod of correction shall drive it far from him" (Prov. 22:15). In
our schools our creed is the Word of God, our conduct is the will
of God; our code, the work of God. Children need to be taught
restraint and basic authority lines.

Our associate pastor and his wife and children were having family
devotions. They gave rigid instructions to their children not to speak
while the Bible was being read or while prayer was being offered.

One little guy seemed very restless. He twisted and turned but did
not speak. The wife kept putting her arm around him and patting him
on the shoulder while the verses were being read. Then one by one
they prayed. At long last it became his turn. Finally he blurted out
his prayer: "God, please tell Mommy she's sitting on my foot." He

had gotten the lesson and dared not speak out or make a motion while devotions were being held.

Finally, we need Christian day schools

VIII. TO TEACH BASIC BIBLE PRINCIPLES

The Bible is filled with principles and facts. We can learn many, many facts from the stories of the Scripture; but the principles are absorbed subconsciously, and there are few of them.

The spiritual or inner man absorbs these basic teachings and gets control of the outer and the physical.

Someone has likened this to a diamond ring in a beautiful box, presented by a young man to his bride. She squealed with delight as she took out the diamond and put it in her pocket and "ah-ed" and "ooh-ed" over the beautiful box. She kept talking about what a beautiful little box it was, completely ignoring the diamond.

So it is with the person who gives all the attention to the outer and the physical, ignoring the precious jewel of the inner man.

We are taught in Scripture that as we absorb the basic principles and observe them, our way will be prosperous and we will have good success.

Some time ago *Christian Century* magazine gave a test to 83 college students to see how much Bible knowledge they possessed. Of the 83, some 68 were Protestant, 11 were Roman Catholic, 3 were no preference, and 1 was Greek Orthodox.

Seventy of them could not name the Gospels; 80 did not know the books containing the Lord's Prayer—8 guessed the Psalms; 74 had no idea what the two great commandments were; 70 had no idea how many books are in the Bible; 81 did not know what Testament meant; 53 did not know the original language of the New Testament; 34 thought the Beatitudes were in the Old Testament; 33 thought the Beatitudes were written by Paul; 35 named Job, Jeremiah, Proverbs or Ecclesiastes as the last book of the Bible; while 52 thought the forerunner of Jesus was Moses.

In evaluating the cost of Christian education, we have come to the conclusion that we have a choice between driving a new car or sheltering our children. I don't know about you, but my children are more important to me than driving a new car, so my choice has been made.

The story was told of a man who came into town with an old buckboard and two horses. He hitched them to the post and began to get provisions out of the general store. Some dogs came along and barked at the horses. Soon they pulled loose and ran out into the street.

Seeing the commotion, the old man rushed out of the store and ran as hard as he could to head them off. The people yelled and hollered, "Get out of there, old man; you'll get yourself killed." "Look out, you'll get hurt."

He continued to run until finally he got hold of the reins and worked himself up alongside one of the horses, throwing himself around between the two, yanking and pulling on their bridles to get them to stop. Then the hoof of one horse caught his foot, and the pain caused him to turn loose. He was trampled and thrown back under the wagon and out into the street.

The large group gathered around him quickly. One man knelt down and put his hand under his head and yelled, "Old man, why did you get yourself killed?"

The old man, gurgling in his dying blood, said, "Look in the wagon! Look in the wagon!"

Someone ran up to the wagon and saw his little four-year-old grandson was waking from his nap. He'd been a crazy old fool up to that point, but now he was a hero.

Friends, I think that the world looks upon us as "crazy fools" by paying extra tuition, building buildings, furnishing transportation, hiring teachers, doing what the government would do for us free. But wait until everybody takes a good look and sees what is really involved. Then they are going to say, "God bless you people! You had more wisdom than we thought."

Chapter 19

The Outcry of the Grassroots

"Is it nothing to you, all ye that pass by?"—Lam. 1:12.

The Weeping Prophet Jeremiah saw the deplorable conditions of the city of Jerusalem. He watched while thousands upon thousands of Jews filed by and observed the problems, yet did nothing. Finally, he got all he could take; and I suppose he screamed out, "Is it nothing to you, all ye that pass by?" (Lam. 1:12).

We have just about lost all our freedoms. One large billboard on the expressway here in Louisville displayed a huge arm and sickle and carried the caption, **WELCOME TO THE GESTAPO STATE!**

Churches all across America have been forced to hire attorneys to keep Christian schools open. In Kentucky, we have been forced to spend thousands upon thousands of dollars that we did not have. The Kentucky Department of Education launched an all-out crusade to close our schools. The preacher who headed up this crusade, while addressing a large delegation of secondary and public school leaders, dropped dead in front of the entire gathering.

The I.R.S. also put on a crusade to impose new restrictions that would force Christian schools out of business in this country. The Unemployment Compensation Department of Kentucky kept us in court several days attempting to secularize our program and refusing to recognize we have a right to exist and exercise our freedoms.

The Christian camps around the country have been struggling in court for the simple rights to carry on their programs free of political, social and secular control.

Church finance houses have gone down and pulled several hundred growing ministries into bankruptcy because of the bureaucratic Security Commission of Washington demanding a grip over their activities.

Forced busing has been crammed down the throats of the Americans against the will of the majority. Rights groups have been lauded and displayed as loyal Americans in the media and in social programs everywhere.

The bureaucrats have cuddled the E.R.A., the homosexuals, the abortion crowd and the socialist groups. Meanwhile, they've been running roughshod over the rights of all of the great majority of moral Americans. The Kennedys, McGoverns, Mondales, Bayhs, and the Frank Churches have been joined by the liberal clergy to make God-fearing folks with high standards and obedient to the laws of the land and the moral people of principle and decency to look like backwoods dumbbells, prudes, ignoramuses and nincompoops.

The F.B.I., one of the greatest crime prevention organizations in the world, and its agents have been pictured as creepy criminals as they gather evidence against the Black Panthers, the communist conspirators and the revolutionaries who burn our flags.

But it looks like we've had enough! We've had it up to here! We're sick and tired of being sick and tired! The sleeping dog is refusing to lie still any longer. The moral American majority has spoken! The grassroots of this land have expressed their concern.

We're upset by their giving away the Panama Canal. We're embarrassed that hostages are still being held captive. We're mad that they want to pass gun-control laws so we won't be able to stop their takeover when the time comes. We're shocked on the insistence of more taxes for stupid giveaway programs. We're amazed at their forbidding prayer and Bible reading in our schools. We're sick of the arrogant attitude of the bureaucrats who come on private property and make demands that go contrary to the Constitution of our land.

We're tired of the Environmental Protection Agency's regulations that choke the economy and bring national bankruptcy. We're bothered at all the oil, coal and natural gas reserves frozen in government lands while we are brought to our knees by third-rate powers around the world and blackmailed with the exorbitant crude oil prices.

We're through in this country with a government of all chiefs and no Indians. Our understanding of government is that it is supposed to be "by the people and for the people." We've been experiencing a "people for the government" arrangement. We've had to decide in this country, "Shall we have controlled citizens, or shall we have controlled government?"

Grassroots fundamentalists have been growing in this country. Christian day schools continue to open at the rate of three per day. For the majority, the great conservative, born-again element—fifty million strong—stood behind Jimmy Carter in his election. But they felt betrayed over and over again, and once was enough.

We have seen the light! We have risen up to speak our piece. Jeremiah's cry, "Is it nothing to you, all ye that pass by?" has been heard. The answer has been demonstrated in the landslide victory of the conservative voter in this country.

In answer to the question, "Does anybody really care?" obviously there is some honest concern. Like Elijah of old, we have paraded into Ahab's office and declared, "You are the cause of all this!" Like Nathan the prophet, we have put our finger in David's face and said, "Thou art the man!" Somebody does care.

Years ago I read a magazine article called, "Careville, U.S.A." It was a beautiful story about a group of concerned people who joined together to meet the needs of people in their area when it was within their power to do so. Everybody lived for others. What a Utopia, a Golden Age, that little town had!

Dr. Joe Henry Hankins used to preach his famous sermon, "Going to Hell—Who Cares?" Brother Hankins pointed out...

1. *GOD THE FATHER CARES.* He quoted, "The Lord is not slack concerning his promise . . . not willing that any should perish, but that all should come to repentance" (II Pet. 3:9).

2. *GOD THE SON CARES,* for He said, "Come unto me, all ye that labour and are heavy laden, and I will give you rest" (Matt. 11:28).

3. *GOD THE SPIRIT CARES.* We see that concern in the statement,

"And the Spirit and the bride say, Come" (Rev. 22:17).

4. *THE LOST IN HELL CARE.* The rich man burning in Hell cried out to Abraham and Lazarus in his bosom, ". . . I pray thee therefore, father, that thou wouldest send him [Lazarus] to my father's house: For I have five brethren; that he may testify unto them, lest they also come into this place of torment" (Luke 16:27,28).

5. *THE SAVED IN HEAVEN CARE.* We are told, ". . . we also are compassed about with so great a cloud of witnesses . . ." (Heb. 12:1).

I. WE NEED TO CARE ABOUT THIS COUNTRY

Conservative Christians everywhere and fundamental Bible believers are elated at the general concern evidenced by the landslide victory of the conservative element in the presidential election. The conservatives are in!

We cannot let this country go down the drain. It is time for all good Christians and loyal Americans to rise up and put on a brand new program of praying for our leaders and giving our moral support to those who will lead us in a direction of righteousness.

We are expecting our Christian liberties to be expanded. We hope to be able to operate our Christian schools without a lot of bureaucratic opposition. Once again we can feel good about rendering unto Caesar that which is Caesar's and relax while we render unto God that which is God's. We expect the I.R.S. and the various bureaucratic agencies of the government to stop trying to act like God.

I'll be honest with you. I had begun to resent paying taxes to a government that would not use my money wisely, and I resented being treated like a second-rate citizen because I wanted to raise my children in a Christian environment and not be told what I had to believe.

We must revive our concern and care for this country and cooperate and work together with our leaders to bring about the development and growth of unity and harmony in the greatest nation on the face of the earth.

II. WE NEED TO CARE ABOUT OUR OWN CITY

It is said of Jesus, "And when he was come near, he beheld the city, and wept over it" (Luke 19:41). He said again, "O Jerusalem, Jerusalem, thou that killest the prophets, and stonest them which are sent unto thee, how often would I have gathered thy children together, even as a hen gathereth her chickens under her wings, and ye would not!" (Matt. 23:37).

Jeremiah carried this same concern over his city. He cried out, "Oh that my head were waters, and mine eyes a fountain of tears, that I might weep day and night for the slain of the daughter of my people!" (Jer. 9:1). He said again, "Mine eye runneth down with rivers of water..." (Lam. 3:48).

We must get the ear of our city by radio and television. We must get the eye of our city through newspaper articles and church papers. We must get into the homes of our city through visitation. We must get to the sick of our city by visiting in the hospitals. We must get to the elderly and senior citizens of our city through working in the nursing homes. We must get to the heart of our city through the message that God has given us in His Word.

A little girl in a railroad station with her grandmother waiting for the train noticed a law-enforcement officer with a prisoner handcuffed to his wrist. The prisoner looked gloomy and dejected. The little girl walked right up to him while her grandmother was not watching and said, "Mister, you don't have to be so sad. Jesus loves you." The man snarled and jumped at her, only to be yanked back to his seat by the officer.

The grandmother quickly grabbed the little girl and cautioned, "The man is very unhappy. You should not bother him. Now you stay away from that unhappy man!"

In a few minutes, the grandmother was busy doing something else, and the little girl once again quietly slipped in front of the man and said, "Mister, please don't be unhappy. Jesus really loves you." The man snarled and growled again.

This time the grandmother got hold of the girl and pulled her away and found a new seat.

For the third time, the girl was able to slip unnoticed from the grandmother's side and repeat her piercing statement, "Mister, remember—

Jesus really loves you, and you don't have to be unhappy!"

It was testified that, after days and nights, weeks and months in a prison cell, that poor, miserable wretch of a human being slipped to his knees by his bunk in a cell and opened his heart to Jesus Christ. . . all because of the testimony of a little girl who reminded him that Jesus loved him.

Like the little girl, we must have a love for the people of our city.

III. WE NEED TO CARE ABOUT OUR CHURCH

Jesus loved the church and gave Himself for it (Eph. 5:25).

While recently discussing some problems with an experienced, seasoned pastor, he looked me straight in the eye and said, "Brother Wallace, do you really love your people?" I thought I did, but I was hesitant to answer the question with boldness and assurance. He sensed it immediately. He gave me some good counsel. I went away from that conference analyzing my feelings with a new realization that God expected me to love the people that He has given me to work with.

We must care about our church.

We must care enough to attend all the services and encourage the fellowship of believers, for we are taught, "Not forsaking the assembling of ourselves together, as the manner of some is; but exhorting one another: and so much the more, as ye see the day approaching" (Heb. 10:25).

We must care enough to sing when the songs are presented, to shake hands with fellow believers and encourage visitors. We must pray for the spirit of the meeting, doing all in our power to add to the flavor and atmosphere of the place.

We need to care about our churches. Over 6,000 Southern Baptist churches had no professions of faith or baptisms recorded during the entire year of 1979. That speaks very emphatically that some are having problems really caring about their church.

IV. WE NEED TO CARE ABOUT CHRISTIAN BRETHREN

We are told in the Word of God, "We know that we have passed from death unto life, because we love the brethren . . . " (I John 3:14).

Paul said, "Brethren, if a man be overtaken in a fault, ye which are spiritual, restore such an one in the spirit of meekness . . . " (Gal. 6:1).

John said, "But whoso hath this world's good, and seeth his brother have need, and shutteth up his bowels of compassion from him, how dwelleth the love of God in him?" (I John 3:17).

In March of 1969, in Venice, California, little four-year-old Mary Elizabeth Lazano was stolen from her bed crying out, "Mommy, Daddy! Help! Help me!" She has never been found. Public sympathy for the sorrowing parents was accompanied by the express thought, "Why didn't they go to her when she called?" The answer was that they thought she was just crying out in her sleep, and both turned over and went back to sleep. On rising in the morning, they found her gone.

To this day nobody has the answers to the questions, "Who did it?" "Where is she?" "Why?" How sad, how sad!

But I'm afraid this is the attitude and problem among Christian believers. So many believers among us constantly are crying out for help because of burdens and problems, while those who could help are not aroused and stirred enough to help meet their needs. They are gone from us. We know not their whereabouts and their plight.

V. WE NEED TO CARE ABOUT CONDEMNED SINNERS, TOO

Jesus said, " . . . but he that believeth not is condemned already, because he hath not believed in the name of the only begotten Son of God" (John 3:18).

Jesus pleaded constantly for His children to pray the Lord of the harvest that He would send forth laborers into the harvest because the harvest is great but the laborers are few (Matt. 9:37,38).

A recent article called "Lost—One Boy" related that the boy had not been kidnaped by bandits and hidden in a cave to weep, starve and raise a nation to a frenzied searching. Were that the case, a hundred thousand men would rise to the rescue if need be. Unfortunately, the losing of the lad is without dramatic excitement, though very sad and very real indeed. The fact is, his father lost him by being too busy to sit with him at the fireside and answer his trivial questions during the years when a father is the only great hero of a boy.

The mother lost him, too, being engrossed in teas, dinners and club programs. The church, also, has lost him. It is occupied with sermons for the elderly and wise who pay the bills and has made no provision to sing songs and give messages on his level.

Now many sad-hearted parents in the church are looking earnestly for their boy. But he is gone! How sad, how sad!

Someone has written,

> There are ninety and nine that safely lie
>   In the shelter of the fold.
> But millions are left outside to die,
>   For the ninety and nine are cold.
> Away in sin's elusive snare,
>   Hastening to death and dark despair.
> Hastening to death and none to care,
>   For the ninety and nine are cold.
> Lord, Thou hast here Thy well-fed sheep.
>   Are they not enough for Thee?
> But the Shepherd made answer, "Millions sleep,
>   On the brink of eternity."
> And these My sheep within the fold,
>   Care not for the dying in sin's stronghold.
> Care not for the dying outside the fold,
>   On the brink of eternity.

Thank the Lord that the grassroots people of this country have risen up to show concern. May it spread like a field-fire through our churches and fellowships to the point where every lost sinner in our towns will know that somebody cares.

Chapter 20

Priming the Pump

(Preached at Missionary Conference at Franklin Road Baptist Church, Murfreesboro, Tennessee, Tuesday evening, January 13, 1981)

"There is that scattereth, and yet increaseth; and there is that withholdeth more than is meet, but it tendeth to poverty."—Prov. 11:24.

There is a wonderful principle here.

If this pastor, Dr. Bob Kelley, were to say tonight, "I want to introduce you to Solomon, one who is known as the richest man of all time," he could tell us that his fortune would have amounted to Paul Getty's and Howard Hughes' added together and multiplied by three. "I will have Solomon come and make one little comment."

I would tune my ear on what Solomon had to say to me.

If Dr. Kelley were to say tonight, "I want to bring to you the man who is known as the wisest man of all time, except for the Lord Jesus Himself," he would introduce Solomon; and Solomon would say, "I am going to give you one statement." I believe the richest and the wisest would say:

> There was a man I knew who went around scattering, scattering, scattering, constantly giving away, but he kept on increasing and increasing and increasing. I knew another man who withheld more than was necessary, and he ended up broke. It tendeth to poverty.

Solomon would then go away, leaving us to chew on those words.

I got to thinking about that principle. The Bible is filled with many, many facts but just a few principles. This principle—what I call a trigger verse in Scripture—goes all the way through the Bible.

I would like to give more money to missions, wouldn't you? I would like to be able to get my hands on more money so that I could give more money in order that I might have more money to give. I have no desire to have money for myself. I got that settled long ago, and God has blessed and prospered me far above my worthiness. I have enjoyed learning how to give. In searching the Scripture to see what God had to say about it, I learned some wonderful things.

The Lord has a lot to say about this. He says, "I am looking for some people who will let Me work with them." He said on one occasion,

"Thou shalt not delay to offer the first of thy ripe fruits, and of thy liquors [or thy juices]: *the firstborn of thy sons shalt thou give unto me. Likewise shalt thou do with thine oxen, and with thy sheep: seven days it shall be with his dam; on the eighth day thou shalt give it me."*—Exod. 22:29,30.

And in Proverbs 3:9,10, we read,

"Honour the Lord with thy substance, and with the firstfruits of all thine increase: So shall thy barns be filled with plenty, and thy presses shall burst out with new wine."

He said again,

"But thou shalt remember the Lord thy God: for it is he that giveth thee power to get wealth."—Deut. 8:18.

He said yet again,

"Thou shalt truly tithe all the increase of thy seed, that the field bringeth forth year by year."—Deut. 14:22.

And again,

"All the tithe of the land, whether of the seed of the land, or of the fruit of the tree, is the Lord's: it is holy unto the Lord."—Lev. 27:30.

Then He said,

"Bring ye all the tithes into the storehouse. . . and prove me now herewith, saith the Lord of hosts, if I will not open you the windows

of heaven, and pour you out a blessing, that there shall not be room enough to receive it."—Mal. 3:10.

Then He said,

"Give, and it shall be given unto you; good measure, pressed down, and shaken together, and running over, shall men give into your bosom. For with the same measure that ye mete withal it shall be measured to you again."—Luke 6:38.

Then He said,

"He which soweth sparingly shall reap also sparingly; and he which soweth bountifully shall reap also bountifully."—II Cor. 9:6.

There are many, many, many other verses like these.

These, in the finance realm, are trigger verses.

There are multitudes of trigger verses on prayer. Someone came into the room tonight and triggered the light switch, and power flowed from the hydroelectric plant by the transmission lines into the transformers; power was distributed into this circuit system and through the wires to these lights so that all that preparation could be channeled in here for our comfort and benefit. But someone had to trigger it to get it all here for us.

Now God has worked out all the arrangements, and He has made every necessary detail ready so you and I can click the switch. He said,

"Them that honour me I will honour."—I Sam. 2:30.

"Ask, and it shall be given you; seek, and ye shall find; knock, and it shall be opened unto you."—Matt. 7:7.

"Give, and it shall be given unto you."—Luke 6:38.

There is always a trigger verse, always a little switch to turn. And if I can just learn the secret of turning those switches, if I can somehow get this straight—that's the answer.

Abraham went up on the mountain; and the Lord said, "Abraham, I want your boy." Abraham consented. Then the Lord said, "I never wanted your boy. I wanted you. Now that I have you, I know what I will be able to work with."

Hannah gave her son out there on the steps that day before he was ever born. Then she fulfilled it by taking Samuel and presenting him to Eli.

The widow gave the bread and the oil; and when she did, her meal barrel did not run empty.

The good Samaritan gave his dollars to help care for that fellow who had fallen among thieves. He put him in the inn and said, "If it costs any more, I will come back and pay that, too."

Peter and John said, "We don't have any money, but what we do have we will give you. In the name of Jesus Christ, rise up and walk."

Mary gave the alabaster box.

The Wise Men gave their gold, frankincense and myrrh.

The boy gave his five loaves and two fishes.

Sixteen parables out of the thirty-five which Jesus gave, deal with finances and money. One out of six verses in Matthew, Mark and Luke deal with giving money.

"God loveth a cheerful giver," says the Scripture. And I say, He also accepteth from a grouch! You don't have to be a cheerful giver, but you will enjoy it and get more out of it if you are.

When God called me to go to school, I nearly starved to death. I made $20 a week from one job, $10 a week from another. I gave my tithes faithfully; then had to buy gas for my visitation ministry, plus giving $1 for missions. Remember, I made only $30. I gave $3 in the offering, $1 for missions over and above that, and it cost me $5 a week for gas.

My wife and I lived on the remainder of that money for two and a half years, and we prayed that God would help us stay involved full-time in the ministry, plus the schooling. I ran completely out of clothes. I triggered God on a Thursday. I prayed, "Lord, I need to go to school, and I pray You will help me to be able to continue. I need some suits."

Friday I prayed again, "Lord, would You please send me some suits?" Again on Saturday, "Lord, would You please send me some suits?"

Saturday evening Bob Coburn from Beckley, West Virginia, asked me to bring my wife and come to his house for dinner on Sunday.

I said, "Bob, I thought your wife had gone to visit her mother."

"She did."

"Well, who is going to cook?"

"I was a cook in the Navy, and I want to cook you both a chicken dinner."

Well, we were going to have beans at our house, and all that went with them; so I gladly consented to go. I was so tired of beans.

Bob cooked a tremendous meal. I said, "Bob, thank you. This is wonderful. I'm glad you were willing to do this."

He said, "This is not the real reason I wanted you to come. Let me show you something." He opened his closet door and said, "Look." There were eight brand new suits!

I said, "Bob, where did you get those?"

"My brother runs a clothing store down in South Carolina. I went down there to visit him last week, and he gave me those eight brand new suits. What size do you wear, Brother Tom?"

I said, "That size right there!"

He said, "Look at this one. What do you think of that one?"

I answered, "That is a beautiful suit!" He gave it to me.

"What about this one?" And he gave me three brand new suits!

I prayed three days and got three suits. I wish I had prayed six days! I learned something about getting from God because I had been faithful and consistent in my giving.

This verse I have read: 'He that goeth forth scattering and scattering and scattering, keeps on increasing and increasing and increasing.' The simple law of the harvest: sowing and reaping.

There is a parallel verse. Isaiah said that no verse shall ever want for its mate. The Old Testament verse always has a New Testament mate.

Almighty God has set the pattern for us in giving.

God, first of all, gave us the Scripture,

"All scripture is given by inspiration of God, and is profitable for doctrine, for reproof, for correction, for instruction in righteousness."—II Tim. 3:16.

Then God gave us His Son:

"For God so loved the world, that he gave his only begotten Son, that whosoever believeth in him should not perish, but have everlasting life."—John 3:16.

Then God gave us His Spirit.

"If a son shall ask bread of any of you that is a father, will he give him a stone? or if he ask a fish, will he for a fish give him a serpent? Or if he shall ask an egg, will he offer him a scorpion? If ye then, being evil, know how to give good gifts unto your children: how much more shall your heavenly Father give the Holy Spirit to them that ask him?"—Luke 11:11-13.

Not only does He give us the Scripture and give us the Son and give us the spirit, but He gives us salvation:

"The wages of sin is death; but the gift of God is eternal life through Jesus Christ our Lord."—Rom. 6:23.

God has set the pattern and said, "Now here is the way it works."

I. GOD WANTS A TITHE

Then He said, "After I have taught you how to do it, then I want you to give Me a tithe." T-i-t-h-e! That is a tenth.

After I talked about the tithe in one of my sermons, one sweet little lady came up and said, "What is this business about *'tithy'* that you want us to give"!

Dan Tolliver lived in a holler in West Virginia, about ten miles away from me; then he moved to Maryland. I tried to win him to the Lord, but he wouldn't get saved.

One day my secretary came into my office and said, "Pastor Wallace, there is a Dan Tolliver in the office to see you."

I said, "Show him in."

He came in and said, "Preacher, preacher, I got awful bad troubles!"

"Dan, what's wrong?"

"Preacher, awhile ago the Welfare Department comed over to my house and tooked away all ten of our little ole young'ns."

"Well, Dan, what in the world do you want me to do about it?"

"Preacher, I thought you might be a willin' to pray."

"I'm not doing any praying."

"Well, what could you possibly mean by that?"

I said, "You don't think I am going to do your praying for you, do you? I have been trying to get you saved, and you won't get saved. Besides, the Bible says, 'If two of you shall agree as touching anything. . .' and I can't do any praying by myself."

"Well, what could a poor fellow like me do about that?"

"You could sit down in that chair and let me tell you how to go to Heaven when you die."

"All right, tell me."

So I told him what to do, and he got saved.

Then he said, "Now can we pray?"

I said, "Where is your wife?"

"The poor li'l thing is over at the house crying her eyeballs out."

I said, "Let's get in the car and go over and talk to her."

Sure enough, she was over there crying her eyeballs out, just like he said. I told her Dan and I were going to do some praying and we weren't about to do her praying for her. She agreed and sobbed and cried her way through the sinner's prayer and got saved. Then we all prayed.

I said, "Now I'll tell you what you are going to do. You are coming to church."

"All right, Preacher, we'll do it."

"When you get there, I want you to walk down the aisle and make a profession and then get baptized."

"All right, we'll do that."

"We will help you get a job now and a bigger house and some furniture. And when you get paid, you are going to give your tithe."

"All right."

Well, he got a job and came up the first Friday and brought his check. "Preacher, Preacher, I have been trying to figure out my 'tide.'" He had it worked out pretty close, and he started giving his "tide" every Sunday.

I began to negotiate with the Welfare Department. They kept checking on the house and kept talking to Dan. As I passed the post office one day something came flying through the glass doors, sailed through the air and landed right in front of me! I looked, and there was Dan Tolliver waving some papers. "Preacher! Preacher! Don't you never let nobody tell you there ain't no God Almighty!"

I said, "Dan Tolliver, I am not in the habit of letting anybody tell me there isn't any God Almighty! What are you talking about?"

"Look'ee here, Preacher! Look'ee here!"

He had a check for $3,875, made out to him and a letter from the Veteran's Administration in Washington. It read:

> Dear Mr. Tolliver:
>   We are so sorry we have had your records mixed up. You should have been getting this money all along. We are happy to inform you that you will be getting a check for $387.50 every month from now on, and we wish you well.
>   Sincerely. . . .

Dan Tolliver said, "Preacher! Preacher! It shore do pay to 'tide,' don't it?"

I forgot that I was pastor of Maryland's largest church, and I said, "It shore do, Dan; it shore do!"

And I am still saying it—"It shore do pay to 'tide,' or 'tithy,' or whatever you want to call it!" Just do it!

II. GOD WANTS TITHES AND OFFERINGS

God taught us how to do it. Then He said, "I want you to give offerings over and above your tithes."

Our daughter Debbie is an English major, a graduate from Tennessee Temple. Debbie came to work with us. After I preach she hands me a paper and says, "Now, Daddy, here is what you said . . . ."

"Aw, shut up, Debbie! God didn't call me to keep straight all that stuff. He called you to do that!"

Anyway, once I said, "Debbie, when a sentence has a subject, a verb, and a predicate, and there is a double predicate with a conjunction, do both ends of that predicate, separated by that conjunction, carry equal weight?"

She said, "Give me an example."

I said, "The Bible says, 'Ye have robbed me' (Mal. 3:8). The people said, 'Wherein have we robbed thee?' He said, 'Ye have robbed me . . . in tithes and offerings.' Now here is the subject—'ye'—and the verb—'have robbed'—and the predicate—a prepositional phrase, 'in tithes and offerings.' I want to know if it is equal to rob in the tithes and to rob in the offerings."

"Sentence-structure-wise, both of those are exactly the same," she told me.

They are both the same: I can rob God of offerings as well as rob God of tithes. I not only rob God of tithes, but I double rob in offerings because I rob God and then I rob myself. I guess maybe it would be a triple robbing because I rob the other people who would be involved if I don't learn this business about giving offerings. Somehow I have to learn what this is. It is what one fellow called "desire giving."

I was riding in a car with a preacher in Knoxville, Tennessee, when he asked, "Brother Wallace, are you a tither?"

"Yes, Sir."

"Are you an Old Testament tither or a New Testament tither?"

I said, "You got me; I don't know."

He said, "Let me check you. Do you get about $100 a week?"

"That's about it."

"Do you get your $100 and then put $10 in the offering?"

"Right."

"If you get another $100, do you put $10 more in the offering?"

"Right."

"You're an Old Testament tither."

"Really! What is a New Testament tither?"

"You put in $10 and the Lord sends you $100; you put in another $10, and He gives you another $100; you put in another $10, and He gives you another $100."

"What is the difference?"

"Well, the way I figure it, the way you are going at it you will always stay at the same level—$100. Could you possibly use $200 a week?"

I said, "I believe I could probably figure out what to do with it."

He said, "Why don't you start sowing for $200? You have been sowing for that $100 all these years, now. You haven't gotten any raises. Maybe you could use $300!"

I said, "Maybe I could!"

"Why don't you start sowing for $300? Maybe you could use $400 or $500! Whatever you could use, why don't you sow for it? Because whatsoever you sow, that shall you also reap."

I looked at that preacher and said, "You know something, Buddy, you just got yourself a convert!"

For six years (three years in school and three years of my first pastorate) we almost starved to death . . . until that fellow taught me that principle. I started giving $25 out of my $100 to the Lord, and the Lord put His hand on me, began to bless me, and I have never had a minute's problem financially since.

Mr. John Beiler was a member of my church in Maryland. One day I called him. "John, I have to fly to Louisville and then fly back into Delaware. Could you possibly help me?"

He said, "I'll be happy to do it."

He picked me up, took me to his home, and I spent the night with him and Mrs. Beiler. I asked, "John, how did you get to be a millionaire?"

He told me a story of how he and his wife prayed on a New Year's Eve and how the Lord burdened them for a certain amount of money which they didn't have; they committed it and let that be priority and said, "We are going to get that much for God this coming year." They set out to do it by faith, over and above the tithe, because God laid it on their hearts.

He said, "Brother Wallace, the Lord sent it to me, and He increased our business that year to the point where we were able to do that without a struggle and we really gained ground for our own personal finances. The next year when we prayed on New Year's Eve and the Lord tripled the amount, it nearly scared us to death! We committed ourselves and made that priority. We pledged to raise that much money and get that much money for God's work and let our own business take second place. We set out to do it, and God sent us that triple amount. He paid off all our bills. I had to get more planes and hire more pilots."

John told how a man sold him a business that was going down, down, down. When John got hold of it, it went up, up, up. He said, "The next year God gave us another great big unbelievable figure; we accepted it, set out to do it knowing we would have to increase our business to make it. And in seven years God made me a millionaire with that policy."

Now you folk know and love John Beiler like I do, and what a testimony he has! And it is based on what God has taught us about giving. "I want you to tithe, then to give offerings according to My leading."

III. GOD WANTS FAITH OFFERINGS

That brings me to another thought. Those offerings must be given completely by faith. We had a "Faith Promise" missionary offering. We asked our people to get the mind of the Lord, write it on a card, and trust the Lord for it. Don't worry about what you have or don't have in the bank; just get the mind of the Lord. We tried to explain what "Faith Promise" giving was.

One fellow who didn't have a cent and didn't have five cents to rub against anything else, felt impressed to write $5.00 on his card. Every week he was going to give $5.00. He was a bus director student with five children. He had been robbed in the west end of our city. Thieves were going to kill him to keep him quiet, but one chickened out, so our director got away.

I asked, "Are you going back on that bus route again?"

"Yes, Brother Wallace. It is kind of like getting thrown off a horse. If you don't get right back on, you are never any good anymore. I have to go back down there and struggle it out until I get my nerve back."

After he made his faith promise commitment, Saturday rolled around, and he didn't have a nickel. He was praying for the Lord to help him find $5.00 somewhere! "Lord, please, will You help me bump into someone who will feel impressed to give me $5.00!" He was looking in the gutters, watching on the street, just looking everywhere hoping to find it lying in the gutter somewhere.

He told me that suddenly a fellow jumped out from behind a building who had been all loaded up with dope the night before. He was shaking and trembling and needing a fix, and he stuck a gun right up in the man's face and said, "Buddy, if you have any money you had better give it to me real quick, or I'm going to blow a great big hole right through the middle of your head!"

Bob said he answered him, "Man, you've got to be kidding! Me, give you money! I have been hunting and praying all morning for $5.00 for myself."

The fellow said, "You have been doing what?"

"Praying for $5.00!"

"What do you want $5.00 for?"

Bob explained the whole bit about the faith promise he had made as the man stood there shaking. After he finished explaining it to the robber, he said to Bob, "I never heard anything like that in my life!" And he reached down in his pocket and got $5.00 and gave it to Bob!

Bob came home and said, "God sent my faith promise offering through a robber!" Well, the Lord has His ways of doing things!

Now God has taught us how to do it. He wants us to tithe. He wants us to give offerings over and above our tithe, and He wants us to do it purely by faith. He wants channels to work through.

God is looking for those He can trust with His money. He needs representatives who will channel it.

Keep in mind, too, that the law of harvest is threefold.

First, you always reap in the same vein in which you sow. If you sow sin, you will reap the wages of sin. If you sow study, you will reap wisdom. If you sow praying, you will reap answers. If you sow apple seeds, you reap apples. If you sow corn, you get one ear for one grain. If you sow wheat, you get a head of wheat for a grain. If you sow money, you get money back. It is as simple as that.

The second law of the harvest is that you always get more than you sow. If you sow one grain, you get one ear.

The third law of the harvest is where we separate the men from the boys, the believers from the unbelievers, those who have faith and those who don't have faith. There is always a time lapse. When I plant in the spring, it is fall before my crop comes in.

Many who get inspired in missionary conferences and in stewardship week emphases decide they will trust God. The testimonies of other believers affect them. Their faith is stirred. But there is a little waiting period, a struggle time. A few weeds grow, or maybe there is a bit of a weather problem until the crop comes in; so many stop planting.

And if somehow I can do what God says, then "they that wait upon the Lord shall renew their strength; they shall mount up with wings as eagles; they shall run, and not be weary; and they shall walk, and not faint" (Isa. 40:31).

So if you will just get the mind of the Lord and follow His leading, then if God impresses you to help somebody, do it. Don't try to figure it into your bank balance. Just do what He says. For when God leads, He is getting ready to bring in a crop, and He is looking for some people to tend the crop for Him. And if He can get some cooperation, then He will care for those.

If you have a real good chicken out there laying eggs and another one not laying eggs, when you want some chicken and dumplings, you pick the one that is not laying eggs. If you have one cow giving milk and one cow not giving milk, when you need hamburger for your freezer, you don't bother the cow that is giving milk.

A friend had a big farm up in Williamsport, Pennsylvania. He had a milk tank that flowed from the cow right to the bottle. You could put your bottle under the spigot, turn it on and get your bottle full of milk. They would serve you a gallon of milk that just came out of the cow, through all those tubes and pasteurizers, right into your jug.

He also had right there a big freezer full of hamburger.

I said to the fellow, "Do you just sell milk and hamburger?"

"Right. We really only want to sell milk, but some of the cows quit giving milk, so we sell hamburger, too."

Now what I am saying in reverse is that God is not going to let anything happen to us while we are producing. Of course, that does have exceptions. But keep in mind that God takes care of producers.

I think I can explain this principle.

We reach up and get what God has to give us, then hand it to those around us who are in need. Then we look back toward God with our hands outstretched to receive more and carry it on to another with a need. As long as we continue getting from God to give to others, He will keep increasing and channeling through us. That is the secret of Christian living.

Do you know what our problem is? We reach toward God and receive His blessings and provisions, then we begin to fill our pockets. We reach for more and fill more pockets. When we continue this act of selfishness, the Lord shuts the valve off. He says, "That is not what I had in mind at all." God will not give a whole lot to us who cram our pockets full.

I heard about a king who dug a big hole in the road, filled a bag with gold, silver and precious stones, and put a great stone over the top of the hole.

A fellow came along and saw it. "Look at that big rock! Wonder what dummy, what clobberhead, allowed that thing to get there! What kind of government do we have here? What is that king doing up in that palace—sitting around in the shade? Why doesn't he get some people down here to move that rock?" He worked his way around the rock and went on down the road grumbling and complaining.

Another fellow came along and repeated the performance.

Still another fellow came along and said, "Goodness! What kind of stupid government do we have! That fat king up there in his palace. . . ." And he, too, went around it.

After awhile an old man came along and said, "That is terrible! That must be awfully embarrassing to our good king." So he found a large stick and a big rock, rolled the rock up next to the huge stone, put the stick under it and made a lever of it and began to roll the stone over and down the bank. Then he threw the stick and the other rock away. He was about to fill the hole when he saw a bag. He opened it up, and there was the gold, silver and precious stones! A gift from the king for the one who cared enough to move the obstacle out of the way.

The obstacle in everybody's life is a lack of faith.

God has a big bag of gold under every one of those stones. The stone is called unbelief. And if I will just get the mind of God and let Him lead me in the matter of giving, if I will just deal with that stone of unbelief, I'll find a bag of gold under it every time!

Now the Lord may lead you this week right into a highway that has a great big barrier. Oh, get your stick out and roll away that stone.

Let us ask the Lord to help us.

Chapter 21

No Place Like It!
How to Make Your Place the Only Place Anywhere Near Your Place Like Your Place

"And when they had prayed, the place was shaken where they were assembled together; and they were all filled with the Holy Ghost, and they spake the word of God with boldness. And the multitude of them that believed were of one heart and of one soul: neither said any of them that ought of the things which he possessed was his own; but they had all things common. And with great power gave the apostles witness of the resurrection of the Lord Jesus: and great grace was upon them all."—Acts 4:31-33.

I read somewhere of a country store along an old dirt road that had a sign hanging on the front porch that read,

THERE IS NO PLACE ANYWHERE NEAR THIS PLACE LIKE THIS PLACE SO THIS MUST BE THE PLACE.

When I read that sign, I said to myself, *Somebody ought to preach a sermon on that.* I thought, *Our church ought to have a sign like that hanging over the pulpit for all to read.*

The grass always looks greener on the other side of the fence. Many times we are too close to our own place to appreciate what we have. If we stop to think it over, we probably would not trade places with anyone else.

I read of a man recently who became so disgruntled and dissatisfied with his house that he decided to sell it. He called a realtor and had it listed. He then began to look in the newspaper to find the house he wanted to buy.

A few days later he saw an ad that described in every detail the house he was looking for. He called about it and was astonished to find that the description was his very own house! He had what he wanted all the time and just didn't realize it.

This is probably the case with many of God's people.

Out in eternity we will have the opportunity to talk to Adam and Eve about their experience in the Garden of Eden. I want to ask Adam what it was like in the Garden before the days of sin. I believe Adam will answer, "There was no place anywhere near that place like that place. THAT was the place." He and Eve really didn't appreciate what they had until they had lost it through sin.

I am looking forward to talking to Noah someday. I want to ask him what it was like to be the only ones left alive at the time of the Flood. I am sure that Noah will say, "There was no place anywhere near that place like that place. THAT was the place." (Of course, all the other places were under water!)

I want to talk to Moses about his unique experience at the burning bush. I plan to ask him, "How did it feel having God Himself talk to you from the fire in that bush?" I am convinced he will say, "Brother Wallace, there was never any place anywhere near that place like that place. THAT was the place."

I plan to have a talk with Abraham, too. I am going to ask him to tell me firsthand about the experience he had on Mount Moriah when he raised his knife into the air to plunge it into the heart of Isaac in obedience to God's command and God suddenly interrupted him. A ram was caught in a thicket by his horns—God had provided and Abraham hollered out in joy, "*Jehovah Jireh!*" ("the Lord doth provide"). I want to ask Abraham, "How do you feel about that place now after all these years in Heaven?" I am sure he will say, "Of all the places I ever went on earth, there was no place anywhere near that place like that place. THAT was the place."

It will be exciting to meet Elijah, who had so many thrilling experiences. Part of the joy of Heaven will be listening to those old saints tell personally about their times of victory. When Elijah begins to relate his story of the fire falling on Mount Carmel, all will be listening with keen interest. And before he is through giving the account, you can be sure he will say, "There is no place anywhere near that place like that place. THAT was the place."

Soon after getting to Heaven, we will meet Paul. I am sure he will still be telling the story of his Damascus-Road experience. The day Paul got saved the world took a turn for the better. Someone will more than likely ask, "Paul, what was it like that day on the Damascus Road? How did you feel when that light shone in your face and that Voice spoke to you?" I believe he will say, "In all of my experiences, there was never any place anywhere near that place like that place. THAT was the place."

When Peter, James and John tell of their trip to the top of the Mount of Transfiguration; when they try to describe Moses and Elijah standing there like great neon tubes, they will share their amazement and wonder of watching Jesus suddenly change into a glowing and glistening Light, too. One of them is bound to comment, "There was no place anywhere near that place like that place. THAT was the place."

I am sure there must be a great number of other experiences in places in the Bible where this same truth can be seen. Someday we will look back upon the place where we are right now and feel the same way as all these Bible characters did about their place.

When the Lord saved me back in 1950, I joined a little Baptist church which had only 35 or 40 members. I still remember the names of almost all of those people. We had many problems and much dissension during those days. But as I look back now upon the work that God gave us to do there, I feel that there was "no place anywhere near that place like that place."

After almost one year in that church, God led me to Tennessee Temple Schools in Chattanooga. We moved out of our new home, left our good-paying job, and I found two separate jobs in Chattanooga paying a total of $30.00 per week. We moved to a stuffy, cramped apartment over a garage. I worked hard and crammed four years of college into two years and nine months. We almost starved several times. I thought I would drop from exhaustion. But in spite of all the trials and hardships, we loved every minute of it. If you ask me now after almost twenty years, I will tell you, "There was no place anywhere near the place like that place. THAT was the place."

Our call to Baptist Bible Church in Elkton, Maryland, came in 1954. There were just a few people, and they were divided. The salary of $50.00 per week was not sufficient. When payday finally arrived, the treasurer would hand me the check and say, "Don't cash it until next Monday; there is no money in our account to cover it." It was hard; there were so many problems and so many growing pains. But God really blessed. Souls were saved, and the work grew. Several times large, well-known churches called and invited me to be their pastor; but each time I felt that the Lord wanted me to stay in Elkton.

Now after all these years I look back at my seventeen years at Elkton, Maryland, and say, "There was no place anywhere near that place like that place. THAT was the place."

I had planned to live and die in Elkton; when the call came to pastor Beth Haven Baptist Church in Louisville, Kentucky, I had no intention of accepting it. But God began to deal with my heart. He showed me in a number of ways that Louisville was my place. After these years of watching the Lord work, I am glad I came. The attendance and the offerings have tripled. Souls have been multiplied, and we are baptizing hundreds more. Now after these years here I have felt, "There is no place anywhere near this place like this place. THIS is the place."

I hope every preacher reading these lines feels the same about your place. Every teacher ought to feel that way about his classroom. Every bus worker should feel that way about his place. I trust that every evangelist, every missionary, every musician, every Christian worker, every deacon feels that way about the place God has given each one to serve.

Now if our place is to be the type of place I have been describing, if we are going to feel like those folk in the Upper Room felt about their place, then there will need to be certain characteristics about our place.

Our place will need to be

I. A PLACE OF PURPOSE

These disciples were not in the Upper Room by accident; they were there on purpose. The Lord Jesus had asked them to go there and tarry until endued with power. The promise of the Father had come, the power had fallen on them, and the preaching was now bringing great results. When God's children do God's work in God's way, there will always be great results.

The main purpose for praying and waiting on the Lord is to win souls. We are to rescue the perishing and care for the dying; we are to snatch them in pity from sin and the grave. Everything we do ought to be designed to win precious souls. All the buildings, the buses, the school programs, the radio ministries, the printing, the bookstores, the organization—all ought to be designed to win people to Christ.

Several years ago I went to the hospital to pray for a man who was to have a limb removed. His other leg had already been taken off because of a diabetic problem. His family had been called to the hospital because of the seriousness of the matter. He wanted to see a preacher before going to surgery. I was called.

I asked the man, "If complications should develop in the operating room, would everything be all right with your soul?"

"I'm afraid not," he answered.

"Would you like me to pray for you to help get the matter settled?"

"Yes, I would," he answered.

We prayed together, he opened his heart, and Jesus Christ came into his life right then and there. His family was very touched about his decision.

The nurses and orderlies soon arrived to take him to surgery. He said good-by to the family. He thanked me for helping him get this settled. Soon they had rolled him down the hall and were gone. He went to the operating room but never came back.

When I conducted his funeral a few days later, the Lord gave us a tremendous service. On Sunday his family showed up for church. They mentioned to an usher in the vestibule that they had come that day to be saved. The usher brought them to my adult class and alerted me about their desire to be saved.

I could hardly wait to get to the end of the lesson and give an invitation so they could all sign up for Heaven! I got so excited that I ran overtime! The other classes began to dismiss, and people were coming from all areas for the morning service. There was nothing to do but save the invitation for the morning service.

The moment I dismissed the class, that family got up and walked out. I was heartbroken. I thought to myself, *Boy, did I foul things up!* I didn't enjoy the preaching service at all. I just wanted to get it all over with and go home.

When we arose and began the invitation, the back door opened and all those people walked in and came down the aisle, with one deacon directly behind them. I greeted them at the front and quickly asked the deacon, "Where did you get these folks?"

"I don't think you are going to believe this, Preacher," he stated, "but I was standing in our vestibule, and these people came up to me and asked, 'Sir, where is the getting-saved room?'" He took them to the nearest room and led them all to Christ. Later he remarked to me, "All of our rooms are 'getting-saved' rooms, aren't they, Preacher?"

We have always kept soul winning the main purpose in our church. Every part of the program, every piece of equipment, every person involved in the organization ought to be dedicated to helping people get to Heaven. If our place is to be the only place anywhere near our place like our place, we must have a purpose that dominates and controls us. There must be a vision; we must have compassion. There must be a goal, a burden for souls. These things must be our purpose.

II. A PLACE OF PRAYER

"And when they had prayed, the place was shaken." Prayer is the key to the amazing and unique experience of the people in our text. If our place will be the type of place that we are looking for, it will need be a place of prayer. When Elijah prayed, the fire fell. When Paul and Silas prayed, the earthquake came. When Solomon prayed, wisdom was given. When Jesus prayed, Lazarus came forth from the dead. The Bible is filled with exciting adventures that resulted from prayer.

The promises of God have not changed. The Bible still promises the same things it did years ago.

The Bible still says, "Call unto me, and I will answer thee, and shew thee great and mighty things, which thou knowest not" (Jer. 33:3).

It still says, "Ask, and it shall be given you; seek, and ye shall find; knock, and it shall be opened unto you" (Matt. 7:7).

It still says, "Whatsoever ye shall ask in my name, that will I do" (John 14:13).

The Bible still says, "If ye abide in me, and my words abide in you, ye shall ask what ye will, and it shall be done unto you" (John 15:7).

It still says, "The effectual fervent prayer of a righteous man availeth much" (James 5:16).

And again it says, "Whatsoever we ask, we receive of him, because we keep his commandments, and do those things that are pleasing in his sight" (I John 3:22).

And then the Bible still says, "This is the confidence that we have in him, that, if we ask any thing according to his will, he heareth us: And if we know that he hear us, whatsoever we ask, we know that we have the petitions that we desired of him" (I John 5:14,15).

When I came as the pastor of Beth Haven Baptist Church in Louisville, I met together with the deacons. The chairman, speaking for all of the men, shared with me that the entire deacon body was ready to follow any program that I might suggest.

I asked them to get me the names of seven of the best men in the church. I then asked those seven men to organize a group of ten or twelve men to meet for an hour of prayer each night of the week. One man would lead his group on Monday night, another on Tuesday, the Wednesday night group would meet after the prayer session, the Thursday night group would come after visitation, the Sunday night group would meet after church.

We have literally bathed Beth Haven in prayer for these years. I am not surprised that when the sermons go forth, an average of one hundred per Sunday come forward to be saved, and an average of fifty are baptized. I am convinced that praying is getting the job done.

When we sold our home and moved to Chattanooga to attend Tennessee Temple College, my two part-time jobs paid $30.00 per week. I visited for our church and then worked as a bus pastor on Saturdays. I worked hard, and we were very happy; but the money just would not reach from payday to payday.

A sign on the wall at chapel was a constant source of encouragement to us.

WHERE GOD GUIDES, HE PROVIDES.

One chapel speaker pointed to the sign one day and said, "And when God leads, He feeds." I was glad to know that. One missionary speaker remarked one day, "Where He leads me I will follow; what He feeds me I will swallow."

On one particular day I came home from classes and said to my wife, "Honey, hurry and fix something to eat so I can get to my visiting."

She answered, "I'll hurry and get something to eat if you will hurry down to the store and get something for me to fix."

I replied, "I'll hurry down to the store and get something to fix if you will hurry and give me some money to get it with."

"Don't be silly," she answered; "you know I don't have any money."

"Well, that makes two of us."

"What are we going to do now?" she asked.

"I think we should play George Mueller."

"How do you play that?"

I told her that I had read of George Mueller praying down eight or nine million dollars' worth of food and clothing for his orphans in England. I believed that the Lord would answer our prayer, too, just like he did Mr. Mueller's.

We began to pray. Suddenly a knock came upon the door. I asked the Lord to excuse me while I answered it. Our next-door neighbor, a little lady from Georgia, was standing on the back porch with two cans of tuna fish. She explained that she was cleaning out her cupboards and found those two cans. "We despise the stuff," she said. "Would you like to have these?" Those two cans of tuna fish looked like two big turkeys in her hands! We found some crackers and ate crackers and tuna fish salad, and it was delicious. We knew God had sent it.

That afternoon I told everybody I met about how God provides for His children. I shouted, *"Jehovah Jireh!"* I quoted Philippians 4:19 all day—"My God shall supply all your need according to his riches in glory by Christ Jesus." When I told one big tall fellow about how God had provided for us that day, he seemed ready to pour cold water on the whole idea. "What do you plan to eat for supper?" he asked.

I pointed my finger at him and said, "The same God who fed me at lunchtime can take care of supper."

He remarked, "Maybe you had better let me help God a little bit," and he gave me a ten-dollar bill! To this day I still think he thinks that was his idea!

That evening I went on an extension meeting. A little white-haired man came up and asked if I would do something if he requested it. I assured him I would. He explained that if I would go the next day at 12:30 and park my car at a certain place, walk up a little alley and knock on some big metal doors on the back of a big building, that a colored girl would come to the door and she would have something for me. I gave him my word that I would go.

When I knocked on those big metal doors that girl came to the door. I explained who I was. She asked me to wait right there. In just a few minutes she came back with a paper plate filled with roast beef. It had a paper plate lid on top of it, and another plate sitting upright was filled with mashed potatoes with a big hole in the middle and some hot gravy poured in it, then a lid on top of that. Another was sitting upright on it with some greens, and then another paper plate lid. Then on top of that another plate was filled with hot rolls and another lid. Then another plate held some banana pudding.

I took that home and greeted my wife with the words, "Honey, look what the Lord has sent us today!" We put those paper plate lids down on the table and ate out of them. Surely God loved my wife and didn't want her to bother about washing dishes. We had plenty of food left over for the evening meal.

I went again on another extension meeting. The little white-haired man came again and asked me if I had done what he had asked. I assured him that I had and thanked him over and over again. He then asked me how I would like to do that again sometime. I assured him that I would be happy to any time he said! He explained that he had it worked out for me to do it every day, seven days a week as long as I wanted to. Of course, I took him up on it.

I went every day, seven days a week for the next two years—over 700 times I banged on that door and every day the girl would bring me something delicious to take home to eat, and every day I realized that it was something from God. All of that came because we believed in prayer. That helped to make our place the only place anywhere near our place like our place.

III. A PLACE OF PREACHING

In our text we read, "With great power gave the apostles witness of the resurrection of the Lord Jesus." They were out telling it, sharing the good news, preaching the Gospel. Three thousand had just been saved through the preaching of Peter; five thousand more would get saved in another few days by the preaching of Peter.

Paul stated, "By the foolishness of preaching" God has chosen to save those who would believe. He said again, "Preach the word; be instant in season, out of season; reprove, rebuke, exhort with all longsuffering and doctrine."

There is a great need for preaching today. We need preaching that will condemn sin, preaching that will convert sinners, preaching that will cleanse the saints, preaching that will comfort souls, preaching that will challenge the servants.

While reading in the Old Testament the other day, in Ezekiel, chapter 37, I saw again the story of the valley full of dry bones. It seems that God called Ezekiel to preach. He took him out into the valley and introduced him to his congregation—a valley full of dry bones. I think Ezekiel asked the Lord what He wanted him to do about the bones. God explained that He wanted him to preach to them.

The Lord gave Ezekiel the sermon on the first Sunday morning on "Unity." His congregation really needed it. They were scattered from their parts—the headbone that belonged to that backbone and that legbone that belonged to the kneebone were scattered in many different directions.

But as Ezekiel began to preach, the bones began to come together. The toebone connected to the footbone, the footbone connected to the anklebone, the anklebone connected to the shinbone, the shinbone connected to the kneebone, the kneebone connected to the legbone, the legbone connected to the hipbone, the hipbone connected to the backbone, the backbone connected to the neckbone, the neckbone connected to the headbone.

Ezekiel's sermon had really brought results.

That evening the Lord gave Ezekiel a second sermon on "Unction." The bones were together, but they had no life in them; so Ezekiel prophesied to the wind, and the Lord sent life into the bones.

On Wednesday night the Lord sent Ezekiel another message. This time he spoke on "Usefulness." The bones had been unified and unctionized; now it was time for them to become useful. Now preaching did all that.

It was said of George Whitefield that as he preached his final sermon, he held up a candle and told the congregation that he would preach until the flame went out. When it did so, he went inside to retire for the night. The next morning his assistants found him dead, on his knees, fully clothed, with the little piece of candle and his open Bible in his hand. He had not retired to bed but to Heaven. The news caption said, "He preached until the light went out."

If our place is to be the only place anywhere near our place like our place, we MUST have a place of preaching.

IV. A PLACE OF POWER

"With great power gave the apostles witness of the resurrection of the Lord Jesus" (Acts 4:33). The place was shaken by the power that was manifest in the lives of these people.

Our Bible promises that the same power is available to children of God in this day.

We are taught, "Ye shall receive power, after that the Holy Ghost is come upon you: and ye shall be witnesses unto me both in Jerusalem, and in all Judaea, and in Samaria, and unto the uttermost part of the earth" (Acts 1:8).

Paul said, "I am not ashamed of the gospel of Christ: for it is the power of God unto salvation to every one that believeth" (Rom. 1:16).

God's power is available to all who will accept it and qualify for it. God's power is necessary if we are to accomplish anything in this day of sin and wickedness.

I heard Dr. Jack Hyles give a message on "Pray for Power" several years ago. I started that day praying for power and have never stopped. It has made a difference in my life and ministry. Jesus promised that the Father would give the Holy Spirit to them that ask Him.

V. A PLACE OF PRAISE

This early church group was continually praising God and having favor with all the people (Acts 2:47). When Peter healed the lame man in the Temple just a little before this experience in the Upper Room, the Word says, "And he leaping up stood, and walked. . . . And all the people saw him walking and praising God" (Acts 3:8,9). When the purpose is right, and the prayer is offered, and the preaching goes forth in power, there will be praise.

David cried out in Psalm 107, "Oh that men would praise the Lord for his goodness, and for his wonderful works to the children of men!"

David told the story of several men who had serious problems and deep burdens, and each time when they came to the end of themselves and had no way to look except up, they called upon God, and He answered and lifted them out of the miry clay and set their feet on the rock. Then again David would say, "Oh that men would praise the Lord for his goodness, and for his wonderful works to the children of men!"

Sometimes when we have an exciting victory in our church, we stand and sing the Doxology—

**Praise God from whom all blessings flow,
Praise Him all creatures here below.**

One church was having a praise meeting, and a lady stood and said, "I really want to praise the Lord; my cup is running over." Another lady stood behind her saying, "My cup is running over, too, and so is my saucer." Way in the back a frail, skinny little lady stood to say, "I ain't got much to be thankful for. I ain't got but two teeth. One is up, and one is down. But praise God, they meet!"

Regardless of how hard things get where we are, there surely ought to be something to praise the Lord for. If our place is to be much of a place, it will have to be a place of praise!

Chapter 22

The Talking Blood

Open your Bibles, please, to I John 5:8,9. Hold your finger in that place and turn to Hebrews 12:24. We will read these two verses tonight concerning the message of "The Talking Blood."

"And there are three that bear witness in earth, the Spirit, and the water, and the blood: and these three agree in one. If we receive the witness of men, the witness of God is greater."—I John 5:8,9.

A witness is one who testifies. Is the blood a witness? Yes, the blood is a testimony. When the blood talks, it has something to say; it has a message.

"And to Jesus the mediator of the new covenant, and to the blood of sprinkling, that speaketh better things than that of Abel."—Heb. 12:24.

What does the blood say? It says there is a better way than the shedding of the blood of a lamb in the Old Testament. It says, "I have a better message than the shedding of the blood of bulls and goats that do not and cannot take away sin." The message? The blood of Jesus Christ has been shed for the sins of the whole world.

It is said that in the English navy they make ropes with a red cord in the middle. If you want to know if a cord or rope is from the English navy, cut the thing in two, look at the core, and see if there is a red ribbon or a red center.

It is so with the Bible. Anywhere in the Bible you will find a red ribbon—running from the very first book of Genesis all the way through the book of Revelation.

Someone said, "Cut the Bible any place, and it will bleed." It is a living Book filled with blood. There are 427 times in the Scripture that we have reference to blood atonement, that without the shedding of blood there is no remission of sins, no covering for sins.

We must trust in the Lord Jesus Christ and His shed blood. It is not His life but His death that redeems us—His death, burial and resurrection. His life serves exactly as the Law. Look upon the perfection of the Lord Jesus Christ, and it is the same as Isaiah looking upon the perfection of the image of God. You automatically see your reflection in the mirror of His example, and you see your own exceeding sinfulness by looking upon the sinless perfection of Jesus Christ. When we look into the Law, it is a mirror, a schoolmaster, to bring us to Christ. The purpose of the life of Christ was to bring deep conviction, but the death of Christ brings redemption and salvation for the soul.

Someone has said that Christ's crimson blood cleanses our crimson sins. Isaiah 1:18 says, "Come now, and let us reason together, saith the Lord: though your sins be as scarlet, they shall be as white as snow"—applied, of course, by the blood.

They tell us that if you take red paper or red glass, put it over a red object, and look at the red through the red, it will appear to be white. When you take the blood of Jesus Christ and apply it to crimson sins, the sins come out white. They shall be made white as snow, not only scientifically but scripturally and spiritually.

We use the word *atonement* in the Bible to talk about blood cleansing or blood remission. The atonement that comes to us is simply the covering. That word *atonement* means "to shelter" or "to put a cover over." The Hebrew word *kaphar* in the Old Testament has a double meaning—"to ransom" or "to cover."

In Genesis 6:14 the word *kaphar* is translated "pitch." It was the pitch or the tar that Noah put in the cracks of the ark to keep the flood waters from where Noah and his family were. You see, the judgment of God cannot get to the persons inside the ark. They are safe there. So it is the blood that keeps the judgment from coming where the sinner is. So *kaphar* is used in talking about the word *pitch*.

Kaphar also has several other meanings in Hebrew. It means "pitch." But it also means "to appease" or "to satisfy." When God looks upon the *kaphar*, the judgment angel passes over and does not stop at that house. He is appeased or satisfied by the blood atonement, our *kaphar*.

The people in pagan lands believed in all kinds of gods—gods of the sun, gods of the trees, gods of food and various other gods. They had a god for everything, and they were continually attempting to appease their gods by making all kinds of human and animal sacrifices. But that word *kaphar* means that our God is appeased when He looks upon the blood of Christ. He is satisfied it has all been done.

The word *kaphar* also means "cleansed." Not only does the blood of Jesus satisfy God, but it has a cleansing effect. *Kaphar* carries with it also the term "merciful." When God sees the blood, He has mercy. If He does not see the blood, He is a God of judgment and fury and wrath.

Kaphar also is translated in the Bible as "pardon." God forgets our sin. He acts as though we were not guilty. When we stand before the Judge and He asks, "Guilty or not guilty?" we have to admit we are guilty—guilty of original sin and also of sin on purpose. The penalty demanded is condemnation forever in the lake of fire. So we are just about ready to be cast off into eternal Hell when suddenly we realize there is another word to be said. The Saviour comes, and He has in His hand a pardon, a pardon that was purchased and paid for by His blood on the cross of Calvary. The pardon is issued; and you and I, with pardon in hand, go free. Guilty—yes—but pardoned and forgiven and walking out free. You cannot pardon an innocent man. You pardon guilty people. The word *kaphar* means "pardon."

It also means "to purge away." The word *purge* carries with it the idea of squeezing out of or burning from. We talk about purging metals of their impurities. We talk about the pressure fires of tribulation and trial that purge impurities from the life of the child of God. So the blood of Christ purges and cleanses the sinner.

Also, *kaphar* means "to disannul." If a marriage is annulled, it means it is broken. When blood is applied, sin's power is broken; and we are delivered from the penalty of sin, from the power of sin, and finally, from the presence of sin—all through the shedding of the blood.

Kaphar is also translated "pacified." You understand what a pacifier is. When a baby cries, you stick a pacifier in his mouth to shut him up. The holiness and purity of God cry for judgment against sin. The Word of God demands judgment. God insists upon it. But blood is brought upon the scene, and God is pacified. Our word *peace* comes from the word *pacify*. So we have peace with God through the blood of Jesus Christ.

We find the word *kaphar* in that well-known passage of Scripture, Psalm 32:1: "Blessed is he whose transgression is forgiven, whose sin is covered [*kaphar*]." Blessed, happy, rejoicing, thrilling is the man whose sins are covered up by the blood.

In the Authorized Version of the Bible, the word *atonement* appears 77 times; but the blood itself appears some 427 times.

Dr. Tom Malone said that when he went away to Bob Jones University (it was in its infant stage in Cleveland, Tennessee), Dr. Bob Jones, Sr., who had been an evangelist on the road, drilled into those young preacher boys the importance of believing, meditating, studying and preaching about the blood of Jesus Christ being shed for sin. He said Dr. Bob made those preacher boys memorize literally hundreds of verses that had to do with the blood.

Dr. Malone gave the testimony that his entire Christian life and ministry had been flavored, anchored and stabilized by the emphasis on the blood. He said, "I attribute whatever little success I have to the fact that I have always been a firm, solid, vocal believer in the necessity of the shedding of Christ's blood for the remission of sins." That is a tremendous statement from a great man of God.

The songwriter says:

> **There is a fountain filled with blood**
> **Drawn from Immanuel's veins;**
> **And sinners, plunged beneath that flood**
> **Lose all their guilty stains.**

E'er since, by faith, I saw the stream
Thy flowing wounds supply,
Redeeming love has been my theme,
And shall be till I die.

We are redeemed, we are cleansed, we are brought nigh by the blood.

Dr. C. I. Scofield gave this old outline that I picked up and thought I would share with you as we talk about the necessity of the shedding of blood. Without the shedding of blood, there is no covering. There is absolutely no salvation without Jesus.

You ask a man, "Are you going to Heaven?"

"Oh, yes," he says, "I believe I will."

"What are you basing it on, friend?"

"Well, I live a good life. I pay all my bills. I belong to the church. I got baptized. I give a strong percentage of my paycheck. I do good deeds. I work and labor for others."

That man is not using the blood.

This is all liberal philosophy and theology that denies a need for the blood. If you check with many, many people, you will find their philosophy and testimony indicate they have absolutely no need whatsoever for Jesus Christ on the cross of Calvary. I have talked to hundreds in this city since I have been here who think they do not have any need for Christ because they feel they are going to make it on this, this, this, or that. But "without shedding of blood [and, of course, the application of that blood] is no remission" of sins (Heb. 9:22).

I. BLOOD IS THE PURCHASE PAYMENT FOR REDEMPTION

What does the blood do for us? Blood is the purchase payment for redemption. God walked up to the counter, put the blood on the counter at the store and was given a package of redemption in return. He gave blood and took redemption. Now He offers redemption freely to all who desire to have its benefits and will accept it. There is not one living, breathing human being who has not had complete payment, complete atonement, made for his sins through Christ's blood. However, people do not get one second's credit and benefit for it until it is applied to the doorpost of their lives. They must do that by faith.

Acts 20:28 says we are "purchased with his own blood"—that is, we are bought, redeemed. Ephesians 1:7 says, "In whom we have redemption through his blood." First Peter 1:18,19 tells us we are "not redeemed with corruptible things, as silver and gold . . . But with the precious blood of Christ." Revelation 5:9 says we are redeemed by the blood. Blood is our redemption.

Remember, if you will, that the Bible does not say that we *may* have redemption or that our sins *might* be covered. The Bible teaches that our sins *absolutely* are covered. God took all the sins of all the world and dumped them into a big pile and covered them with Jesus' blood and said, "That takes care of that! It is finished!" Now He says, "Anybody who will believe and put his confidence and trust and faith in the blood of Jesus Christ will be saved." Redemption means all sins are completely, once and for all, paid for.

Someone said, "Nothing to pay." Thanks be to God, the matter is settled! And the price was the blood.

> **The blood of the victim**
> **A ransom divine;**
> **Believe it, poor sinner,**
> **And peace shall be thine.**

It is settled. We are redeemed. But anyone who does not believe it, even though his sins are all paid for, still cannot go to Heaven without the application.

II. BLOOD IS THE GROUND OF FORGIVENESS

Notice again: blood is the ground of forgiveness. In Ephesians 1:7 it is "through his blood." In Colossians 1:14 it is "through his blood." In Hebrews 9:22, "without shedding of blood is no remission."

Notice the Bible says all transgression is covered. Many people say, "Preacher, we will accept that statement with one stipulation or with one alteration—that we talk only about past sin."

The Bible speaks about *all* transgression. It does not say all past transgression. Our future transgressions are also under the blood. The present transgressions are under the blood as well as the past. Redemption is for past, present and future. The beautiful part about this thing is that not one conceivable, possible circumstance can arise within the universe that can ever cause me to lose the redemption that is now mine. I cannot go to Hell. I will always be on my way to Heaven. That cannot be changed.

III. BLOOD IS THE BASIS OF OUR JUSTIFICATION

There is a third thing. The blood is the price of our redemption. The blood is the ground of our forgiveness. The blood is also the basis of our justification. The Bible says we are justified by the blood. *Justified* means "just as if I had never sinned." In the eyes of my heavenly Father, I am spiritually like a clean baby, I am completely forgiven, completely clean. I am as though I had never sinned.

In Romans 5 we have a description of both the grounds for and results of justification. This passage makes three statements about the basis of our justification. It is "by his blood" (vs. 9), "by faith" (vs. 1), and Christ's resurrection is proof of the Father's acceptance.

Justification comes by His blood; justification comes by our faith; justification comes by Christ's resurrection (Rom. 4:25). You cannot separate the three. They are all hooked together, and Romans 5:8 and 9 drives it home: "But God commendeth his love toward us, in that, while we were yet sinners, Christ died for us. Much more then, being now justified by his blood, we shall be saved from wrath through him."

IV. BLOOD IS THE GROUND OF OUR PEACE

The blood is also the ground of our peace. The Bible talks about all basic peace being settled in and on the blood.

I can say, "I cannot ever go to Hell. I will always be on my way to Heaven. What a satisfaction! What a relief! What a contentment is mine! It does not matter so much what may happen. I may break a leg, but that does not change where I am going when I die." So I can have peace because the blood of Jesus Christ paid for my sins.

I am satisfied eternally because of my redemption through His blood.
Someone has said:

> I praise Him for His precious blood
> That will never lose its power;
> He keeps and saves and satisfies
> Every day and every hour.
>
> I am grateful for the peace He gives,
> It fills my heart this day,
> For deep, abiding, eternal joy
> That shall never pass away.
>
> I would not change my lot
> With angels in the sky;
> For I have known redemption's song
> Redeemed by His blood am I.
>
> A tent or a cottage, well, that matters not,
> So content to let the world go by;
> A home in Heaven is waiting for me
> Because redeemed by His blood am I.

Our salvation is settled forever, and as a result, we have wonderful peace. What a blessing to be able to relax! While others chew their fingernails, pull out their hair and say, "I sure hope I don't die," you and I, born-again believers, can say, "Man alive! Wouldn't it be wonderful to go home to Heaven!" Peace, peace through the blood!

We talk about "making our peace with God." You say to a man, "Have you made your peace with God?" Cross that statement out of your vocabulary. Listen! God made the peace; we didn't. God made the peace through the blood. We accept the peace which God made.

We picture ourselves walking up and saying, "Lord, I apologize. I am sorry. I am ashamed. I am a terrible, wicked sinner. O Lord, would You please. . . ?" No, that is not the way it is. The Lord is standing here saying, "Look, here is peace, bought and paid for by the blood. Could I please give you this? Will you please take it? Come on, friend, open up your heart; let Me give you this."

God is continually seeking whom He may save and trying to get us to take His gift of salvation. God is reaching out to us. We do not have to make peace with God. We have to let God make peace with us. And He is trying His best to do it. He is trying to persuade:

"How often would I have gathered thy children together, even as a hen gathereth her chickens under her wings, and ye would not!"—Matt. 23:37.

"Come unto me, all ye that labour and are heavy laden, and I will give you rest."—Matt. 11:28.

"Come; for all things are now ready."—Luke 14:17.

"Come unto the marriage."—Matt. 22:4.

All through the Scriptures it is "come," "come," "come." "Though your sins be as scarlet, they shall be as white as snow." God is bidding, pleading, begging us to come. We do not have to make peace with God.

V. BLOOD IS THE GROUND FOR OUR CLEANSING

It is also the ground for our cleansing. Not only do we have peace and justification, not only do we have forgiveness, not only are we redeemed, but we are cleansed. The Bible says, "We are washed in the blood." Don't you enjoy a country boy up in the mountain singing, "Are you *warshed* in the blood of the Lamb?" I get mixed emotions when I hear a country boy sing like that. I wish he would say *washed* instead of *warshed*, but after awhile I get to enjoying what he is saying so much I quit listening to how he is singing it and say, "Amen, I am glad I'm *warshed* in the blood, too!"

We have a fellow up in Maryland who used to say, *Hallelujer!* I used to wish he would straighten that out, but after awhile I got to the place where I wanted to join him! He had something real. It was coming out all over, and everybody knew it. So I thought, *Fiddle, let him say it the way he wants to; it is what is in his heart that makes the difference.* So every once in awhile I, too, would say, *Hallelujer!*

VI. THROUGH THE BLOOD WE HAVE ACCESS TO GOD

There is something else that comes besides cleansing. Because we are washed in the blood, the Bible says we have access to God. Without the covering of the blood, not one person could ever enter into God's presence. In the Old Testament, the result of entering the presence of God by the high priest without the blood would have been immediate annihilation. No priest dared crawl under that veil— that veil that led into the Holy of Holies where the ark was and where the cherubim sat facing each other over that golden ark of the covenant.

But when the blood was in the hand of the priest and sprinkled on the mercy seat, it satisfied God. It gave access for that priest into the Holy of Holies. Without that blood he dare not go there because it would mean his death.

Remember the belching smoke and fire and volcano reaction that took place when God came down and touched Mount Sinai, when the holiness and righteousness of God came in contact with the sin-cursed earth? The same thing would be true if any person stepped into the presence of God without the blood covering.

When you and I go to God now, we do not ask our priest to crawl under the veil with a bucket of blood and sprinkle it on the mercy seat. When Jesus died, that veil was rent from the top to bottom. The phrase in the Scripture is "rent in twain," or ripped in two. That big linen veil was ripped by a giant hand like a hundred telephone books together. One great muscled arm ripped that thing apart. It divided and separated. Hebrews 4:16 says, "Let us therefore come boldly unto the throne of grace . . ."—through the blood, of course. Without the blood, you and I would not dare walk through that ripped veil; but Jesus Christ has given us personal access.

So when I want to go to God now, I do not come through any human priest; I go boldly to the throne through the blood-covered veil and say, "My Father, I have come to ask You to forgive and cleanse me. I pray for wisdom, power and love. Lord, please bless our people over at the church. And please bless our family."

I have about four hundred preachers and Christian workers for whom I pray daily. I pray for all the people who have gone into full-time service from our ministries, and on and on. To have access to God is a beautiful and wonderful thing.

VII. THROUGH THE BLOOD WE HAVE FELLOWSHIP

Through the blood we are brought nigh, and that brings us fellowship. The basis of Christian fellowship is the blood. "Can two walk together, except they be agreed?" (Amos 3:3). We go out into society and say, "Friend, are you one of us? Are you like I am, and am I like you are?"

Where do we draw the line? Well, there is one thing sure: if we break down on blood atonement, that is a hot spot. Any fuzzies in the blood atonement make a fellow of a different world.

When a church begins to be modern and liberal, the first thing it does is clean out its song book racks and get new books which have no songs about being washed in the blood. If you go to a liberal church, you will not find "Power in the Blood" in their song books. You will not find "Are You Washed in the Blood?" You may not even find "On a hill far away, Stood an old rugged cross." These songs are eliminated, and others which teach works, etc., take their place. So the way a man thinks about the blood atonement is a test of faith.

I read last evening the story of the owner of a Swiss chalet or hotel. He looked at the clock on the wall, then walked over to a window and peered out. One of his guests had taken off to climb a rocky, steep mountain. While he was gone, a snowstorm had settled into that area; and now they did not know his whereabouts. They wondered if he had taken refuge in one of several cabins up on the mountain. Where was that young man? Had he found shelter, or was he out there exposed in that blizzard?

They knew a human being would only expose himself to the elements if he tried to find him. So the owner of the chalet got his Saint Bernard dog that had been trained for this, turned him loose and sent him out in that direction. That dog wandered up through those valleys, up into those mountains; he got into those snow areas and for hours tracked that man. Finally he came upon the body lying in frozen snow. The man's life was just about drained out.

The dog got hold of the back of his shirt and shook him the best he could and just kept shaking him, trying to wake him. He dragged the man a long ways. The dragging along the ground and shaking him stirred the man's blood up enough to make him conscious. He was not quite conscious enough to realize what was happening; and thinking he was being attacked by wolves, he grabbed for his knife and with his last bit of strength sliced into the dog and cut him up. The warm blood began to flow from the dog as the man fainted in despair and dropped the knife.

The dog turned loose of him and began to make his way down over the hills, dragging himself along. Finally he got out of the snow and dragged himself across the meadow up to the door of the chalet. He rooted himself in one spot and slapped his tail against the door until the man came; then the dog flopped over dead just inside the door.

The owner, seeing his dog bleeding, realized he needed to follow the trail. He followed the blood all the way in the snow and came upon the body of the man. They brought the man back and did what they could to help him thaw out. He was badly frostbitten.

When the man regained consciousness and learned what he had done, he cried out bitterly, remembering how affectionate and trustworthy that Saint Bernard dog had been. He said over and over again, "He came to save me, and I killed him! He was my friend, but I treated him like an enemy!"

You and I have heard another story just like that. The Lord Jesus Christ, in mercy, tenderness and grace, came because He loved us; but our sins drove the nails, the spear, the crown of thorns into His body on the cross of Calvary. Our sins, responding to His love, brought about His death on the cross of Calvary. It is exactly the same story.

I read years ago an old story about an evangelist who had preached a powerful sermon one night. A man in the congregation walked up to him afterward and said, "Sir, I want to ask you some questions. Would it be possible for you to come home with me after the service?"

The evangelist said, "Sir, if you will wait until I counsel with the rest of the people and shake hands and sign Bibles, I will be glad to go with you."

In a few moments the pastor of that church slipped over and said, "What did that man say to you?"

"He said he wants me to come home with him."

The pastor said, "Don't! Please don't do it."

"Why?"

"He is the most wicked man in these parts. He had as soon kill you as to look at you. He is up to no good. Don't trust him."

The evangelist said, "But I promised him I would go. I cannot lie. Besides, I sensed a note of tender concern. I believe that man has something he wants to share with a preacher."

The pastor insisted he not go.

But against the advice, he went on. The fellow took him way down the street and through a little alley. He came to a back door, opened it and entered a smutty kind of office in a back street. He closed and bolted the door. He reached into his pocket, pulled out a revolver, held it in his hand, and said, "This gun has killed five people. Now I want to ask you something. I heard what you said tonight. I want to know if you meant what you said."

The preacher, a little nervous, said, "Well, yes, I meant everything I said. But what particular part are you referring to? I am not exactly sure what you are talking about."

He said, "You made the statement that the blood of Jesus Christ cleanses from all sin. Sir, did you really mean that?"

The preacher said, "Yes, that is what the Word of God teaches. The blood of Jesus Christ cleanses from all sin."

The man said, "But let me tell you—I want to show you something." He opened the door and walked into a big tavern. "Do you see this tavern? Men have spent their very last in here. We have killed two or three men because of arguments over taking their money at this counter. Wives have come in here to get their husbands, and I have had both them and their husbands thrown out. I have taken every penny of a man's paycheck, knowing his wife and children would go hungry for a whole week. Man, is there any forgiveness for that?"

The preacher looked at him and said, "Sir, the blood of Jesus Christ, God's Son, cleanses from all sin."

This wicked man said, "Come, let me show you something else." He opened another door and walked into a gambling parlor. "When people get out of the place where they have been drinking, if they have any money left, we get them in here by persuasion and take every penny they have. Several times we have drained men. Everything in here is as crooked as the Devil. All the cards are marked. All the wheels are magnetic. We have it all rigged. We have robbed and cheated. We have taken tens of thousands of dollars off innocent men who have gone out of here to face their families in shame and despair. Many a man has left this place broke and committed suicide. We have killed those people. Is there any forgiveness for a man like that?"

That preacher looked in his face and said, "Sir, the blood of Jesus Christ, His Son, cleanses us from all sin."

The man continued, "Sir, let me ask you one more thing. Look across the street. Do you see that brownstone home over there? That is my home. In that home is a frail woman in ill health. There is a little thirteen-year-old girl who is very nervous and chews her fingernails and cries herself to sleep at night. They are my wife and daughter. I went up to Pennsylvania and met her. I told her that I was a stockbroker, a very successful businessman. I courted her. I even told her I was a Christian. She married me. I brought her back and showed her my taproom and my gambling hall. We were already married, and she was gracious enough to stay with me. But I have treated her like a tramp. I lied to her. And the little baby was born and has been brought up in this hell on earth. I want to know if there is any forgiveness for a man like that."

That preacher said, "Sir, the blood of Jesus Christ, God's Son, cleanses from all sin."

Again he continued, "Let me tell you this. The other night when I came home, my wife and I got in a fight. She tried to plead with me. I swung at her and struck her across the cheek. As I did, my little girl ran in, and I brutally hit her with my fist, knocking her against the stove and burning her arm. Her arm will be disfigured forever. There are ugly scars, and the bones had to be refixed. She is a beautiful little girl. I have literally killed my wife; her health is gone. I have marred the body of my child. Preacher, is there any forgiveness for a man like that?"

And that preacher said, "The blood of Jesus Christ, God's Son, forgives and cleanses from *all* sin."

He said, "Sir, tell me what I must do." And that man got on his knees and prayed and asked the Lord Jesus to save him.

The next day the preacher was asked to come back again. As he walked into the gambling hall, he saw that the man had taken a big axe and chopped up the gambling wheels and burned all the cards. The preacher walked on into the taproom, and there on the floor were broken pieces of bottles and split-open kegs of beer. The place had a terrible stench because of all that alcohol, beer and wine flowing around through the cracks and boards and the sawdust there at the rail which the owner had put there to take up all the drippings from those drunkards. Everything in there was broken and crushed and crumbled. The newborn man said, "I want you to come across the street to see my wife."

The preacher went across the street with him and heard the ending of the story. When that blood-washed sinner had returned home the night before, the little girl had hidden under the bed and the woman had gone back into the bedroom, quietly hoping she would not have to face her husband.

He sat down in a chair and called for his little girl to come. Finally, he coaxed her out from under the bed and got her to come sit on his knees. He got his wife to come and ordered her to sit on his knee, too. Then he put his arms around both and began to sob, saying, "I want you to know you have a brand-new husband and a brand-new daddy because *the blood of Jesus Christ cleanses from all sin.*"

It is still true. It still works exactly the same way.

Chapter 23

"On the Wrong Side of the Log"

(Preached Thursday morning, January 19, 1984, at the Southwest Sword of the Lord Conference on Revival and Soul Winning, Garland, Texas)

From Proverbs, chapter 16, verse 25, I would like to share with you a basic Bible principle.

Suppose I were able to step up to this podium and announce, "I have a delightful and very unique surprise for us. I have arranged to bring someone along with me who is now in a side room waiting to be introduced. He has the distinction of being the richest man who lives today. He is also the wisest man who ever lived outside the Lord Jesus Christ Himself. He has another appointment in downtown Dallas and must leave immediately, so he is going to come out here and give us just one little nugget of advice before he goes. I introduce to you now—King Solomon!"

King Solomon comes across the platform in all his splendor and royalty and says, "Ladies, gentlemen, and young people from the school, let me share with you just one of the greatest distilled verses of wisdom that I was ever able to write in all of my three thousand proverbs." Then, let's suppose he quotes for us verse 25 of Proverbs 16: "There is a way that seemeth right unto a man, but the end thereof are the ways of death."

Now, with all that impressiveness of who he was, how much wealth and wisdom he had stored away, I believe I would have those words inscribed indelibly on my mind and would think about them a long time. What he said would impress me to the point where I would not be able to get away from it. And I believe these words would sink into my philosophy: "There is a way that seemeth right unto a man, but the end thereof are the ways of death." That says, "It may seem all right, but it is not all right; it brings tragedy and sorrow."

Years ago I read the account of a man and his friend in Arkansas who were sitting on a log up on the side of the hill. He was on one side of the log and his friend on the other side. They were just chatting. The man had on cowboy boots and was raking a boot along, subconsciously digging with his heel while talking to his friend. In a moment, when his heel caught on a root that was running along underneath the surface of the soil, he began to press against it real hard; and his leg straightened out. The force caused the log to roll back about two inches. Realizing what had happened, he released his leg and the log rolled back into its little rut. Then it rolled out again. Because of the motion of the log, his friend on the other end fell off. The thrust of his falling body gave the log a push. The man who had been digging with his heel jumped off on the front side of the log and began running as hard as he could go, with the log rolling after him. The other man got up, brushed himself off and, looking about, saw the log overtake the man and crush him to death. The newspaper article said one man was on the right side of the log and one man was on the wrong side of the log.

I. CAIN AND ABEL

That story hung in my memory. One day I was reading in the Bible the story of two young fellows who were born of the same parents, lived in the same environment, had everything exactly the same. One turned out to be a shepherd with many sheep out in the field. The other turned out to be a gardener who grew corn, squash, beans and tomatoes.

These boys were Cain and Abel. From the time they were little, bitty fellows, once a year Mom and Dad would get them together and say, "Boys, it's time for the sacrifice. We're going to go out and do exactly what God told us to do again this year." Those little boys would probably ask a lot of questions. Cain would say, "Mommy, Daddy, are we going to kill another one of those little lambs?"

"Yes, we are."

"Are we going to make the blood come out of it like we did last year?"

"Yes, we are."

"Why do we take its skin off and cut it up in pieces like that? Will the fire come again and devour it?" They asked all kinds of questions.

As they grew into their primary and junior years, they watched. Every year they would ask, "Why do we do this every year?"

Adam or Eve would always answer the same way: "Because this is the way God said to do it." That satisfied them.

They were great big teenagers now. This year they had a surprise. Adam and Eve called the boys in and said, "Now, boys, this year you are old enough and have learned enough. It's time to make your own sacrifices."

Abel said, "It will be easy for me. I'll just go out and get one of my lambs and make my sacrifice."

Cain said, "What am I supposed to do? I don't have any lambs."

They suggested, "You'll have to make some sort of trade or arrangement with your brother and get one of his lambs to sacrifice."

Cain thought about that for awhile. The boys were out maybe behind the house or over in the edge of the field when Cain said, "You know, Abel, I've been thinking about this. It looks to *me* like... the way *I* look at this thing... *I* think God ought to be willing to accept what I have grown in my garden rather than my having to take what I've got, trade it to you and get what you've got to sacrifice."

Abel said to Cain, "I don't think you had better change it. You need to do it God's way—the way God showed our mom and dad, the way God told us to do it."

Cain said, "I don't look at it that way. I tell you what I think. *I* think... *I* believe... here's the way *I* feel."

Somebody had better say to Cain, "There is a way that may seem all right, but the end thereof will end up being the way of death."

You know the story. Those boys made their sacrifices with Abel always saying, "Cain, I think you're making a bad mistake."

"Aw, no. I have thought this thing through. I have my own ideas about things."

"Okay, you can have your own ideas, but remember—if you make a mistake, you will have to live with it. Your chickens will come home to roost. Whatsoever a man sows, he will have to reap."

They made their sacrifices. I will not belabor you with details, because the story is so well known. God accepted Abel's sacrifice, but not Cain's. Cain got so frustrated and so angry that he became very hard to live with.

The next day out in the field they got to talking about it. Abel said something like this, "I told you it wasn't going to work." Cain probbly got real, real smart about the thing. Abel said, "All right, I didn't mean to get you upset, but you ought to have known that you were supposed to do it the way Mom and Dad taught us to do it, because that was the way God said do it." Cain got so angry that he rose up and, getting hold of some kind of blunt instrument, slew his brother in the field. Now we know it is true: "There is a way that seemeth right unto a man, but the end thereof are the ways of death."

When I read that story, that old newspaper account came back to me about the log. I thought, *Yes, one fellow was on the right side of that log and one on the wrong side.*

II. JACOB AND ESAU

I kept reading through the Bible; and I came upon the story of two more fellows, both born in the same home to the same mom and dad, in the same environment, with the same hereditary factors. Their names were Jacob and Esau. One was an inside fellow; the other, an outside fellow. One day that outside fellow—Esau—had been out in the field or the woods, and he had gotten famished with hunger. He came in out of all that fresh air and crispness; and when he walked through the door, he smelled something cooking. Jacob was cooking a bowl of red pottage—chili to us. Now, a hungry fellow smelling chili has something happen to him.

He asked, "What in the world are you cooking?"

"Aw, I'm making a pot of chili," answered Jacob.

With his mouth watering, Esau said, "Listen! I've just got to have some of that! Please, Jacob, give me a bowl of that chili."

Jacob said, "Look, I'll be glad to arrange for you to have some of it—only it will cost you."

"Cost me what?"

"I'll sell it to you."

"How much?"

"The birthright."

"The birthright?! Who cares about a dumb, silly old birthright? Man, that's way, way off. That's way out there somewhere. I'm not worried about way off out there! I'm worried about right now. If I don't get something to eat *right now,* I'm going to die. Man, listen! You can have that dumb old birthright for a bowl of that chili!"

Jacob said, "Okay, buddy; sign right here," and he got it down in black and white. Then he gave him his bowl of chili.

Esau ate his chili and went away. Then he began thinking about the terrible, terrible mistake he had made.

Now, for the young people's sake, I want to explain something. Just before my mother died two years ago she called me into her bedroom and said, "Tom, I want you to double-check my Will. Be sure now that every one of the six kids gets exactly the same thing." She had just a small house, a car, some furniture and a little savings in the bank. She lived near Philadelphia.

Almost all of us want it that way, don't we? We made out our Will not long ago. We made sure that our four children would be treated equally. Almost all of us think that way.

But in the days of Jacob and Esau, it was entirely different. The oldest boy got the deed to the house, all the fields around the house, all the sheep and goats, cattle and camels in the fields, all the grain in the barns, all the furniture in the house, all the money in the bank. He also got the title of President of the Clan. Esau was in line for all that.

Jacob said to Esau, "I will make a trade with you. For a bowl of chili you give me all that property, those sheep, those goats, those houses, this and this and this. . . ."

Hold it, Esau! Hold it, hold it, hold it . . . ! "There is a way that may seem all right to a man, but the end thereof will be death." You had better not do that.

But Esau said, "Aw, fooey. I got my own way of looking at this. Man, right now is important. What good does it do a man to get a whole lot of things in a birthright if he is dead from starvation? Give me the bowl of soup and you can have the whole birthright."

You dummy! You dummy! You dummy! But he did it. All of you will agree that he was a first-class idiot.

I know hundreds of people who are selling out their entire eternity, with the mansions of glory and the presence of all the holy angels in all eternity, for ten or fifteen minutes of pleasure or a little puff of marijuana or a little sex or a bit of illegal money or for some popularity or some little pleasure—yes, trading off their entire birthright.

Do you see what I am seeing in my story? One of those fellows was on the wrong side of the log, and the other fellow was on the right side.

III. THE WISE MAN AND THE FOOLISH MAN

I kept reading through the Bible until I came to a story that Jesus was telling in the Sermon on the Mount about two fellows who built a house. He said that one built his house on the sand. He was the foolish man, because he didn't take into account that there might be some problems out ahead—the winds might come, the rains might fall, and the sea might rise. Neither did he make any preparations. He just hurried into it and built his house on the sand. Then when the winds blew and the rains came and the floods rose up, his house fell with a great smash!

Jesus says there was a wise man also. This fellow put down a solid rock foundation, then built his house on top of it. Then when the winds blew, and the rains fell, and the floods rose up, his house stood the test.

As Jesus told the story of the foolish man and the wise man, He was again repeating our truth and our Bible principle: "There is a way that seemeth right unto a man, but the end thereof are the ways of death." In the interpretation of that simple truth in the Sermon on the Mount, we have the story of a fellow who rushes into church membership or baptism experience or a "start to do good" or a "throw away some bad habits and clean up the act and hope everything will be all right."

Are you born again? Are you washed in the blood? Are you saved? Do you know for sure your name is written in the Book of Life?

"Well, I don't know about all that, but I am doing the best I can. I'm building my life."

Yes—but building on the sand! And when the testing times come, your house will not stand the test. You are making the same mistake Esau made, the same mistake Cain made.

"Well, I'll tell you what, Preacher; here is the way *I* look at that. Here is the way *I* feel. Here is the way *I* think. Here is the way *I* believe...." "There is a way that seemeth right unto a man, but the end thereof are the ways of death."

IV. THE RICH MAN AND LAZARUS

I kept reading, and I came to the story of two men who died. One was Lazarus in Luke 16. The other man we call Dives—the Bible refers to him as "the rich man." He lived in the mansion on the hill, while Lazarus was down at the gate begging. Both men died the same evening. One landed in the lake of fire—Hell, Hades. "And in hell he lift up his eyes, being in torments" (Luke 16:23). He saw Abraham, and over there with Abraham was his beggar friend, Lazarus. The Bible says that Lazarus died "and was carried by the angels into Abraham's bosom" (vs. 22)—the place we call Paradise.

Now, these fellows could see each other, and there was some conversation across the great gulf. The rich man said, "I am tormented in these flames. Send Lazarus over here with a drop of water to put on my tongue. I am suffering." Then Abraham said, "Son, you had your opportunity in your lifetime, and you threw away your birthright. You had your own way of looking at it. You felt differently about it then. You didn't bother to listen to the preacher. You didn't pay any attention to the Bible. Now you have sealed your eternal doom. Nobody can help you. Nobody can get across the gulf." But Lazarus was comforted in Abraham's bosom.

Here we have the same story—two men on a log. One was on the wrong side of that log and the other was on the right side.

V. TWO MEN AT THE RAPTURE

I kept reading, and I came to the story of two men at the rapture. The two were out in the field, and suddenly the trumpet blew and the voice of the archangel was heard and the dead in Christ rose up. One of those men just disappeared up into the sky, his body being transformed, his corruptible suddenly putting on incorruption, his mortal suddenly being made immortal. The other fellow was standing there scratching his head, rubbing his eyes and wondering what happened. If we look back a little, we will see that one had repented of his sin and believed on the Lord Jesus Christ and had become a child of God, while the other had said, "Now, I have *my* way of looking at that. I don't see any sense in that fundamental, Bible-believing approach. I believe if a person does the best he can. . . ."

These two fellows obviously were on opposite sides of the log— one on the right side and one on the wrong side. And we feel like saying to that poor fellow over there, "There is a way that may seem all right to you, but the end thereof will be the ways of your eternal death." He missed it.

VI. THE PHARISEE AND THE PUBLICAN

I kept reading, and I found two men praying. One was out there in the street with his hands raised up, looking up to God and saying, "O God, I want to thank You that I am not like all these other people. I fast twice in the week. I give tithes of all that I possess. I am so thankful that I am not like this old Publican over here." Then Jesus said the other fellow, that old Publican, smote on his breast, bowed his head and begged, "God be merciful to me a sinner" (Luke 18:13). Jesus said, "One of those fellows—the old Publican—was justified, while the other fellow was not."

There were two men, one on the right side of the log and the other on the wrong side of the log. "There is a way that seemeth right unto a man, but the end thereof are the ways of death." Even though it looked all right to that poor fellow and he felt all right about it, it was the way of death.

VII. THE TWO THIEVES ON THE CROSS

I kept reading, and I came to two more men. One was hanging up on a cross over at Golgotha outside the city of Jerusalem. He is a thief and has been caught in the act. He has been sentenced to death by crucifixion on the cross. Over on the other side is another thief, guilty of the same act. Both are thieves; both are guilty; both know they are guilty, and everybody else knows they are guilty; both are paying their price.

Right between those two stands a huge log, sticking right up out of the ground. There is a crosstie on it, and a Man has been nailed to that log. He calls Himself the Son of God. As He hangs there, one thief suddenly begins to speak. "If You really are who You claim to be, why don't You get down off that cross with Your magic powers? We are a party to all this with You; why don't You save us? I don't want to die; I've got some things I want to do." He had his mind on NOW—more life, more sin, more of all the rest of it.

The other thief over here said, "Man, don't you fear God?"

"Hold it! You mean to tell me you think that's God hanging there?"

The fellow answers, "Yes. He said He was, and I believe Him." Then that same fellow said to Jesus, "Would You remember me when You come into Your kingdom?"

Jesus answered back, "To day shalt thou be with me in paradise" (Luke 23:43).

One fellow was on the right side of that log. He repented; he received Christ as his Saviour; and when he died, he went right straight into Paradise where Lazarus, David and Abraham were. That other fellow died and went straight into the place called Hades or Hell where the rich man was. One of those men was on the wrong side of that log and the other on the right side. There was a way that may have seemed right to that one man: "If I could just get down from here and go on and live a little bit. . . ." Wait a minute, man! The end thereof are the ways of death.

VIII. TWO FAMILIES

I was visiting in a hospital in Elkton, Maryland, some years ago. I walked into the room where one of our members was lying over against the window. Over here was another gentleman who was turned facing the wall, with a sheet up over his ears. I said to my church member, "I have come to pray for you." I was just ready to bow my head and pray when he said, "Just a minute, Preacher. Would you take a moment to try to help that guy? He has more troubles than anybody I have talked to in a long, long time."

I went over to him and said, "Hello. Listen, I am Tom Wallace, a pastor out here at a Baptist church. My buddy here tells me you have a lot of trouble. Anything I can do to help you?"

He said, "No. You can't help me. But you might help my wife, if you want to."

"What is it about your wife?"

"Aw, she found her a boyfriend. She said she's gonna have herself a good time for the first time in her life. I have been so upset about it that I have just come apart at the seams." (He was having trouble with ulcers, and his nerves were coming apart. He was so angry that he shattered. They hauled him into the hospital to try to calm him down.)

I said, "Let me ask you something. Do you know Christ as your Saviour?"

"Yes, I do. I got saved a long time ago. Now, I have to confess that I haven't been going to church or paying much attention to the Bible. I am not much of a Christian, but at least I'm saved."

"You know the Bible says, 'That if two of you shall agree on earth as touching any thing that they shall ask, it shall be done for them of my Father which is in heaven.' You make peace with God and get on praying ground, then I'll pray and you can pray. Together the two of us will agree, then I'll talk to your wife; I believe then we can get things going.

He replied, "No, no. I'm not interested in that. Go straighten her out if you can, then I will take care of that."

"That's not the way the Bible says do it."

"Well, I have my ideas about how to do it."

I said, "Man, look. You need to do what the Bible says."

"I don't care what the Bible says," he replied.

I said, "Look, man. If you're going to get anywhere with God, you must humble yourself and submit and do it God's way."

"I don't care anything about that. Just quit bothering me, Preacher. If you want to help me, then go straighten the old lady out."

I said, "Okay." I had prayer for the fellows, got in my car and drove about six miles to the Howard Johnson's Restaurant in Newark, Delaware, right across the Mason-Dixon Line. The hostess came and said, "May I show you a seat?"

I said, "No, Ma'am, I'm not here to eat, but would you introduce me to Mrs. C_____ P_____?"

She said, "That's her, right there," and motioned to her. This very attractive lady came over and the hostess said, "This gentleman would like to meet you."

I said, "Mrs. P_____, I'm Pastor Tom Wallace from over here at the Baptist church. I was visiting in the hospital and your husband told me you two are having some real problems."

She said, "We certainly are."

I said, "Mrs. P_____, would you let me have an appointment with you sometime today?"

She said, "I get off work in two hours, and I live two blocks down the street. If you'd like to come by the house, I would be happy to talk to you. I'll have to pick up our teenage daughter at school, and I can be there at 3:15."

When I pulled up in front of the house, she pulled up right behind me. I followed both of them inside and said, "Now, Mrs. P_____, your husband tells me that you two are having some real problems."

She said, "He may be having some problems; but, Preacher, I have found a wonderful man who tells me he loves me, and I believe I love him. We have something wonderful, and I am leaving my husband. I am going away with this fellow; and for the first time in my life, I plan to start living."

I said, "Ma'am, I don't want to disagree with you, but I think you're getting ready for a tragedy. You are getting ready to make a bad, bad mistake."

"That may be your opinion, and I don't agree with you at all. I am going to have a wonderful time."

"Ma'am, do you know what the Bible says?"

"I don't care what the Bible says."

"But, Ma'am, let me ask you something. Are you a Christian?"

"No, I'm not."

"Well, you know the Scripture teaches...."

"I am not interested in becoming one either," she added.

"Ma'am, do you realize that God loves you?"

"No, I am not interested. Don't go preaching to me."

I tried to get to the place where I could give her the plan of salvation, but she kept saying, "No, I don't want any of that. I don't care anything about that." Soon she said, "Look, we have a piano lesson coming up in a few minutes. If you will, please leave."

Now, folks, I can take a hint! So I said, "Okay," and I left. She didn't care.

Two days later while I was driving down the road and listening to some music, the radio announcer cut in and said, "Ladies and gentlemen, we interrupt this broadcast to bring you this news bulletin. This afternoon a man walked into the Howard Johnson's Restaurant in Newark, Delaware, pulled out a revolver and shot and killed one of the waitresses. He then walked back into the kitchen and shot and killed the cook. That man is Mr. C_____ P_____. The Delaware State Police have now arrested him."

I said, *Oh, my soul! Mr. P_____ got out of that hospital, got his gun, went down to that restaurant and blew that woman out into eternity, also killing her boyfriend in cold-blooded murder.*

I went to the House of Corrections, where they had placed him, and walked into his cell. He was sitting there with his face down in his hands. I said, "Mr. P_____, what in the world did you do?"

He looked up and said, "Preacher, I killed 'em! That's what I did—I killed 'em both!"

I said, "You did more than that. You put both of them in the lake of fire to burn for all eternity. Is that what you wanted to do—send them out into eternal Hell forever and forever and forever?!"

He just put his face back in his hands and wept uncontrollably. Since I couldn't even communicate with him after that, I turned and left.

Three or four days later my phone rang. A weak voice was on the other end. The lady said, "Preacher, this is Agnes Butcher. Could you please come to our house quick—as soon as you can?"

I asked, "What's wrong, Agnes?"

"Denver just left the house with a pistol in his front pocket. He said he's going downtown and get loaded up on liquor; and as soon as he gets his nerve up, he's coming back and blow my brains out! Then he's going to put the gun up to his head and blow his out! Preacher, his brother did the very same thing a few years ago, and he has that on his mind. He'll do it, Preacher! He'll do it! Come and help me, please!"

When I pulled up in front of that house, Agnes was waiting in the doorway. I walked in and said, "Now, Agnes, are you sure Denver has that gun?"

"Yes, I am. He showed it to me."

"Now, you believe he has enough nerve to come back and do that?"

"I know he'll do it!"

I said, "Now sit down. [She was chewing her fingernails, pulling her hair, and wringing her hands.] Agnes, if he does come back and blow your brains out like he said, where will you go—Heaven or Hell?"

"Preacher, I would go to Heaven. I got saved in a tent revival years ago, but I never got baptized. I haven't been going to church nor reading the Bible. I haven't given any tithes or offerings. Neither have I tried to win anybody to Christ. I haven't done anything that a

Christian ought to be doing. I would be so ashamed and embarrassed to meet God like this!"

I said, "Well, I recommend that you get down on your knees right now and let me read to you I John 1:9. We'll do our best to get you right with God, and if he does come back and carry out his threat, at least you won't have to worry about not being in tune with God."

She just dropped down on her knees. I read her the verse, "If we confess our sins, he is faithful and just to forgive us our sins, and to cleanse us from all unrighteousness." She did exactly what the Bible said—she asked the Lord to forgive her. Then she said, "O Preacher, I feel so much better! He'll still probably kill me, but at least I can go Home not being ashamed and embarrassed. I've tried to get it all fixed up."

Just about that time I heard a car pull up in front of the house. I thought, *Oh, my soul! I hadn't planned to be here when all this took place! How did I get in this? I can just read tomorrow morning's headlines:*

"MAN WALKS THROUGH THE DOOR, PULLS OUT A PISTOL, SHOOTS AND KILLS HIS WIFE AND A PREACHER, THEN KILLS HIMSELF!"

I thought, *Everybody in town will try to figure out what the preacher was doing there and why the guy killed him. How in the world did I get in a situation like this!*

I heard him coming up the sidewalk. I reached over and took hold of the door; when he reached for the door, I just opened it. He looked up in surprise. I said, "Hello, Denver."

He said, "Preacher, what in the world are you doing here?" (That's what I was trying to figure out!)

I said, "Denver, Agnes told me about your troubles. Come on in and let me talk to you a few minutes."

He walked right in. I said, "Denver, let me ask you something. I realize you have a lot of troubles, and I realize how upset you are. I don't want to do anything to cause you any more burden. But, Denver, I have to ask you a question. I want you to know, first, that Agnes and I have just been on our knees praying, and she has just gotten right with the Lord. Now if you do blow her brains out, I want you to know that she is going to Heaven having confessed it all to the Lord. But I need to ask you: if you do blow your brains out, what's going to happen to you?"

He just straightened his shoulders and said, "Preacher, you know what would happen to me. I would bust Hell wide open!"

I said, "Denver, do you think it's very smart for a fellow to blow out his brains and bust Hell wide open?"

"That wouldn't be very smart, would it?"

"Denver, eternity in the fire is a long, long time. Why don't you sit down on the couch here and let me take my Bible and show you what you can do to change the whole picture. What have you got to lose, man?"

"Nuthin."

"Okay, please sit down there." He sat down. I took this Bible, and I went the old familiar route: Romans 3:23, Romans 6:23, Romans 5:8, Romans 10:13, then I said, "Denver, I'm going to get right down on my knees beside your couch and ask the Lord to come into your heart and save you. Is that all right with you?"

"Yeah, that will be all right."

I got right down on my knees, then I looked up at him and said, "Denver, will you get down on your knees with me?"

That old boy, with his face beginning to twist up a little bit and some tears beginning to well up in his eyes, fell right over on his knees and began to cry. I prayed for him, and he prayed and accepted Christ as his personal Saviour.

Then when I got them both on the couch, I said, "Now, I want you two to make me a promise. Promise me that both of you will get down on your knees tonight, hold hands and pray out loud together. Will you promise me that?"

Old Denver looked over at Agnes; Agnes looked at Denver, and then she said, "Well, now, I will if he will."

He said, "I will if she will."

She looked back and said, "I will if you will."

He said, "Well, you know I will if you will."

So they willed!

I said, "Okay. Now there's something else I want you to do. Promise me that you will come to church and sit together Sunday morning in the service."

He looked over at her, and she looked at him. He said, "Well, now, I will if you will, Agnes."

She said, "I will if you will, Denver."

"Well," he said, "I will."

She said, "Well, I will, too."

I said, "Now, there is something else I want you to do. Promise me that after I get through preaching, you will walk down to the front and let me introduce you to the folks and tell them what happened to you. Will you do it?"

She looked at him and said, "I will if you will."

He said, "Well, I will if you will."

She said, "I will."

He said, "I will."

They showed up Sunday morning. They sat way, way in the back where the teenagers used to sit in our church. (We bring them down front now.) I watched old Denver. He put his hand up on the back of the pew. He was just holding on to the pew. But in a few minutes, he just sort of pulled his hand over on her shoulder. That was all right. Then he cupped his hand around her shoulder, and I noticed that he began to pull her a little bit. Then, first thing you know he was just a hugging on her to beat the band! She was looking at him smiling, and he was looking at her smiling. They were just enjoying that! If that had been some of our teenagers, I would have said, "ALL RIGHT! ALL RIGHT BACK THERE! Some of you deacons go and sit between those kids!" But when I saw them doing it, I thought to myself, *God bless him! I hope he kisses her!*

I finished the message, then I said, "Let's stand." And on the first note of the first verse of the invitation song, they stepped out holding hands and came down to the front. They followed the Lord in believer's baptism and went out of the house of God rejoicing in the Lord because they did what the Bible says.

Now, do you see where I am going with this? Here is one man, C_____ P_____, who says, "I don't care about that, Preacher. I got my own ideas. Look! Let me handle it my way. Go straighten her out, then I'll get right!"

"Yeah, but wait a minute, wait a minute. The Bible says...."

"I don't care about that! I got my way of lookin' at it. If you'll get her straight, then that'll help me enough!"

"No, no, that's not the way God said do it. That's not what the Bible says about it, Mr. P_____."

His wife said, "I don't care about that. I have my own ideas! I'm going to be happy and have a good time for the first time in my life."

"Wait a minute, Mrs. P_____. The Bible says...."

"I don't care what the Bible says."

"Yeah, but Mr. P_____, Mrs. P_____, there is a way that seems all right unto a man, but the end thereof are the ways of death."

"Agnes, here is what you ought to do."

"Okay, Preacher, if that's what the Bible says, I'll do it."

"Denver, here's what God says you ought to do."

"Okay, Preacher, if that's what God says, that's what I'll do."

"Solomon, what do you think about this?"

"Well, there is a way that seems all right, but it's not. The end are the ways of death."

One way is just flat humanism—"*I* think," "*I* believe," "Here's the way *I* look at it," "Let me have *my* way." The other way is, "What God says I will do."

Every junior high and every senior high student in this school, every member of this church, every preacher, every person who has come into our meeting this morning will face this truth many times a day: *What will I do? Will I do what the Bible says? Or will I do what I think I want to do?* Which side of the log will you be on? Everyone in this room will face this simple principle that Solomon has given us: *Will I do what God says about it? Or will I do what I think, the way I feel, the way I look at this?* Young folks probably have a lot more trouble with it than some of the others, because they haven't yet had an opportunity to absorb as much basic Bible principle as some who have been studying for forty years. But think on it: *What will I do? Will I do what God says? Or will I do what I think?*

"There is a way that seemeth right unto a man, but the end thereof are the ways of death."

Chapter 24

Crystallizing the Gospel

Preached at National Sword of the Lord Conference on Revival and Soul Winning, Highland Park Baptist Church, Chattanooga, July 25, 1984)

"But when he saw the multitudes, he was moved with compassion on them, because they fainted, and were scattered abroad, as sheep having no shepherd. Then saith he unto his disciples, The harvest truly is plenteous, but the labourers are few; Pray ye therefore the Lord of the harvest, that he will send forth labourers into his harvest."—Matt. 9:36.

Take some honey or syrup, put it for a time on a shelf, and under the right conditions it will crystallize and turn to sugar.

There is a formula in these three verses that will turn to success and become sweet.

I see seven words.

The first is *visualize:* "he saw."

The second word is *tenderize:* "he was moved with compassion."

The third word is *analyze:* When He saw them scattered, when He saw them fainting, He looked to see what was causing their problem.

The fourth is *vocalize:* "Then saith he...." He began to speak.

The fifth word is *agonize:* "Pray ye...the Lord"; real praying will be agonizing.

Sixth is the word *evangelize:* "Pray ye therefore the Lord of the harvest, that he will *send forth....*"

And seventh is the word *jeopardize:* Our Scripture says, "...the labourers are few."

Now how do we get this formula to come together? Dr. Bob Bevington at Knoxville Baptist Tabernacle used to tell about the tongue-tied man who sat in church and enjoyed it better than anybody. He couldn't say it right; but he said, "Every sermon I hear just gets thweeter and thweeter."

He said that one day the man got a little dizzy and went to the doctor. The doctor found some sugar in his blood. And the man said, "Doctor, I knew it was getting thweeter and thweeter, but I didn't think it would ever turn to thugar."

Well, this verse does turn to "thugar" if you get these seven steps together.

First, look at this word

I. VISUALIZE

"When he *saw* the multitudes." He got the vision; and the Scripture says, "Where there is no vision, the people perish." There must be a vision. Unless I can see something that will make me feel something, get me burdened down deep in my heart, I'll not really ever do anything because there will be nothing pulling on me, nothing pushing and pressing on me to make me different, extra, out of the ordinary. I must see that thing myself and let it grip my heart.

I heard of an old preacher who took a church that was about defunct. He was determined to stir that place up and make things happen. He had talked with God about it. He began preaching with great compassion and concern. He placed this sign across the front:

WHERE THERE IS NO VISION, THE PEOPLE PERISH.

But his members did not respond. They had been sitting so long, he could not get them up and out. They wouldn't come to visitation nor help him start bus routes. They took no interest in the missionaries who came to the church.

After a long, hard attempt at getting them going, he stood before the people and announced: "Since I cannot get you to do what my heart is so burdened about, I offer my resignation effective this morning. I feel I have failed here."

He closed his Bible; and as he started down the aisle, a loud noise was heard. All eyes had been on the preacher; but as they looked back toward the front, they saw that the W had fallen off the sign; and they saw now only,

HERE THERE IS NO VISION, THE PEOPLE PERISH.

Where there is no vision, the people *will* perish. A vision is a mental picture of the unsaved. Like faith, it is the substance of things hoped for, the evidence of things not seen. Vision arises out of a sense of need. Vision leads us into action and causes us to do something. Isaiah the prophet talked of a people who had eyes but did not see.

Now you preachers know, because you're out there among them, that people live and die not knowing anything for sure. They're not sure why they're here. They don't know where they've been. They're not sure where they're going. They just don't seem to know what it's all about. I see them, and you see them, sitting in the pew.

But, thank God, every once in awhile somebody gets some faith based on vision; they get stirred in heart, and something happens. We've heard many testimonies here and read them in THE SWORD OF THE LORD of those catching a vision and going out and doing something unique and unusual.

While I was holding a meeting at Gibraltar, Michigan, running around the church was a little man whom everybody called "Busby": "Busby, would you check the bathroom over there? The tissues are gone." "Busby, help the man get his car started." After the service— "Busby, make sure the song books are put in the right places." It seems everyone was throwing orders at Busby—just a little balding fellow.

About the third day of the meeting, Busby came to me and said, "Brother Wallace, I'd like to take you on a tour of my plant."

The pastor standing nearby said, "Brother Wallace, go with him. It will be worth your while."

I said I would be glad to go.

The next morning he came by the motel. As I got into his little Jaguar, I wondered how in the world a fellow who takes care of the toilet tissues and the song books could drive a Jaguar. I got in, and we roared down the road. Soon we came up to the gate of a big plant. I saw a chimney sticking up in the air. When we came up to the gate, the guard tipped his hat as he said, "Good morning, Mr. Busby."

We went inside. Everybody was bowing and scraping to that man. He took me into a room as big as my auditorium back home. There were computers, red lights blinking, flashing signs, and all sorts of gauges. There must have been a dozen men, all with spotless white outfits on and wearing white gloves. This was a very, very intricate operation—a nuclear power plant. Everybody was saying, "Good morning, *Mister* Busby."

In just a few minutes, I found that Mr. Busby was a nuclear physicist and in charge of everything. Back at the church, though, he was the janitor; and everybody enjoyed calling him just "Busby."

We walked over to a desk with a little red button. He said something like this:

> Nobody fools with that button but me. If I'm off the base, I carry this little piece of equipment with me. I can give orders to push it down or leave it up. The molten metal flows through certain pipelines, heating water and turning it into steam; that steam turns the turbines, which create the electricity; and it flows out over the biggest part of Detroit here. All is fired by nuclear rods that create nuclear fission that heats the metal.
>
> If anything goes wrong, I push a little button down and all these gauges stop. All the lights quit blinking. Everything becomes dead. But when I pull that little button up, every operation begins again. All of the clicking, all the moving of the metal, all the moving of the steam, and the turbines and the electricity start going.
>
> Preacher, do you know what that little button is? That little button is faith. Just believing opens up everything toward God. It opens up the Bible.

Folks, that is exactly what vision means. When we have only a little vision, it still opens up everything. We can see something others do not see. We can lead out into the areas that nobody else seems to care about because we can see it out there. We have a little red button called faith. We believe God is in it, and we see past what other people see. We see Him who is invisible, as the book of

Hebrews teaches us, while the natural man receiveth not the things of God. We are different.

Jesus told Nicodemus, 'Except you are born again, you cannot even see the kingdom of God.' But when we get our eyes open to the Gospel, it changes everything. And when we get our eyes open to what God has called us to do, then we can go forth and make things happen.

There must be visualizing. And visualizing in its proper setting will automatically bring

II. TENDERIZING

When Jesus saw, He had compassion; He became very tender.

The word *compassion* comes from two words: *suffer* and *with*— "to suffer with." It's like the word *paraclete*, which means that the Spirit of the Lord "comes alongside of" us, for us to lean on. He carries part of our weight or burden.

The Scripture says that the compassion of our Lord Jesus Christ caused Him to weep over Jerusalem. "O Jerusalem, Jerusalem, thou that killest the prophets . . ." (Matt. 23:37). It was His compassion that caused Him to work: "My meat is to do the will of him that sent me" (John 4:34). The compassion of our Lord Jesus Christ drove Him to prayer. A great while before day, He went out to a solitary place and there prayed. It was the compassion of our Lord Jesus Christ that caused Him to go to the cross of Calvary and suffer for our sins. Without compassion we wouldn't have all those aspects of our Lord Jesus Christ.

A ship was crossing the Atlantic. The captain was very rigid about the schedule. The word came, "Man overboard! Man overboard! Man overboard!"

They ran up to the captain's deck and announced, "Sir, there's a man overboard, and we must turn the ship around."

The captain replied, "Nothing doing! We're not to get off schedule. Besides, the fellow has probably drowned by now." He would not budge.

Several pleaded and begged with the captain, but he said, "You don't know what you're asking. My reputation is at stake. We always arrive on time."

But they kept pleading. "Please, sir. The man is overboard. He is drowning. We believe we could save him."

The captain replied, "It will take over an hour to turn this ship around, search the waters for the man, and get back on our route." After much begging and pleading, finally he said in disgust, "All right. All right. We will start the search."

The captain gave the order, and the big ship made a wide circle. The man was bobbing in the water, unconscious, his lungs filled with water. The workers put a grappling hook in the back of his shirt, pulled him up on deck and began working to get the water out of his lungs. Finally they turned him over on his back.

The captain walked through there in a storm of disgust, looking at his watch and checking everything out. Then he looked down on the deck to see the face of his own son! He fell down beside him, with tears of compassion flowing. Now he said, "Why didn't you tell me it was my boy! Why didn't you tell me it was my boy!" It became different then.

If we could see what Jesus saw, our hearts would get tender quickly. It would change us if somehow we could understand.

I made a call one night in Elkton, Maryland, in a little red Volkswagen. The snow was already five or six inches deep and still falling. That Volkswagen went along on the snow very well. I wanted to see the man who operated a taproom. His wife was a sweet Christian, and they had two beautiful children who came faithfully to our services. This fellow wouldn't come, though he was a nice guy. We had talked to him several times.

He came to the door. "Preacher, what in the world are you doing out on a night like this?"

I said, "Paul, I thought I could catch you home. May I come in and talk to you?"

"Why, sure. Anybody who would venture out on a night like this can talk to me."

I sat down with him and said, "Paul, listen now. You've just got to get this thing settled."

He said, "Preacher, we've talked about this before. You know if I get saved, I'll have to give up my business. And I just cannot afford to do it. I'm making more money than I've ever made before."

I said, "Paul, you're going to Hell, and these beautiful children will become frustrated and go the wrong way. Later you will pay and pay and pay. You've got to correct it now while you can." I pleaded and begged, but being stubborn, he held his line.

I gave him the Gospel again. "Paul, I want to get on my knees and pray."

"Help yourself. Pray if you want to," he replied.

I thought he might pray after I did. I prayed. But when I offered to pray along with him, he said, "I told you I'm not going to do that."

I stayed on my knees. "Paul, would you just get down on your knees with me?"

"Well, if it would help you, I will. I appreciate your concern. You know that I'm all stirred up inside. The conviction has built up to the point where I'm about ready to explode. But I can't see my way through this thing."

He did get on his knees. His little wife Nellie and his children were on their knees. In a few minutes, after I had prayed again, I heard a sniffling sound. In a few minutes it turned into an audible sound. Little Nellie Mullins looked up, opened her eyes and said, "Paul, if you don't get saved, I think I'll die!" As she sobbed and pleaded, Paul burst into tears. "All right, Nellie, I'll do it." And that old boy gave his heart to Christ and got saved!

Of course, he sold his beer garden and got out of business and came on to church and got baptized. But what I couldn't do with the message that I had, and what I couldn't do with my example of going out in the snow and working at it, those tears did.

Tenderizing compassion will do it. "Weeping may endure for a night, but joy cometh in the morning" (Ps. 30:5).

William Booth got a letter from one of his captains who wrote: "I'm having a hard time in my place. I can't get anybody moving. I can't get the programs established in this church. What do you advise?" Mr. Booth sent back a two-word telegram: TRY TEARS.

That's good advice. "He that goeth forth and weepeth, bearing precious seed, shall doubtless come again with rejoicing, bringing his sheaves with him" (Ps. 126:6).

Look at the third word,

III. ANALYZE

They were fainting, and they were scattering, and they were groping, and they were stumbling, and they were drifting, and they were burned out. They were tired. They had no direction. They had become empty.

Every pastor who has been around a church through one season knows something about that. You have had it in your own life and have seen it in the lives of others who burn out or who get tired or who begin to drift or who begin to scatter. They're groping. Things get in a mess. In today's society things are so bad we wonder whether we're doing any good.

A couple of days ago I began to realize how much the liquor business is growing and spreading. New figures this past week said that, as of January, 1984, it is evaluated by new studies that 91 percent—not 50 percent like we've all quoted over and over again—of fatal accidents on the highway are caused by alcohol.

The drug traffic is completely out of control. The music culture has become demonic across the country. Humanism is flowing like lava out of the volcanoes in Hawaii. The attitude toward morals is sickening. It just makes one heartsick to think about what is happening. How are we going to make a dent with the Gospel?

Dr. Everett Koop, the U.S. Surgeon General, said, "Because of the great increase of lung cancer, I recommend that America somehow become a tobacco-free nation by the year 2000." I thought, *What a statement!* But Governor Hunt of North Carolina said, "Anybody who would make a statement like that ought to be fired from public office because of reckless irresponsibility." I've got my idea about who ought to be fired!

It's a mess out there. Socially we're losing the battle.

But we see something they don't see. There's something we feel that they don't feel. We know something they don't know as we analyze and look this thing over. We're seeing some things happen underneath. It's like yeast spreading through a mushroom bed or like yeast in a loaf of bread.

Years ago when we were struggling with some of these things on the coast in Maryland, we invited Dr. John R. Rice to come and bring Dr. Jack Hyles for a Sword of the Lord Conference. Our people didn't know either one, but the preachers in that area did. And we packed the place! If you could get five or ten preachers together up there in those days, you were doing really well; we had 166 pastors!

Dr. Hyles once said something like this:

> I put a hook on my line and got a fish. But this thing is too slow for me. I put a second hook on there, thinking I would catch more fish. I did catch a few more, but not enough to suit me. Finally, when I put on a third hook, I began catching more fish. There I'm fishing with three hooks on one pole, getting them all tangled up, but doing better than I was.
>
> I got to thinking, *I have only one hand occupied. Man, I've got another hand over here not doing anything.* So I bait three more hooks and put them on another pole. Now here I am with two poles and six hooks, catching more fish than anybody ever caught. Nobody can do any more fishing than this.
>
> Suddenly I realized there was a man out there in the middle of the river in a boat. He would move up a little bit, throw out an anchor, pull up a line, take off a fish, throw it in the boat, bait it again, put it back in the water, then pull up his anchor and row a little bit. He would take up another one and go through the process again. He would move up a little, do it again, move up a little more. That crazy guy had one hundred hooks on one line! I thought, *With six hooks I'm doing more than anybody could ever do.*
>
> I began to think about my church back in Hammond. I went back to my people and told them, "Look, folks, we're going to start a trout line here. I want every deacon to be a hook, every Sunday school superintendent and every teacher to be a hook, all the Christian day school people to be a hook—I want everybody to be a hook. Sunday when I give the invitation, I'm just going to pull up the trout line, and you had better have a fish on your hook."
>
> Our people got caught up in that. I preached that Sunday (it was Christmas Sunday) on "Mary Had a Little Lamb." I didn't preach on how to go to Heaven. I didn't talk about the Romans Road of

salvation. But when I gave the invitation, 84 people whom our people had on their hooks came forward and made their professions.

Our church in Elkton, Maryland, became a soul-winning church
because they heard that.

Dr. Rice got up after Dr. Hyles and said, "Brother Wallace, I want
to organize a fire company."

I said, "Now, Dr. Rice, if you want to organize a fire company,
you do it."

He said, "Would you be one of my firemen?"

I said, "If you think I could be a fireman, I'll be happy to be one."

He said, "Now, we have a lot of sitting-around time; so while we're
sitting around here waiting on a fire, could I give you another job?
Will you shine the fire truck? Would you make it the prettiest fire
truck in any fire department?"

I said, "I'll take care of it, Dr. Rice."

He looked at our song leader and said, "Brother Jack, will you also
be a fireman?"

"Yes, Sir!"

"Brother Jack, I've got a second job for you. Go up and make up
the bunks until we have a fire."

"All right, Dr. Rice."

Dr. Rice said, "Now I need another fireman." He picked one of
the other staff members and asked him, "Are you willing to be a
fireman?"

"Yes, Sir!"

Dr. Rice said, "I want you to shine the fire pole so that when those
fellows in the bunk room hear the bell ringing, they can slide down
that pole without any friction and jump on the engine and roar away
to put the fire out."

"Just as you say, Dr. Rice."

"Now," says Dr. Rice, "we've got our fire department organized,
and I'm the captain."

All of us firemen salute and say, "Yes, Sir. If you want to be the
captain, you be the captain."

The fire alarm sounds: "Ding-a-ling-a-ling-a-ling-a-ling-a-ling-a-ling-a-ling-a-ling!" Dr. Rice says, "Hey, there's the fire bell! Let's go, Brother Wallace!"

I balk: "I'm not going, and you're not taking that fire truck out. I've only got one fender shined. We are not taking that thing out and messing it up. Look! Wait until I get through shining that fire truck. I know there is a fire, but you told me to shine the fire truck, and I'm not finished with that job."

Dr. Rice says, "O my goodness! Go on and fool with the thing. Come on, Brother Jack, let's go!"

Jack balks. "No, sirree! Only six of my bunks are made, and I've got six more to go. I'm not leaving until the job you gave me is done."

Dr. Rice again says, "O my goodness! Let's go put the fire out. Never mind about the bunks."

"No, no! You told me to fix the bunks!"

And Dr. Rice turns to the other fireman and says, "Come on, Buddy, let's go!"

"No, no. I have only three feet of the fire pole shined. As soon as I get it all done, I'll be glad to go."

Then Dr. Rice looked at one and all and said, "Everybody knows that the job of a local church is to keep people from burning in the fires of Hell."

Dr. Rice said, "Somebody says, 'But my job is singing in the choir.' No, your job is to put out the fire! Never mind about the fire truck. Never mind about the teaching. Never mind about the singing. Never mind about the offering. Never mind about the buses. Let's not get sidetracked in all these other jobs. The main business of a church is to keep people from burning in Hell!"

The members of my church got hold of that.

We fundamentalists have seen our churches grow, and we've gotten occupied with all of our problems and away from the main business. And because of it, we see something happening. A Sword of the Lord Conference is the best thing I know of to keep soul winning right in front of us and to keep us from getting away from it.

Check back in the first century. They had soul-winning churches. "Daily in the temple, and in every house" (Acts 5:42). But after that first century, that passed off the scene. In Revelation, chapters 2 and 3, we see those churches going through their suffering periods, their various apostasy periods, their compromise periods. Then they come into the Philadelphian revival period. That was mass evangelism but not soul winning. The difference was that they were now being saved *in here* rather than being saved *out there*.

About fifty years ago Dr. Rice and J. Frank Norris and a few others began putting emphasis on going house to house. Dr. Norris put it into effect with Louis Entzminger's plan in Fort Worth, and Dr. Beauchamp Vick carried it out up in Detroit. Then the world's two largest churches came into being through returning to biblical soul winning. Then a lot of others picked it up.

Fifty years ago THE SWORD OF THE LORD began to promote it, began to push it. When I came to Highland Park Baptist Church to the Thursday night visitation—I saw it in action—300 or 350, sometimes 400 people going house to house. That was soul winning. When the invitation was given, down the aisle they came. I worked at it for two years—*out there*. I always won all mine *out there*. And when Dr. Roberson gave the invitation, we brought them *down here*.

Then Dr. Hyles at the Pastors' School began banging and hammering on that theme of visitation. The Sword of the Lord Conferences were going on everywhere, and a lot of us got caught up in it and began building large church memberships. Things really were happening.

Then when it became necessary to work with many of our new members on their marriage problems, to deal with family problems, the social problems they were confronting, and other problems which we face in this day, we got pulled away from soul winning. We stayed evangelistic as much as we could; but after dropping down to evangelistic, the next step is evangelical. We are evangelistic in name only. We get away from soul winning to evangelism, then go to evangelical; then we become orthodox, and the next step is dead orthodoxy, which we now find across this country. Then from dead orthodoxy comes liberalism. And from liberalism comes modernism. And from modernism comes radicalism. And from radicalism come riot and revolution. Then the same thing always happens over again. Study church history and see. Folks will get all shocked to their teeth and wonder what is happening. Realizing what it is, we get that red hot soul-winning program going again.

I think the difference is whether it is *out there* or *in here*. And I believe the greatest thing about the Sword of the Lord Conferences and our kind of churches is the emphasis on soul winning. So we need to analyze. After we have visualized and tenderized, we need to stop long enough to analyze. Then after analyzing, it's time to

IV. VOCALIZE

Al Smith, I think I read the story of this hymn in your new *Stories of the Hymns*. Mrs. B. C. Slade wrote a song called

TELL IT AGAIN

Into a tent where a gypsy boy lay,
Dying alone at the close of the day,
"News of salvation we carried," said he;
"Nobody ever has told it to me!"

Tell it again; tell it again;
Salvation's story repeat o'er and o'er
Till none can say of the children of men,
"Nobody ever has told me before."

"Did He so love me, a poor little boy?
Send unto me the good tidings of joy.
Need I not perish, my hand will He hold?
Nobody ever the story has told."

Bending we caught the last words of his breath,
Just as he entered the valley of death:
"God sent His Son—'Whosoever,' said He:
Then I am sure that He sent Him for me!"

Smiling he said as his last sigh he spent,
"I am so glad that for me He was sent!"
Whispered while low sank the sun in the West,
"Lord, I believe; tell it now to the rest."

We need to vocalize it, to tell it again and keep on telling the old, old story.

I read again this morning II Kings 7. The four lepers were sitting outside the gate. Inside there was no food to throw over the wall to them. Almost a year before, Benhadad had come from Syria and had surrounded the city of Samaria. The food supply was very low. To eat a donkey's head—all there was left to eat—would cost eighty pieces of silver. About a pint of dove's dung was five pieces of silver.

Two ladies came to the king and said, "Oh, king, we have a problem."

The king inquired, "What aileth thee?"

One of them spoke: "I made a deal with this woman that we would eat my baby first, then kill and eat her baby today. I kept my end of the bargain. Now she refuses to kill hers. King, make her do it!"

And the king put sackcloth and ashes on himself and cried out. Then the prophet came on the scene and said, "King, you really don't need to be upset because by this time tomorrow everything will be fine. You can buy all the wheat and barley you want for just pennies."

Someone standing alongside the king said, "If the Lord should make windows in heaven, might such a thing be?"

Well, during the night an angel of the Lord came and made sounds like an army of horses, scaring the daylights out of the people who were encamped around the city. The Syrians got up and ran as hard as they could go, leaving the place quiet.

These four fellows sitting out there were reasoning with themselves. "What are we going to do? Why sit we here until we die?"

One fellow said, "Look! If we go back in the city, we shall die there, for the famine is in the city. If we sit still here, we die also. If we go over to the Syrian camp and they save us, we shall live; and if they kill us, we shall but die. But if we do nothing, we're going to starve. Let's take our chances. They just might feed us over there at that camp."

And so the four lepers got up and hobbled over to the camp of the Syrians. When they got there, behold, there was no man there; but food was everywhere. There were horses and all kinds of equipment and baskets full of everything—more than they could ever dream of! They ate and drank and sat around with bloated stomachs. Then one of them said, "We do not well."

One of the others said, "What do you mean? Man, this is the best we've ever had it!"

And the fellow said, "Our wives, children, all of our friends, the king and everybody back there are starving to death; and here we have this abundance. We're not doing right. We ought to go tell them."

And the Scripture says they agreed that was the thing they ought to do.

If I ever read a story that speaks to me, that one does! I have abundant life. I have the peace that passeth all understanding. I have joy unspeakable and full of glory. I have everything anybody would want! And out there are people, like a bunch of lepers, dying in their sins; and I do not well unless I go and say, "Listen, folks, let me tell you, there's food everywhere." There's abundant life.

We've got to vocalize it.

Then notice the word

V. AGONIZE

"Pray ye therefore the Lord of the harvest" (Matt. 9:38); "The effectual fervent prayer of a righteous man availeth much" (James 5:16). And Matthew 7:7 says, "Ask, and it shall be given you; seek, and ye shall find; knock, and it shall be opened unto you."

That sounds rather easy. We can get on our knees and just say, "Lord, now don't forget about this promise. I'm asking, I'm seeking, I'm knocking."

But there is more to it than that. The Greek rendering is, "Ask, and keep on asking. Seek, and keep on seeking. Knock, and keep on knocking." That is where the agonizing comes in. That is where we separate the men from the boys. This is where we have the difference between the natural and the supernatural. This is where we either see it humanly speaking or we see God step through the door. It is the difference between continuing in prayer and breaking of bread. Jesus in the Garden sweat as it were great drops of blood. We don't know anything about that. We have never gotten involved in anything like that. There must be some agonizing.

I keep thinking about the story of the old man who had been janitor at the church for maybe twenty years. A pastor friend came to the pastor's office and said, "By the way, let me see your auditorium while I'm here."

They walked into a big, beautiful auditorium. An old man was working his way back and forth through the pews with a vacuum cleaner. He had been up and down one whole section. He had gotten the aisles and worked under each pew. After three or four hours of work, he was about two-thirds finished.

The visiting preacher asked his friend, "What's wrong with that thing over there?"

"What do you mean?"

"I see that old man, but I don't hear the vacuum cleaner running. Do you have some special sound effects in here?"

"Oh, no," said the minister. "Let's go over and see."

They went over where the old man was. He had been at it for almost four hours now. When they looked over to the wall, they noticed that the plug was some distance away from the receptacle.

The old man had been going through the motions. He was doing his job, he was right in his place; nobody could criticize him—except he was not plugged into the power, so he was accomplishing nothing.

If I ever heard a story that fits us, it is that one. Most of us just go through the motions. We've gotten a disciplined program, and we're doing it day after day, night after night; but much of the time we're not plugged in; nothing supernatural is happening. The difference is simply in the matter of agonizing. And if there is no agonizing, there is not going to be any real power.

And then we come to the word

VI. EVANGELIZE

"Send forth labourers." To get it to crystallize or turn into sugar, to make the recipe work, we must get the ingredients right; and one of the ingredients is *evangelize.* "Send forth labourers." We must go where they are. We are not sent to civilize; we are to evangelize.

The emphasis today is on the happiness cult. Bookstore shelves are full of books: *How to Be Your Own Best Friend*. There is *Mood Swing*. Have you read that one? And then one called *How to Deal With How You Feel*. Then there's *The Strategy of Self-Esteem*, and the book on psychocybernetics, *Study Your Mind*.

When one fellow got up and said, "I want to talk to you about psycho*ceramics*," one raised his hand and said, "Excuse me. You meant to say 'psychocy*bernetics.*'" "No, I want to talk about psycho*ceramics*—about 'crack pots.'"

There's a book out there on the shelf that you can buy called, *Self-Fulfillment*. The best seller, they tell me, is a book called, *Looking Out for Number One*.

Do you see what is happening? We're turning inward instead of outward. The New-Age movement, involving thousands of groups, says we are eventually all going to become gods. Literally hundreds of cults started in oriental-based religions, and all of them turn inward and say, "We eventually (many of them through the process of reincarnation, others through self-improvement and accent on deeper life) will become better and better, until we become gods."

That whole philosophy is humanistic to the core, and we must get back to the realization that it is not a matter of improvement; it is a matter of miracle conversion, a matter of the filling of the Spirit. There is a basic egocentric philosophy involved in all of that.

I got this very important invitation to a meeting at the town library in Elkton. I told the lady I thought I could come.

She said, "We hope you can come. You're going to be very important to the meeting." When I asked who would be there, she said, "A lot of the folks who carry the responsibility of our county."

I went. There were about twenty-five chairs. Right in the middle of the room, right in the middle of the other twenty-five, was another chair. I thought, *I don't know what will be going on, but I feel for whoever gets in that chair!*

The county sheriff was there. The head of our medical department was there. All the various groups of leaders—everyone who had any kind of important social responsibility—were there. All were walking around shaking hands.

Then the lady said, "It's time for us to have our meeting." She walked over to me and said, "Reverend Wallace, could I ask you to sit in that chair in the middle?"

I said, "You've got to be kidding! What kind of a meeting is this?"

She said, "We'd like to ask you some questions."

I went over and sat down in that chair.

She explained: "Reverend Wallace, we have talked this out ahead of time. You are the only one who doesn't know what is happening. We have been going out to places like Muddy Lane, Far Creek, Dogwood Road—all these places where the houses are in shambles, where mud is in the front yard and no flowers are growing, where the shutters are falling off the windows, and no paint is on the trim of the houses. We want to put on a self-improvement program. We would like to get into these homes and talk to the mothers about how to care for their babies. We would like the teenage girls to know how to do certain things. But when we approach these people, they close the door on us. We can't get to them. We have seen your buses running up and down through there and your people going out there knocking on doors. These people invite them in. Then they get on those buses and go to your church. We want to know how we can get in there like you do. So would you please share your plan with us?"

I said to myself, *Goody, goody, goody!* Then I stood up and said, "I'll tell you how. Does everybody here know Bob Jones, Sr.?"—the town drunk of Elkton, Maryland—not the one in Greenville, South Carolina. All shook their heads up and down. The sheriff knew him (he had arrested him 30 times). The Welfare Department leader knew him (they had fed the wife and children thousands of dollars' worth of food).

I said, "Sure, everybody knows Bob Jones. Well, it all started when Mrs. Jones came to church. Their children came first on the bus. They got saved, and Mrs. Jones came to see them get baptized; then she got saved. Now they have been coming to church for a long while. We decided to have a prayer meeting down at Bob's house to try to get the Lord to really deal with Bob Jones' heart. The only hope we had to get that confirmed alcoholic saved was a supernatural touch of God."

I said, "While we were having this prayer meeting in his living room, Bob, about 30 percent loaded, stumbled up on the porch, opened the door, and stuck his head in. When he saw all these people, he backed out and closed the door. Then he went down the sidewalk and alongside the house. About that time I felt very impressed of the Holy Spirit to peek! So as I raised my eyes, I saw him go by one window; then I saw him go by another window. I got up and went to the kitchen; and when he came around to the kitchen door, I opened it for him and said, 'Come on in, Bob.'

"He said, 'Preacher, what in the world's going on here—you having a prayer meeting in my living room!'

"I said, 'We are in there praying for you to get saved, Bob.'

"He said, 'Really?'

"I said, 'Come on in. Sit down here, and let's talk while they pray.' And while they prayed, I led the fellow to Christ!

"I went in there, and I said, 'Hey, folks, you can quit praying now. Bob got saved!'

"And like folks treated one Rhoda in the Bible, they said, 'Sh-h-h; be quiet, Preacher. We're right in the middle of our praying.'

"I said, 'You don't need to pray anymore!'

"They didn't believe it. And then Bob came smiling through the doorway. Oh, you talk about a *beautiful* experience!

"Well, Bob Jones got a job immediately. He was put in charge of a big trucking operation. Fifty men were working for him. He bought a house down on the west side of the city, cleaned it up, put in grass, and painted that thing. He bought his wife new dresses and dressed the kids up. It was all so beautiful." (Everybody in the whole town knew about that, including this group.)

I said, "Folks, you know what happened to Bob Jones? He was born again by the power of the Spirit of God through the teaching of the Word of God."

That wasn't exactly what this group expected, but they had to realize that was the answer. And I said, "Folks, that's the only answer to it. Take the Gospel out where the folks are. Then you'll see the social climb pick up."

We had to dismiss the meeting, but they got the message!

We have to evangelize. We really don't know what is happening. But I can see Bob Jones coming Sunday after Sunday, getting up at daylight to make sure the bus tires are inflated and there is gas in the bus and taking care of our money, later on becoming the superintendent of that Sunday school. We can see all that, but a lot we don't see, and it discourages us because we don't see some of the things that are happening.

I preached in Perth, New York. The pastor said, "Brother Wallace, would you go with me to make a call? We'll eat after awhile, but let's stop by to see this guy whose wife has been in the meeting both nights, but he won't come. He is a graduate of a Bible school, but he is absolutely out of fellowship, completely backslidden. He is miserable, bitter and angry. His wife is a sweet Christian. Let's go see him."

The fellow we went to see was as friendly as he could be. We shook hands, sat around and talked about Bible school, about his move up to Perth. Finally he said, "I'll try to come. Really, I've gotten so far away from it all, I am already in the hogpen. But I appreciate you fellows coming by."

We talked a little while longer, had prayer and left. Seeing no results, I didn't think we had accomplished anything.

Fifteen years went by.

I was down in Alabama preaching. After the service a fellow came up grinning, stuck out his hand, gripped mine and said, "Do you remember me?"

I said, "I don't know—I may have seen you somewhere, but—"

"It's been a long time, Preacher. I doubt if you'll remember me. Up in Perth, New York, you came to my house."

I said, "I do remember going to a fellow's house. After a service?"

"Yes."

We talked on a little while. He said, "What you didn't know was that that night two times I had pulled off my shoe, sat my shotgun down on the floor, and had leaned over and stuck the barrel in my mouth. I put my toe in the trigger housing, and two times I came within a fraction of a second blowing the top of my head off. I backed out both times because I thought about my wife coming home and finding me there in blood and mess. But I intended to do it. Then you fellows came to the house. I don't suppose it was what you said; it was just that you cared. It started something happening. After my wife and I had a chance to talk it through, we moved and got back into school. I now pastor this Baptist church over here. Would you come sometime and hold a meeting for me, Brother Wallace?"

I went home saying, *We don't know what we're accomplishing. We don't realize what God is doing in hearts. Oh, if we could somehow understand that He is back there working behind the scenes!*

But there is one more word in this text, and it is

VII. JEOPARDIZE

After we've visualized and seen it; after we've gotten tenderized with compassion; after we've analyzed and seen the fainting and the scattering; after we've vocalized and given the message; after we've agonized and backed it up with prayer; after we've evangelized and gone out there where they are; then there's the sad word *jeopardize*. The laborers are so few.

We could do so much if we would, if we knew our potential. It's terrible if we could and we don't.

Dr. Bob Jones, Sr., saw a sign on a wall somewhere, and he began putting it into his little sayings:

> "I'm only one, but I *am* one. I can't do everything, but I can do something. And what I can do, I ought to do; and what I ought to do, by the grace of God, I *will* do."

That is what it is all about. I've got to make up my mind that I *will* do it. And I need to realize it is important that I do it here while God is working in the atmosphere of our services.

Jesus, the Soul Winner's Example

(Preached in the Second Baptist Church, Festus, Missouri, August 30, 1982, in a Sword of the Lord Conference on Soul Winning and Revival)

I would like to read in John 4:1-26, the entire twenty-six verses:

"When therefore the Lord knew how the Pharisees had heard that Jesus made and baptized more disciples than John, (Though Jesus himself baptized not, but his disciples,) He left Judaea, and departed again into Galilee. And he must needs go through Samaria. Then cometh he to a city of Samaria, which is called Sychar, near to the parcel of ground that Jacob gave to his son Joseph. Now Jacob's well was there. Jesus therefore, being wearied with his journey, sat thus on the well: and it was about the sixth hour [about twelve o'clock]. There cometh a woman of Samaria to draw water: Jesus saith unto her, Give me to drink. (For his disciples were gone away unto the city to buy meat.) Then saith the woman of Samaria unto him, How is it that thou, being a Jew, askest drink of me, which am a woman of Samaria? for the Jews have no dealings with the Samaritans. Jesus answered and said unto her, If thou knewest the gift of God, and who it is that saith to thee, Give me to drink; thou wouldest have asked of him, and he would have given thee living water. The woman saith unto him, Sir, thou hast nothing to draw with, and the well is deep: from whence then hast thou that living water? Art thou greater than our father Jacob, which gave us the well, and drank thereof himself, and his children, and his cattle? Jesus answered and said unto her, Whosoever drinketh of this water shall thirst again: But whosoever drinketh of the water that I shall give him shall never thirst; but the

water that I shall give him shall be in him a well of water springing up into everlasting life. The woman saith unto him, Sir, give me this water, that I thirst not, neither come hither to draw. Jesus saith unto her, Go, call thy husband, and come hither. The woman answered and said, I have no husband. Jesus said unto her, Thou hast well said, I have no husband: For thou hast had five husbands; and he whom thou now hast is not thy husband: in that saidst thou truly. The woman saith unto him, Sir, I perceive that thou art a prophet. Our fathers worshipped in this mountain; and ye say, that in Jerusalem is the place where men ought to worship. Jesus saith unto her, Woman, believe me, the hour cometh, when ye shall neither in this mountain, nor yet at Jerusalem, worship the Father. Ye worship ye know not what: we know what we worship: for salvation is of the Jews. But the hour cometh, and now is, when the true worshippers shall worship the Father in spirit and in truth: for the Father seeketh such to worship him. God is a Spirit: and they that worship him must worship him in spirit and in truth. The woman saith unto him, I know that Messias cometh, which is called Christ: when he is come, he will tell us all things. Jesus saith unto her, I that speak unto thee am he."

The setting is very familiar, and I will point out one thing that you might or might not have thought of. We have a privilege in this setting which the Lord Jesus did not allow His disciples to share. He picked a time when they had gone to get physical provisions before He came to the setting of this woman at Sychar, depriving them of the opportunity of witnessing her salvation. But we are not deprived of that privilege. We see what they didn't see. Something here makes me feel sort of privileged of God.

Jesus had said to His disciples before this, in Matthew 4:19, "Follow me, and I will make you fishers of men," or "I will teach you, show you—I will make you into . . . ." It is not, "I will touch you and cause some miraculous thing to happen," but "I will expose you to various examples." But for some strange reason He deprived them of this example.

"Make" in this verse means something I have heard Dr. Curtis

Hutson say over and over again: soul winning is *caught*, not *taught*. Once we get around it and it is talked about and we begin to experience it and see it take place, it gets hold of us. Then soon we begin thinking in that direction. The fever builds up, and something exciting begins to happen.

Now in these verses just read Jesus is showing us how He did it. In verses 35 to 38 He tells us to go out and do it.

"Say not ye, There are yet four months, and then cometh harvest? behold, I say unto you, Lift up your eyes, and look on the fields; for they are white already to harvest. And he that reapeth receiveth wages, and gathereth fruit unto life eternal: that both he that soweth and he that reapeth may rejoice together. And herein is that saying true, One soweth, and another reapeth. I sent you to reap that whereon ye bestowed no labour: other men laboured, and ye are entered into their labours."

Some people have sown a lot of seed, and we have come to the point when reaping is right before us. "The fields are white unto harvest," the Bible says. What a thrilling time in which to live, when we can reap the benefits of all the preaching that has been done, all the books that have been written. We are sort of going along on the coattails of Dr. John R. Rice and all the others who have set the pace for us!

In Matthew 28:19 and 20, we are reminded that Jesus gave us a general commission to go out into all the world and preach the Gospel to every creature, baptizing them in the name of the Father and of the Son and of the Holy Spirit. And He promises, "Lo, I am with you alway, even unto the end of the world" (Matt. 28:20).

He came here for that purpose—"to seek and to save that which was lost," says Luke 19:10. We may be talking to a different person than the woman at the well—or it may be a different time or place or setting; yet there are some similarities in this story that relate to every one of us. And this should help us to see how easy it is to bring someone into the family of God.

On one occasion Dr. Bob Gray got so burdened about winning someone, so he prayed early in the morning that the Lord would give him a soul that day. He had that on his heart as he drove to his early morning radio broadcast. As he got out on the expressway in Jacksonville and headed downtown, he saw a fellow sticking out his thumb. The Spirit of the Lord seemed to say, *There's your man.* So Dr. Gray pulled over and said, "Jump in, fellow. Where are you going?"

"I'm going downtown."

As Dr. Gray started back out on the expressway, he said to him, "I didn't mean, 'Where are you going *today*?' but 'Where are you going when you die?'"

The fellow said, "I haven't thought much about that."

Dr. Gray engaged him in conversation about it. The man listened intently. Then Dr. Gray asked, "Do you mind if I pull off the highway and explain this to you?"

"I'll be glad for you to," he answered.

They did so; and Dr. Gray took out his New Testament, showed him some verses and led right up to the point where he said, "Why don't you bow your head and let's both pray. Then you can receive Christ as your Saviour."

The fellow did it. Then as he wiped a little tear out of his eye, he reached into his pocket, pulled out a revolver, laid it on the seat and said, "Sir, as I hitchhiked I had determined that whoever picked me up, I would make him pull off the highway. Then I would kill him and steal his car, dump his body and go on my way to another state. Sir, if you hadn't talked to me about this, you could have been a dead man by now!"

Dr. Gray said, "It pays to be a witness, doesn't it!"

Now I want us to see in this story:

I. JESUS HAD A GREAT INTEREST AND CONCERN FOR *ONE* INDIVIDUAL

He was not concerned that there be a great host of people like this. Jesus was interested in one, solitary, isolated, individual soul all by herself—one on one. When going through the book of Matthew, I was amazed to find sixteen private interviews between the Saviour and one individual. In the book of John I found seventeen places where the Saviour talked to one isolated individual. In Luke 15 there is *one* lost sheep that gets all the attention. Ninety-nine others are left over there, but just one do we give our attention to. Though there were several other coins, the *one* coin got the attention. The *one* son who wandered away from home got the attention. The other good boy stayed home and minded his own business and did what he should; yet the one individual, the prodigal, got the attention. In Mark 8:36, the Bible says, "For what shall it profit a man [one man], if he shall gain the whole world, and lose *his own soul?*"—one individual.

I read again this week the wonderful story about Ed Kimball, a Sunday schoolteacher. He won a young fellow to the Lord and got that one stirred up. The new convert got the secret of the Lord's power upon his life. He became the well-known D. L. Moody.

The story says that after evangelizing America, D. L. Moody started on England. There in England Frederick B. Meyer heard his message. One of the illustrations that Moody used did not at first stir Brother Meyer. Then one of his Sunday schoolteachers came to him and said, "Brother Meyer, the illustration that that preacher gave in our church the other day stirred my girls so much that there has been a lot of weeping, confession and testimony. We are sure that the Holy Spirit has come among us; and we have had an experience in our class that you won't believe!"

F. B. Meyer was so affected by the testimony of that teacher and those girls that he got off by himself, and soon it began to grip him in the same manner. His ministry began to open up and spread, and as it did, he was invited to come to America.

He came and went to Furman University to preach. One young fellow in the student body had decided to quit the ministry and go back to a secular job. But the message by F. B. Meyer was given with such fervor and flame that the young fellow stepped out, came forward and renewed his vow to his calling. He became the great R. G. Lee.

Then F. B. Meyer went on to preach at another location. In that service a young fellow caught fire and began to evangelize. His meetings spread out all over the areas of New England and the mid-

Atlantic coast, until they were bulging at the seams. J. Wilbur Chapman, set on fire of God through the preaching of F. B. Meyer, began to stir up the whole northeastern coast.

Then, because of Chapman's preaching, he was invited to speak at a certain place. His ministry was changing, and he needed someone to move in on those citywide crusades that he was holding. Someone said, "The man you want is the young convert, Billy Sunday."

Billy Sunday, influenced by J. Wilbur Chapman, got into the ministry and went to Charlotte, North Carolina. There a group of laymen got so inspired and so stirred up that they organized a committee to invite other evangelists back. One invited was Mordecai Ham from Louisville, Kentucky. He preached in a meeting, and Billy Graham got saved. Billy Graham became a renowned evangelist around the world—all because Edward Kimball—one nobody—won one other nobody and started a series of dominoes falling that ended up with millions saved in Moody's ministry, hundreds of thousands in Meyer's ministry, hundreds of thousands more in Chapman's ministry, hundreds of thousands more in Lee's ministry, and hundreds of thousands more in Graham's ministry. All because one fellow won one soul to Christ!

That is why Jesus spent so much time talking to this one poor woman at the well. This story needs to be indelibly impressed upon our minds so that we might be influenced and affected, and some will catch fire by this one story and go out blazing to win one hundred thousand more to the Lord.

So it's a matter of one on one here. A chain reaction starts, and no one knows where it will end. Let's take time for just one.

Then notice:

II. JESUS HAD TO GO OUT OF HIS WAY

It was not convenient for Him to go through Samaria. All the Jews went across the Jordan, up through Moab, then back over the Jordan into Galilee again. They did not go through Samaria primarily because the Samaritans were the scum of the earth to the Jews. To go through Samaria meant one had to stop and eat at their homes, sleep in their homes; and the Jews wouldn't do that under any circumstances. They felt toward the Samaritans then somewhat like the Jews feel toward the P.L.O. today. They had no dealings with them at all. Yet Jesus went through that area because He had something pressing upon Him. It was a matter of taking the time, working it into a situation regardless of whether He had the time or could afford to go that way or not.

I am saying this: we are not going to win anybody if we wait for them to stumble across our path. We must make a point to go out of our way and give of our time and energies. We have to be concentrating and hunting for the experiences just like Jesus was.

Then think also about:

III. THE COMPULSION THAT WAS IN JESUS' HEART

The Scripture says here, "And he *must needs* go through Samaria." That word *must* is the same as the word in II Corinthians 5:14 where it says, "For the love of Christ *constraineth* us."

There was some sort of pressure on Jesus, a leading of the Holy Spirit. And let me say that nobody can be an effective witness without being under the influence and direction of the Holy Spirit.

A fellow was giving out tracts. He would knock on a door; and when the people came to the door, he would smile, hand them a tract and say, "I would be very grateful if you would read this," then knock on the next door and the next and the next.

He came to one house; and when he knocked, nobody came to the door. He knocked again; nobody came. He knocked a third time; nobody home. So he put the tract in the screen door and walked away.

But something compelled him. It seemed that the Spirit of God said, *Don't go off this porch! Go back up there and knock again.* He felt silly, but he walked back and knocked again. Still no answer. As he started to walk away this time, the feeling came stronger. So he went back and knocked again.

This time the door suddenly opened, and there was a man standing there saying, "WHAT DO YOU WANT?!"

"I got the wrong house." He was shaking when he handed the man the tract. "Sir, would you please read this?"

The man snatched it out of his hand and slammed the door.

He walked off the porch unnerved. It took him two or three houses before he got his composure back. Then he finished that block and another block and went home.

His name, address and phone number were on the bottom of each tract.

Late that evening the phone rang. "Sir, are you the man who was giving out the little papers over in a certain area today?"

"Yes, I was."

"Is it possible for you to come by and talk with me?"

"Sure. Give me the address."

He copied down the address and quickly made his way over there. It was the same house where he had knocked several times!

The fellow said, "Come in. I want to show you something." He took him up in the attic. The man said, "I was getting nervous for sure then!" There in the attic, on the rafters, hung a rope with a noose; and a basket was sitting right under the noose. He didn't know what to think about it.

The fellow said, "This afternoon I heard your first knock. I was standing on that basket with that rope around my neck, planning to end it all. When I heard you knock a second time, I thought, *I'll wait just a moment; and when the man goes away, I'll jump.* You knocked a third time. Then it got quiet. I was ready to jump when I heard you knock again! I figured I had better go see who it was. After you gave me that tract, I sat down and read it in its entirety. I must have read it fifty times this afternoon before calling you. I need what that is talking about."

I am glad that one in the tract ministry was sensitive to the leading of the Holy Spirit in his life. Jesus "must needs go." He had no choice. If somehow we, too, can understand the impression and the guidance and the leading of the Holy Spirit, it would greatly help us. Romans 8:14 tells us, "For as many as are led by the Spirit of God, they are the sons of God."

There is another thing for us to see:

IV. JESUS WAS FRIENDLY AND SYMPATHETIC TO THIS WOMAN

He didn't walk up to her and say, "Look here, you wicked harlot!"

He didn't walk up to her and say, "You're the lady who has had five husbands and are now living with a fellow who's not your husband! What kind of a wicked soul...! You're going to bust Hell wide open!" He didn't use that approach. He was friendly and sympathetic.

Neither was He reserved and distant. He was friendly. It wouldn't hurt fundamental Baptists to be friendly, would it? He was not arrogant or curt or blunt toward her. He was not too busy, not too preoccupied. He was just simply, in an everyday way, friendly, sympathetic and understanding. The poor soul was a sinner who needed something, and He knew what. So He approached her in a kind and friendly manner.

Then I want you to see:

V. JESUS ENTERED INTO AN ORDINARY SITUATION

He took advantage of the ordinary, everyday circumstances to open the conversation. He said, "Excuse me; could I bother you for a drink of water?" It was just beautiful.

She said, "Why, Sir, I will be glad to give you a drink of water ...but aren't you a Jew?"

"Yes."

"Well, why would a Jew like you be asking of me...? Don't you realize I'm a Samaritan?"

"Well, that's all right."

There was an ordinary setting in which Jesus stepped in and used it to an advantage. Jesus was weary. He was thirsty. And she came along. It was an ordinary thing—just like all of us live in our everyday routines. That is the place to win souls, the place where we get folks saved. He turned a disadvantage into an advantage.

Dr. Walter Wilson wrote a book in which he gave several examples of how he personally went at this. This medical doctor later preached more than he practiced medicine. I guess he was like the two Dr. Browns. One was the preacher; one, a medical doctor. One was the father; the other, the son. The phone rang. The grandson answered it. The caller said, "I would like to talk to Dr. Brown." The grandson asked, "Do you want the one that preaches or the one that practices?"

Dr. Walter Wilson said that when he would get on an elevator, it was his custom to say to the elevator operator, "Do you go up and down like this all the time?" To which that person would usually say, "All day long, eight hours a day—up and down." "When you die, are you going up or down?" He said the operator would open his or her mouth and gawk at him. Then he would usually be able to lead that one to Christ on the elevator.

To a bookkeeper he would ask, "Are your books balanced?" Then he would talk about the books, then ask about his or her eternal books.

When he would meet a lawyer, he would usually ask him, "What will the verdict be for you at the Great Judgment?" Boy, he probably hadn't thought much about it, but he started to, then.

Then when he met a laundryman, he would take an old dirty shirt or a pair of trousers that had a big spot, show it to the laundryman and say, "Do you think you can get this spot out of this pair of trousers?"

The person would usually say, "Why, sure, we can handle that."

He would say, "Do you think maybe blood would take that out?"

The person would say, "No, I don't suppose it would."

"Blood removes stains. The Bible says . . . , " and Dr. Wilson would give a verse of Scripture and win the laundryman to Christ talking about how blood cleanses from sin and takes care of the stain.

When he would meet a policeman, he would usually ask, "Do you realize that you are a minister of the Lord?" Then he would quote Romans 13:1. This was his way to win souls.

When he went with an undertaker on one occasion, he looked over at him and asked, "Sir, would you have any idea what that verse of Scripture means when Jesus says, 'Let the dead bury the dead'?" He won the man to Christ.

Jesus just went right into the situation of a well, some water, and a poor woman with a bucket when He didn't have a bucket. It was ordinary, an everyday circumstance.

Then He did another thing:

VI. JESUS ASKED HER FOR A FAVOR

What a beautiful lesson—just to open a conversation with a simple question! People usually like to be asked questions: "Could you tell me the way to the post office?" Nine out of ten would be so happy to tell you.

My wife and I were traveling through a little town in Indiana. The highway came into this little town and went right back out the other side of it; and we were hungry. I said to my wife, "Pull over right there where that man is." Here was a sharp-looking businessman. She wheeled over to the curb. I opened the door, stepped out and said, "Excuse me, sir. Could you help me find a real good family restaurant?" He smiled real big and said, "Just a block and a half down there is the best restaurant in town." That fellow was delighted to help me find a restaurant. People will always help us find restaurants, post offices, etc.

One preacher checked with a little boy one day and said, "Excuse me, son. Do you know where the post office is?"

The boy said, "Yeah. It's two blocks down this way."

"Now you have helped me. Let me help you. Son, let me tell you how to get to Heaven."

"Oh, no. You don't even know the way to the post office!"

I don't know how many times I have asked people for change for the telephone when I had plenty of it in my pocket. People like to help you. If I can find some way to ask somebody for something, then I can get the conversation started and break the ice. It's a matter of practicing and working at it. "You've been kind to me. Let me be kind to you . . .," and we could do what Jesus did here.

Then I want you to see another little thing, and that is:

VII. HE TALKED TO HER ALONE

He didn't wade into her while two or three people were there. When people are with their peers, they are different from when they are by themselves. If you see four teenage boys out playing, there is no use walking up to them and saying, "Hey, boy, let me ask you something. Where are you going to spend eternity?" You will get wiseacre answers.

Don't talk to folks when they are in crowds. Isolate them and get them out. Jesus got this woman when she was by herself. He made sure that the disciples had gone before He touched this woman's life. Otherwise she would have been super-sensitive. Can you imagine Jesus' talking to this woman with twelve disciples all gawking and staring, seeing what her reaction would be? Each time Jesus asked a question, she would have looked at all twelve. But He talked to her when she was alone.

I think there are exceptions. When there is death in the family, sometimes you can deal with the whole family because everyone is affected by that same mood. In the hospital where two or three people are around, perhaps you can talk to them together.

One occasion was a delightful exception for me. My phone rang; I answered. The fellow on the other end said, "Tommy? Is that you?"

I said to myself, *My soul! I don't know who this is, but it's been years and years since I have been around this guy!* (I was called "Tommy" until I graduated from high school.)

I said, "Who is this?"

"Tommy, this is your cousin Donald."

"Don Paisley! It's been years, Don. Where are you?"

"I live in the next town, over here at Newark, Delaware," which was just across the state line from Elkton, Maryland, where I pastored.

"Well, Don, what can I do for you?"

"I need your help. Now I understand you are pastoring a church in Elkton, and I need a preacher."

"I'll be glad to help you if I can."

"My wife died this morning, and I wonder if you would help with the arrangements and hold her funeral?"

"Don, I will be glad to. Tell me where you live. I want to come by the house and meet your children."

They were three and a half miles from our church, and I drove to their house. Here was my cousin Donald and his sister Lillian. There were two or three of his children, and several were around a big table. I sat right down at that table and drank a cup of coffee. There were ten of us now—nine others and me. I said, "Don, let me ask you about your wife. Was she a Christian?"

"Oh, she was a wonderful Christian! She read her Bible all the time. She went to church before she got sick. She was a real good Bible believer. There is no question about the fact she's gone to Heaven."

"Don, how about you? Are you saved?"

"No, I never did get saved."

"Lillian, are you saved?"

"No, I am not saved."

"How about you, young man? Are you saved?"

"No, I'm not saved."

"How about you, young lady?"

"No."

"What about you?"

"No."

"How about you?"

"No"..."No"..."No"..."No"—nine "No's."

I said to Don, "Now tomorrow I will preach and talk about your wife being in Heaven. Do you hope to go to Heaven and be with her again?"

"Oh, yes, I'd like to get that settled."

"How about you, Lillian? Would you like to get that settled?"

"I sure would."

"How about you, son?"

"Yes, I would."

"How about you?"

"Yes, I would"—nine "Yeses."

I read Romans 3:23, and I said, "What about you? Do you believe that?"

"Yes."

"What about you?"

Nine times we went down that one verse. Then I went to Romans 6:23," 'The wages of sin is death. . . .' Now, you realize that, if you die, you will have to go to Hell?"

"Yes, sir."

"You have to go to Hell?"

"Yes, sir."

"Where would you go?"

"I'd have to go to Hell."

"How about you?"

"I'd have to go to Hell."

Nine of them going to Hell.

Then we went to Romans 5:8, "But God commendeth his love toward us, in that, while we were yet sinners, Christ died for us.' Now, did Christ die for you?"

"Yes, He did."

"Did Christ die for you, Lillian?"

"Yes."

"How about you? Did He die for you? Do you believe He died for you?"

He died for all nine of them!

Then we came to, "For whosoever shall call upon the name of the Lord shall be saved" (Rom. 10:13). When I read that, they all said they believed it; and they believed it would work for them—nine times.

So I said, "Well, we will pray together if it's all right. I'll pray, and then I'll help all of you pray." I prayed first. Then I prayed with Don, and he got saved. Then I prayed with Lillian, and she got saved. Then I prayed with the next one, and that one got saved. I prayed all the way around, and all nine of them got saved!

The next Sunday morning, when I gave the invitation, they all came right down to the front and made a profession; and all got baptized.

But that is the exception. Usually it is just one on one, and usually while that one is alone. I don't have anything against mass evangelism and great services like we had here yesterday; but it is still one on one. We have to do it when they are alone.

Then I want you to see this:

VIII. JESUS OVERCAME NATURAL BARRIERS

There was a barrier of sin. Here He is—the holy, sinless, perfect, righteous Son of God; and here she is—immoral adulteress, wicked, vile scum of the earth. Sinner and holy Son of God—what a barrier!

Then there was the barrier of race—He a Jew, she a Samaritan.

Then there was the barrier of sex—He a male, and she a female; and nobody ever talked to the opposite sex in public in that area in that day.

Then there was the barrier of religion—she worshiped at Sychar; He worshiped at Jerusalem.

Sometimes I get to feeling like, *Man, you can't get that fellow saved because he's a Catholic,* or, *You can't get that person saved over there because he has this problem....* We let these little barriers stand up in front of us and shake us to the place where our faith is weak. We do not believe the Bible any longer. We shy away and don't enter into that conversation.

I think Jesus is giving us an example here. The reason He did it like He did was so we can understand that we can overcome four major barriers! We are making excuses when we could get over those walls really easily if we had the filling of the Holy Spirit. We could move right in there in boldness, confidence and assurance and win some of the most impossible cases in the world to the Lord Jesus Christ.

Then:

IX. JESUS CAPTURED HER CURIOSITY

He said in verses 10 through 13, "Would you really like to have some unusual and unique water? I don't have a bucket like you do, and I can't get any of this water out of this well like you can. But I have some water that would bubble up from inside and would bubble into everlasting life." She got curious about that! That sounded exciting!

I think He is giving us a lesson here in trying to talk a little about the beauties, the blessings, the joys of Heaven so that people might get excited and interested in what's waiting for them. If we can whet their appetite a bit, if we talk to them about how happy people can be after they get Heaven settled, I believe they'll want to get saved, just like she did. Jesus created curiosity and interest.

Then I see another thing I want to mention:

X. JESUS DIDN'T SCOLD HER OR REPROACH HER

He didn't give her a sermon on adultery. She was guilty, but He didn't blaze away at it. He didn't talk to her about the problems of divorce; she had already been through it five times now. He didn't bring up the possibility of VD or anything like that; He just pointed her to God, saying, "Lady, God is a Spirit, and they that worship Him must worship Him in Spirit and in truth."

I am not saying he didn't talk about her sin, but He eased into it. First—"Lady, would you give Me a drink of water?"

She answered, "Why, You're a Jew!"

"Yes, I know, but if you knew about the water that I have . . . ."

"But look! You don't have any bucket. How are You going to get water? The well is deep."

"The water that I am talking about is different."

Then second, He said, "Hold it. Before we talk any more, maybe it is better if you go get your husband." Oh! There He dealt with her sin problem. He didn't avoid that, but neither did He jump on her and give her a hard time about adultery and divorce and other matters. He led her to the Lord. He spoke about the only thing that would meet her need. He began to talk about everlasting life and salvation.

Suddenly she said, "I know! I know! I am waiting and hoping that the Messiah will come! We're waiting on Him; and when He comes, everything is going to be great!"

Then He opened the whole thing up by revealing Himself to her. Right then and there it was all settled.

While thinking about this yesterday, I said to the Lord, "Lord, I want to give myself over afresh and brand new, and I want to ask You, Lord, to let me be Spirit-filled; and I am going to dedicate myself to winning somebody to Christ just like You got this woman saved. Lord, I don't know who it is, where they are, what I will say. But, Lord, I am available. Would You please help me? Lord, I will try my best to get somebody this week. Please help me!" I felt like He would, and I accepted the challenge.

We had a number of people saved in the service last night. Then a fellow came up to me and said, "I've got to talk to you, Preacher. My name is Luke Jones. This is my wife, Sue. Could we go somewhere and talk?"

We went back in my office. Luke said, "I was a Mormon, but a fellow out of your bus directors' school led me to Christ. I told him I had already been baptized. Because I didn't get baptized like I ought to, it caused doubt to come. I resisted the Lord there, and I resisted Him again. Now I have a problem about whether I am still saved or not."

We talked for a few moments. Then he realized exactly who he was and where he was. He was born again and saved, but was disobedient. He came out with real assurance that he was really saved. He began to beam.

I looked at his wife and said, "Mrs. Jones, are you saved?"

"No. . .but. . .but. . .but, Preacher, I sure would like to be." There mine was! Just a little while before I had asked the Lord to use me if He would. I didn't try hard nor work at it. I just became a yielded vessel, and the Lord seemed to set one up there. I had to have some initiative. I had to bring up the question, but He put things together.

I am convinced that the Lord would like to do that day after day after day for every one of His children. He wants people saved! He wants to use us! The Bible teaches that when we receive the Spirit of the Lord into our lives and then yield ourselves so we have the filling of the Holy Spirit, then we begin to have a boldness and an assurance like Peter and John had. Then the Lord gives us wisdom and discernment and insight, and He puts us into the right place at the right time, and we win souls all over the place! These Conferences help us to understand how to be filled with the Holy Spirit and how to win others to Christ. And we have our prime Example.

May God help us to be able to win somebody to the Lord.

For a complete list of books available from the Sword of the Lord, write to Sword of the Lord Publishers, P. O. Box 1099, Murfreesboro, Tennessee 37133.